For the people of West Virg

and disregarded—their flagship univ
a source of pride, a shining representative for their state on the national
stage. So when native son and head coach Rich Rodriguez led the
Mountaineers to an unexpected Sugar Bowl victory at the end of the
2005 season, behind a youthful roster that included electrifying freshmen
Patrick White and Steve Slaton, West Virginia fans figured the best was
yet to come.

Instead, the seasons that followed served up endless, stomach-churning
drama, pivoting around one of the most earth-shattering upsets in college
football history—to be known forever by its final score, 13-9. Successes
came the Mountaineers' way, including three Bowl Championship Series
victories in seven years. But so did turbulent coaching changes that
splintered the fan base, looming uncertainty caused by ongoing conference
realignment, power struggles that forced some into highly embarrassing
acts, and enough backstabbing and subterfuge to fill a Shakespearian
tragedy. The Mountaineers emerged from the turmoil to face a bright
future in a new conference, but would the old demons still haunt them?

As a sportswriter for the *Charleston Daily Mail*, Mike Casazza has covered
the Mountaineers for more than a decade; he's lived WVU football
from Nehlen to Rodriguez to Stewart to Holgorsen. In *Waiting for the
Fall*, Casazza has written the definitive document of this unprecedented
period for West Virginia University football. You'll also read an insightful
foreword from ESPN play-by-play announcer and native West Virginian
Mike Patrick, who broadcast that infamous loss to Pittsburgh.

Waiting for the Fall is an epic tale that captures the events and emotions
that defined an era for West Virginians who experienced it firsthand.
It's also a must-read for football fans who watched with interest as the
sport's most successful team without a national title became a soap opera
disguised as a major college football program. And if you're a sports fan
who simply loves a great story told well, *Waiting for the Fall* is just the sort
of page-turner you'll love.

WAITING
FOR THE
FALL

Praise for *Waiting for the Fall*

"Strap on your clown shoes, crank up that calliope, and relive the Bill Stewart Epoch all over again. It's all right to laugh now. Laughter heals."

> — Holly Anderson, editor of the SI.com
> college football blog and contributor to
> Every Day Should Be Saturday

"In *Waiting for the Fall*, Mike Casazza does the impossible: He writes about his alma mater as an informed and incisive observer, rather than a pom-pom toting alum. (As a Northwestern alum who doesn't cheer from press row, I can relate.) Mike tells you everything you need to know about West Virginia football from the role of Richard III and RichRod to the mystifying management decisions made by Andrew Luck's dad."

> — Teddy Greenstein, *Chicago Tribune* college
> football reporter

"If you are looking to read about Mountaineer football in the last decade, you have got to check this book out! Has all the behind-the-scenes scoop you need to know about."

> — Mike Gansey, Cleveland Cavaliers scout and
> former WVU basketball star

"I moved away from Morgantown in 1991 but my heart never really left. A disproportionate share of my good and bad days are still influenced by strange men half my age wearing gold and blue jerseys—and I love it. I wouldn't be half as connected to the comings and goings at Mountaineer Field if not for the smart, insightful, and even sometimes uncomfortably honest reporting of Mike Casazza. After RichRod and Grandpa and Ollie and all the chaos and carnage of the past decade, I've thought more than once, "That guy should write a book." And, finally, he did. A book every bit as smart and insightful and uncomfortably honest as his newspaper work. Only much longer, which is a good thing. The chapter about the dark days after the Fiesta Bowl is going to haunt me for years. At least until Dana and his golden mullet deliver me a national title. Let's Go Mountaineers!"

> — Josh Dean, Author of *Show Dog:*
> *The Charmed Life and Trying Times of a*
> *Near-Perfect Purebred*

"College football is all about the dreams of those who play and coach and the fans who watch, and it's also about the drama of each game, each season. West Virginia has had its share of dreamers and drama, and reporter Mike Casazza has been there to expertly chronicle the ups and downs of the last decade in real time and now in this book. Casazza tells the story of West Virginia football, a state's love affair with the program, its joys and often its heartaches, and the coaches—primarily Don Nehlen, Rich Rodriguez, Bill Stewart, and Dana Holgorsen—whose names, no matter what, will always be tied to the Mountaineers. To understand the last decade of West Virginia football is to have lived it. Casazza has as the beat writer, and that's allowed him to weave an untarnished, well-researched story that football fans not only in West Virginia but across the country will understand. Why? Because there's the ultimate message of hope and that success is the price of hard work, and that the past is always intrinsically tied to the present through tradition and pride. Finally, it's because college football is about dreams and drama and the Mountaineers have had their share of both ... and everyone can relate to that."

— Angelique Chengelis, *The Detroit News*

"From the Rich Rod years to the bizarre circumstances surrounding Bill Stewart's hiring and firing along with the behind-the-scenes dealings that earned West Virginia an invitation to the Big 12 Conference, this is the quintessential book for West Virginia fans on Mountaineer football from an insider's view that only Mike Casazza could provide."

— Brett McMurphy, CBSSports.com
national columnist

"Casazza's book sheds light into the personalities and figures making up the drama surrounding West Virginia—which really has been as wild as any program I can think of—with humor and clarity. The book isn't as behind-the-scenes-Rich-Rodriguez-cried-into-his-hands as John Bacon's book on Michigan, but Casazza has watched the WVU program carefully and leaves no major turn unreported. I enjoyed the book a great deal."

— Chris Brown, Smart Football

"... it isn't so much a 'recommendation' as it is 'demand.' If you haven't read *Waiting for the Fall*...do it. Right now. Like, if you don't buy it in the next 10 minutes, I'll be personally offended.

"Really, it's impossible for me to tell you how good this book is...I doubt you have any idea how many truly wild things have gone down within the program over the last 10 years...Forget Tennessee, USC, Michigan or anywhere else: it is West Virginia which has been the most volatile and fascinating program of the last decade."

— Aaron Torres, Crystal Ball Run

"If you live and die by what happens to WVU football like I do, or if you just want an insider's view of the last decade's craziness, then this book is an absolute MUST read."

— The Smoking Musket, SB Nation WVU Blog

"It's a full-color picture of WVU football during those amazing years, from the amazing successes to the underpinnings of impending disaster...[Casazza] has good sources and is thoughtful and fair at a time when both seem to be in short supply. It was comforting to know that the trials and tribulations of my beloved Mountaineers were in capable hands."

— Brandon Priddy, The Signal Caller

"I would highly recommend [it] to anyone that loves college sports. My being from WV, I think he certainly captured how myself and many others from WV feel about the state and the team."

— Amber Fillinger, WVU fan

"Insightfully titled, the book chronicles the WVU football program beginning at the end of Coach Nehlen's career, and accurately describes how many fans feel about West Virginia football and the emotional roller-coaster it never lets us exit. The text reminds everyone that WVU is the winningest Division I football program (#15 all-time) without a national championship!

"The team's history, detailed in this book, explains why I sat nervously awaiting the second half of the Orange Bowl, worrying that the Mountaineers might find a way to lose despite a 49-20 halftime lead."

— Dr. Stanley Toompas, Amazon.com review

"You don't have to be a WVU fan to enjoy this book, and you may even find it more insightful if you are not a diehard Mountaineer. Casazza details a rollercoaster ride of a decade for a fanbase (and as it turns out, athletic department and coaching staff as well) filled with constant paranoia because they always come up just short. It describes how the pressure and demands of college football caused good people to make mistakes that cause serious consequences. From coaching drama to inexplicable losses to changing conferences, no team has had a decade quite like West Virginia."

— M. Smith, Amazon.com review

"What a fun read. Let's face it, this story is like a tragic opera, and Mike has captured it faithfully."

— Phillip, Amazon.com review

"...the pages will turn quickly for any fan of college football. Notice I said 'college football' and not 'Mountaineer fan.' Casazza writes about an athletic department that is simply entertaining. In it, you have bona fide characters...Rich Rodriguez, who is the talented, successful character who decided he was worth so much more ...Bill Stewart, the home grown but in-over-his-head fool...Oliver Luck, the decision maker who essentially rules with an iron fist...and Dana Holgorsen, who represents the hopes and dreams of the fans. If I were to compare this book to others in the marketplace, I would compare it to a John Feinstein book but without all the 'filler.'"

— Cam, Amazon.com reviewer

"The book is a perfect illustration [of] why Casazza has become the premier beat writer covering the Mountaineers."

— Jeff Woolard, Amazon.com review

WAITING
FOR THE
FALL

A Decade of Dreams, Drama and
West Virginia University Football

BY MIKE CASAZZA

FOREWORD BY
ESPN's MIKE PATRICK

Version History
Paperback and electronic versions published March 2012.
Version 1.1, September 2012

ISBN: 0985200901
ISBN-13: 978-0-9852009-0-9

Cover Layout and Design by Peter Stults
Interior Layout and Design by Tom Heffron
Copy Editing by Leah Cochenet Noel and Rick Jensen

Contents

Foreword

With apologies to to any English Lit teachers I ever had, was it Wordsworth or Longfellow who asked, "As high as we have risen in delight, in our dejection do we sink as low?" The answer is yes, and if you are a Mountaineer fan, the answer is, "Oh God, yes." It may be wholly unfair that the losses hurt so much more than the joy brought by wins, but they do.

As a kid growing up in Clarksburg, West Virginia, West Virginia University football was a part of my life as long as I can remember. My first crushing memory of it was the 1954 Sugar Bowl against Georgia Tech. The Mountaineers—who had an incredible 18 players on that roster who would be drafted into the NFL over the next three years, including Hall of Famers Sam Huff and Bruce Bosley—had beaten Pitt and Penn State that season and had been ranked as high as No. 5 during the campaign before a late loss to South Carolina. It was a chance to show the nation what Mountaineer football was all about.

Oops! Georgia Tech 42, WVU 19.

The next 57 years would follow that theme. Enough good moments to keep you away from the suicide hotline, and then the crushing blow to bring you to your knees.

Most of the joy came during Don Nehlen's great run from 1980 through 2000, highlighted by the only two unbeaten seasons ever. That 1988 club, of course, would lose to Notre Dame in the national championship game, but I am convinced, to this day, that if quarterback Major Harris hadn't been hurt, the Mountaineers would have won.

I nominated myself for the Stupidity Hall of Fame that day after inviting my broadcast partner, former Irish quarterback Joe Theisman, to watch the game with me and my wife, Janet. Gee, how could that have turned out badly?

It was during Nehlen's tenure that I had a chance to do Mountaineer games as an announcer. Each game was a daunting task. Here I was, a fan who couldn't cheer, couldn't scream at the referees, couldn't leave if it all went wrong. It was my job to be fair and impartial, and if anything, I went overboard. For three and a half hours I had to ignore the emotions that had been part of my life. Somehow it was worth it, just to be part of a big game, even the one that hurt the most.

It was the night of December 1, 2007. The Mountaineers were huge favorites against Pitt with a place in the national championship game on the horizon.

What went wrong? What didn't? When it was over and my job was done, I walked into a recently emptied room and screamed my heart out.

Maybe everyone goes through the same things we do as Mountaineers. But does everyone do the right thing by hiring Bill Stewart after the miracle win against Oklahoma and then force him out three years later with the best winning percentage in school history? I think not.

But read on, my fellow sufferers, and find out why things seem to conspire against us and who the conspirators may have been. If knowledge is power, then this is a powerful book.

—Mike Patrick

Mike Patrick, who joined ESPN in 1982, is the play-by-play voice for many of the network's top events, including college football, NCAA men's basketball and the NCAA Men's College World Series.

Preface

The details of July 27, 1980, are totally absent from my mind. I was a few weeks old and not yet in the habit of toting a pen and steno pad wherever I went.

That was the date I was baptized in Hamilton, Ohio, the very place I was born 28 days earlier to Marie and Eugene Casazza. Had I not been an infant, I would have found it quite unforgettable—not for the baptism, but for the fact that Hamilton was shaken by a 5.2-magnitude earthquake that day.

Hamilton. Metro Cincinnati, southwest Ohio. Not California or Alaska. Not Mexico or South America or Asia. Hamilton, Ohio.

There was no real damage. No one was hurt or harried or even really shaken, so to speak. But understand the effect this has on one's life. Beginning with the very first opportunity in my life, it was apparent that celebrations often come with circumstances.

I've thought about this a whole lot in my life. Don't get me wrong; I've had a lot of events and causes to celebrate. A few have even gone off without a hitch. Yet as a kid who played sports, and later as an adult who covers sports for a living, I am often reminded of this unsettling reality, that what is bad often accompanies what is supposed to be fun.

It would be easy, though painful, to go back through my many years spent reinforcing this thesis. I could, for example, say the only championship trophy I proudly remember winning was in T-ball when I was five years old.

Today, as I have friends with kids who play T-ball, it occurs to me everyone gets a trophy. I'm forced to wonder if the triumph I still cling to was actually a farce of good sportsmanship.

I instead submit my most vivid case for cautious celebrations. I married my wife, Erinn, on August 25, 2007. The days leading up to the wedding featured beautiful weather, surprisingly reasonable temperatures, and acceptably crisp afternoons that transitioned into cool-enough evenings. It was entirely tolerable.

On the day of the wedding, the heat was absolutely brutal. The temperatures soared into the 90s. I remember seeing one thermometer that read 98 and then hearing the radio announcing we were approaching record highs. The only part that surprised me was that the temperatures hadn't set, or demolished, the previous record.

And that had nothing to do with everything that went wrong that day—it merely made matters worse.

The groomsmen and I made it from our hotel to the church with no trouble. We boarded a classy city trolley and scooted up and down the road without incident. My groomsmen and my parents enjoyed a few light, albeit sweaty, moments in the shade provided by a gazebo outside the church.

The time neared three o'clock, and we headed inside to join the more than 160 others who were waiting for the ceremony. I waited in a back room so I wouldn't see my bride-to-be. But as we got closer and closer to the 3 p.m. start, a quick peek revealed no one from the other half of the wedding party had arrived.

Then my phone rang. It was the matron of honor. "Mike," Jennelle said, "I have some bad news."

I had no idea what that meant. I had no idea what to think. I only knew nothing good could follow those words on your wedding day. Never before had I even considered the wedding might not happen. I was in no way prepared to consider that possibility at that moment.

I eventually remembered to breathe, and that got my ears working again. Jennelle explained to me an utterly inexplicable story.

The same trolley that left us at the church had then traveled to our apartment, where it was to pick up Erinn and her bridesmaids and parents. That part went as planned.

As the driver steered out of our gravel driveway, he clipped a phone line above the trolley that ran parallel to our apartment building. The line was wedged into a corner under the roof and the trolley was stuck.

Rather than back up and adjust and try again, as most everyone else would do, the driver tried what nobody else would do. He slammed the gas pedal to the floor.

The trolley lurched forward and the phone line sliced under the roof. You can only imagine the reactions, everything from alarm to terror. One bridesmaid abandoned the trolley, certain it was a power line and everyone's life was in danger.

The driver somehow freed himself from that mess, but the damage was done. As the trolley sped along the road to the church, aerodynamic drag peeled the roof off the top of the trolley like a lid on a can of sardines.

The driver, who, I kid you not, was the company's employee of the month, pulled over the crippled trolley and stopped alongside a major four-lane road in town. The sun beat down on the blacktop and cooked the poor girls in their exquisite dresses. Jennelle told me they were slowly finding their way to the church thanks to guests and even complete strangers who witnessed this scene on the side of the road.

After I hung up with Jennelle and took a moment to digest that story, I started to tell my groomsmen and the other friends and family members who'd come to surround me and my astonishment during that phone call. They were delighted. Not because everyone was fine and on their way, but because the wedding had been delayed and defined by chaos.

We were past three p.m. at this point, and people in the pews were beginning to look around, wonder, and whisper. Never before had I been able to read minds, but at that very moment the power came to me. I could sense people thinking, "Ooh! I've never been to a wedding that was called off! Is this going to happen? What about the open bar?"

We decided to tell people in the back of the church what was happening and encourage them to tell those near and in front of them. Ideally, the message would get to everyone and they'd all calm down. It also spared me from having to make the embarrassing announcement to the entire audience, which would be caught on someone's video camera to live forever. I was consciously afraid of that. My family is ruthless; they'll appreciate reading here just how scared I was of what they might do with that footage.

The message made its way to the front of the church, but with the sort of results I should have expected. This convoluted game of telephone twisted and turned the story until the last people to get the message were told a tale of a grisly accident and bodies all over the road.

Eventually, the bridal party arrived. Erinn showed up last in a pickup truck, which is probably not how she ever envisioned arriving to the church on her wedding day.

Mercifully, the wedding did happen. It was a lovely ceremony followed by a spirited reception. Again and again that evening, and in all the days and occasions to retell that story that would follow, I was complimented on the calm way I handled the drama. Impressed and amused, people wanted to know how I held it all together, how I maintained a smile and a good mood in light of an incident that probably should have ruined my big day.

The answer: I was ready for it. OK, you never expect such an event, but you can condition yourself for the low moments and the low blows life throws at you. And thanks to sports, I've had a lot of practice.

My early life was spent in Ohio, which is my excuse for liking the professional sports teams in Cleveland. I know them as the Browns, the Indians, and the Cavaliers. You know them as the NFL team that last won a championship in 1954 and was devastated by John Elway, The Drive, and The Fumble, and later moved to Baltimore; the baseball team that hasn't won a World Series since 1948, got painfully close in 1995, and lost a lead in the ninth inning of Game Seven in 1997; and, of course, as the championshipless NBA team that Michael Jordan regularly humiliated and that later embraced and developed a homegrown, once-in-a-lifetime talent in LeBron James, who then publicly divorced himself from his past by taking his talents to South Beach.

It would be wrong to say the city hasn't won anything lately. In 2004, ESPN was so kind as to crown Cleveland as "America's Most Tortured Sports Town."

Time hasn't been kind to the place or its people, either. Society and industry have taken their hits through the years. Trade and manufacturing aren't what they once were. Cleveland defaulted on federal loans in 1975, something no other U.S. city had done since the Great Depression. The mayor at the time was Dennis Kucinich, and he was so unpopular that the local mafia wanted him dead.

The city had its comeback in the 1990s as the downtown area was redeveloped with a new baseball stadium and a basketball arena. The hit movie *Major League*, which focused on the Cleveland Indians, felt good for a time, but we all winced when we heard about the sequel, which was predictably awful. The Rock and Roll Hall of Fame opened and served as a reminder that the city had some culture and history that didn't include race riots or a burning river.

I have friends and family in Cleveland, and they love it, but you get the idea they're never out from under it. People point and laugh at Cleveland from afar, mostly because they've never been there or never cared to understand the situation and perhaps come to find their perception isn't the reality.

The city needs to win something. It needs the affirmations of the doubters. It needs those who point and laugh to one day nod and smile and say, "Cleveland got it right, man."

Until then, the city and its people are, in sports and in society, underdogs. They are spooked by the past. They are desperately waiting for something good but preparing to deal with the bad that so often comes in its place.

They wait for the other shoe to drop.

* * *

I feel just as strongly that I've been a part of something similar in West Virginia, where I have lived since 1998, where I was an undergraduate student, and where I have covered the West Virginia University athletic program full time since 2002.

West Virginia has its societal and economic troubles. Its industries and businesses have suffered through the years. There is poverty. There is crime. There are things outsiders hold against the state and its people, both fair and unfair.

West Virginia is full of wonderful, proud, committed, and passionate people. One of them is Bob Huggins, the men's basketball coach at the university. He was born in Morgantown, played basketball at WVU, and returned to West Virginia to become the coach in 2007.

He frequently tells a story about a conversation he had in 1977, when he started as a WVU graduate assistant, to illustrate a point about the people of the Mountain State.

"One of the football coaches came up to me—he was a West Virginian and a great guy—and he put his arm around me and he said, 'Huggs, just remember this: the greatest resource in the state of West Virginia isn't coal. The greatest resource is its people. We are the greatest people in the world.' I never forgot that, and I've always believed that," Huggins recalls.

West Virginia is deeply invested in its Mountaineers. There are no major professional teams in the state. Many cheer for the Pittsburgh Steelers or the Cincinnati Reds or the other teams from nearby states, but they know these teams aren't really their teams. Their teams are the ones that play on campus at WVU.

The devotion West Virginians hold for their Mountaineers is a reflection of their loyalty and how important that loyalty is for people of this state. It's one reason Huggins is held in such high regard, and why he was signed to a lifetime contract after the 2007–08 season.

West Virginians suspected they had something similar years earlier when former WVU safety Rich Rodriguez was hired in 2000 to succeed Don Nehlen as the head football coach. Although WVU was 3-8 in Rodriguez's first season, the team went 9-3 in his second regular season.

Then in 2005, WVU began a remarkable run of unprecedented success. The team announced its arrival with only its second bowl victory in its last 13 tries, an improbable upset of Southeastern Conference champion Georgia—in a BCS bowl, no less—behind a promising roster chock full of talented and speedy underclassmen. It seemed that WVU would soon, finally, reach the pinnacle of college football.

But on the cusp of a berth in the BCS championship game at the end of the 2007 season, WVU lost its last regular-season game at home against archrival Pittsburgh, a game that will forever be known for its final score, 13–9. Some considered the loss the biggest choke in college football history, but for West Virginia fans it was only the first of a series of shocking, frustrating, and perplexing events. Rodriguez fled for the head coaching job at Michigan within days, the team bounced back to score a historic victory in the Fiesta Bowl, and interim coach Bill Stewart was hired virtually on the spot.

Thus began three tumultuous years for Mountaineer football, ending only with an even more tumultuous transition of power to offensive guru Dana Holgorsen, new athletic director Oliver Luck's handpicked coach. By the summer of 2011, a first-time head coach was in charge of the main moneymaker for the self-supporting athletic department and the top target of a state's affection. The people held their collective breath, hoping for the best but preparing for the worst.

That trepidation is a constant condition in the lives of many WVU fans, and one that's been in my life, too. It's why I wanted to write this book. What is found in the chapters to follow will probably rub a lot of people the wrong way. That's not my intention. I know the uneven relationship WVU fans have with their sports teams. I know it can be a painful existence; even on the occasions when the people are filled with hope, they can be left empty.

As a professional journalist, I don't—I can't—root for WVU's teams. To be totally honest, though, I do sometimes feel for the participants. Because I can relate to their plight, I just refuse to believe something good will never, ever come from their unwavering dedication and unbeatable spirit.

Are we about to revisit some bad times? Yes. That's not the goal, though. The point is to remember where you've been, because when you get to where you want to go, it will be as unbelievable as it will be satisfying.

I know this not because I've covered it, but because I've lived it.

Introduction

The excitement that West Virginia football fans had feared was gone during the last few years under coach Don Nehlen, what they'd thought was possible during the early seasons with Nehlen's successor, Rich Rodriguez, arrived by surprise in 2005 with a program-altering, perception-changing, triple-overtime victory at home against Louisville. A bright, full moon hung over the field that night, almost like a message from above that illuminated the WVU players and reminded them, "Hey, there's still time on the clock. You're Mountaineers. You're not done yet."

This was a game that had everything. A backup quarterback who saved the day in relief of the injured starter. An impossible fourth-quarter comeback. A controversial call on an onside kick that swung the game in the home team's favor (with the Big East Conference later admitting to a missed penalty on the play that would have never allowed it to happen). And decisive clutch plays by the Mountaineers.

WVU was just about left for dead in that game, so much so that when the players entered the locker room at halftime, behind 17–0 after being dominated in all meaningful aspects, Rodriguez tried to encourage his players by asking them to think about climbing out of a well, a little at a time until you get your head above water.

"I don't know if they believed me or not," Rodriguez said in the *Dominion Post* after the game, "but they shook their heads like they did."

Things were no better, and actually looked worse, when the Cardinals answered WVU's first score with one of their own. Then starting WVU quarterback Adam Bednarik left the game with a foot injury on the first possession of the fourth quarter.

It was at this moment that freshman Patrick White stepped off the sideline and into the hearts of WVU fans. Fellow freshman Steve Slaton, a running back, had come through earlier in the season in the team's lone loss to Virginia Tech, but now the combination of White and Slaton was like a chemical reaction, creating light and heat and firing up an offense that had been sluggish all season. White, with his icy-cool demeanor under pressure, kept several drives alive with scrambles and precise passes, while Slaton shook some defenders and smashed others as he racked up yards.

A touchdown, a field goal, and another touchdown later, the game headed to overtime, where Slaton scored three more touchdowns for a Playstation-esque total of six, a WVU game record. The final score was 46–44. WVU scored all of its points after halftime, despite not scoring a touchdown in the second halves of the previous three games. This great victory, this unquestioned turning point for the team and for the program, happened in front of a home crowd that had dwindled dramatically at the end of the third quarter, when, for all practical purposes, the game was over. Fans of the Mountaineers can quickly grow disenchanted and bail on the team they love. That was the case in that Louisville game. Tens of thousands of people left the game to get a head start on the postgame binge or the drive home, either of which would take them far away from another sad Saturday at the stadium. During the comeback, some of the loudest cheers actually came from the crowded parking lots beyond both end zones.

At that time, I lived in an apartment down the road from the stadium. The deck out back overlooked Route 705. Before every home game, the football team's bus travels down 705 before turning toward the stadium to deliver the players.

Every game, my wife and whoever was at the apartment's tailgate that day would serenade the bus as it rumbled down 705, confident their screams and cheers of "Let's go, Mountaineers!" would make a difference that day. Things like that happen everywhere in Morgantown on a game day.

One of my college roommates was in town to be a part of it all. He bought a ticket online and drove up the day of the game from Roanoke, Virginia. He crammed in as much of the pregame atmosphere as he could, which would be a problem for him later. Just like so many other fans who got fired up for the game, he left early when the Cardinals took a commanding 24–7 lead.

When stunned and euphoric people flooded the apartment sometime later, they shook and awoke my old roommate on the couch. "Jay," they said, "how about that game?"

"Enough!" he said as he rolled away from the noise and balled up in a corner of the sofa where there was no light and no harassment. "I can't believe I came here for that."

He was sleeping off a loss and another disappointment delivered by the team he loved. He never saw the comeback happen and was instead passed out on our powder-blue sofa with a pink floral design. Quite a picture. But in the future, when the conversation turned to the comeback and how it changed the fortunes of WVU football, he could say he was there.

Nothing was the same after that game. Rodriguez's fifth WVU team—and, people forget, his third straight to win or at least share the Big East championship—went on to outscore its final four opponents of the season 156–39. The reward was a Bowl Championship Series berth and a date with the University of Georgia in the Sugar Bowl on January 2, 2006.

* * *

The 11th-ranked Mountaineers were familiar with bowl games, in particular with losing them. Since 1987, the year before an 11-0 record earned a spot in the Fiesta Bowl and an opportunity to play Notre Dame for the national championship, WVU had played in 12 bowls and lost 11. Rodriguez was 0-3 so far, by scores of 48–22, 41–7, and 30–18.

WVU rarely gave itself a chance in those debacles. Virginia led 28–10 at halftime of the 2002 Continental Tire Bowl. Maryland led 24–0 at the half of the 2004 Gator Bowl. Florida State needed all of five plays to inflict more of the same in the 2005 Gator Bowl. The Seminoles scored on a 69-yard touchdown run on the first play from scrimmage and then recovered a fumble on the ensuing kickoff before kicking a field goal.

"They flew those planes over the stadium in Jacksonville, and before they landed we were down 10–0 to Florida State," Rodriguez recalled for the *Dominion Post* in the days before the Sugar Bowl. "We have to get off to a good start for our guys to get confidence and keep their fans from getting too boisterous and just play ball."

At the end of 2005, the Mountaineers had a 10-1 record and had compiled six straight victories. WVU had a veteran defense, but its youth on offense was exciting for the present and the future. In addition to White and Slaton, guard Ryan Stanchek was a freshman, fullback Owen Schmitt and receiver Darius Reynaud were sophomores, and receiver Brandon Myles, guard Jeremy Sheffey, and center Dan Mozes were juniors.

Rodriguez had been recruiting speedy and skilled players, often luring them away from bigger programs in better conferences by promising them a chance to play on offense. Other times, WVU just lucked out and found a player on whom others had given up. Across the depth chart, WVU was a story of succeeding despite the circumstances—like an "island of misfit toys" in the landscape of collegiate football, as Rodriguez would describe his team in a *USA Today* article in 2006.

The timing couldn't have been better, either. Miami and Virginia Tech left before the 2004 season for the Atlantic Coast Conference, and Boston College followed a year later. To compensate, the Big East accelerated Connecticut's entrance into the conference and welcomed Cincinnati, South Florida, and Louisville. None of those four had as much to offer as the schools that left. The Big East had a bruised reputation, and even if WVU was winning, the experts, the pundits, and even the fans were underwhelmed.

The Big East champion was fortunate, it was said, to have a spot in the BCS, and that spot was in peril. In the first seven years of the BCS, the Big East was 3-4, with all the wins and only one loss belonging to the Hurricanes, including their 1-1 record in national championship games. Virginia Tech lost the 2000 national championship to Florida State. Pitt represented the Big East in the first season after the departure of the ACC defectors and lost badly to Utah in the Fiesta Bowl—and then Pitt watched its coach take a job at Stanford in the Pacific-10 Conference.

The Mountaineers were carrying the flag of the Big East and hoping to spare the conference further shame. On top of that, the sports media by and large discounted the Mountaineers as too young, too small, and too underrecruited to play with the mighty eighth-ranked champions of the Southeastern Conference. WVU was reminded of this throughout the week of interviews that preceded the game. It may have been the best thing to happen to them.

"No one likes to hear they can't win or don't belong," Georgia coach Mark Richt said to the *Dominion Post* before the game. "The older I get, the more I coach, the more I believe in the psychology of the game."

What's more, the Sugar Bowl had been relocated to the Georgia Dome, after Hurricane Katrina devastated New Orleans and the Louisiana Superdome, the bowl's longtime venue. Georgia's campus was about 90 minutes from the Georgia Dome, making the Sugar Bowl a virtual home game. The Bulldogs had won the SEC championship game with a 34–13 victory against No. 3–ranked LSU four weeks earlier in that very stadium. Had LSU beaten the Bulldogs, LSU might have been chosen to play in the BCS championship game. Instead, Georgia had destroyed them.

The Mountaineers opened as nine-point underdogs, and though the line dropped to six-and-a-half points before kickoff, 83 percent of the readers who picked a winner on ESPN.com picked Georgia.

So WVU had the geographical disadvantage of playing the game in Atlanta, the perceptional disadvantage of being merely a Big East team up against the SEC champ, and the historical disadvantage of its terrible record in bowl games.

Events back in West Virginia added further emotional weight. The day of the Sugar Bowl, 13 coal miners were trapped below the earth by an explosion at Sago Mine, in Upshur County.

The mine had been closed for New Year's Day, but the first crew was rolling along in the mantrip on the familiar rails at around 6:30 a.m. on January 2, some 14 hours before the Sugar Bowl. An explosion trapped the miners behind the rubble, and they were unable to work their way to safety. In 2005, the U.S. Mine Safety and Health Administration had issued 208 "enforcement actions," basically citations for problems discovered during inspections, against the mine.

The MSHA acknowledged afterward that "several involved significant violations that were the result of high negligence" but would also say less than half of the 208 citations were what it called "significant and substantial." While accurate, 96 is still a big number, and well above the 68 *total* citations issued the year before.

The news was nothing new. Mining was and is a dangerous job, a truth so many West Virginians know because their fathers and grandfathers knew it before them. It's a family trade in so many parts of the state, a profession the people across the 55 counties identify with, whether they personally know a coal miner or not.

This was a tragic story in the state and then throughout the nation. News crews from the major networks and newspapers descended upon Sago. Rescuers would have to wait some 12 hours before it was safe enough to begin their work. By kickoff, there was no news on the miners, only hope.

"It's only football, but we wanted to do something to lift our people's spirits," Rodriguez said. "We always want to play well, but tonight especially."

That merely added to the burden the players already carried into the game. West Virginia's governor at the time, Joe Manchin, a former quarterback for the Mountaineers, met with the team the day before the Sugar Bowl and had a simple message.

"I told them when they put that uniform on they carry the love and respect of the people of West Virginia," Manchin relayed to the *Dominion Post*.

That was an enormous responsibility, but the Mountaineers took all the doubts and all the reasons to be discouraged and combined them to make a decisive psychological advantage. They sprinted to a 28–0 lead early in the second quarter, rebounded from a Georgia rally, and escaped on a daring fake punt late in the game's final drive. In a 38–35 win, White completed 11 of 14 pass attempts for 120 yards and had a touchdown. He also added 77 yards rushing, leading the team under pressure like a seasoned veteran, not a redshirt freshman starting only his fifth game. Meanwhile, Slaton ran for a bowl-record 204 yards and three touchdowns.

"The thing is," Rodriguez said in the press conference after the game, "Pat and Steve should keep getting better."

That was frightening for teams who would be on WVU's schedule the next two or three years, as well as the fans of those unfortunate teams. It was really invigorating for WVU's fans, the ones who hadn't experienced much of this degree of nationwide adoration but couldn't get enough of it.

On January 20, not three weeks after the game, Pat Forde, a national columnist working then for ESPN.com, picked the Mountaineers as his preseason No. 1 team for the 2006 season. He highlighted Slaton and White, but astutely added, "They have plenty of other offensive weapons to rely on." Mozes was one of them, and he'd prove as much by winning the Rimington Trophy the next season as the best center in the country. He said what so many others were thinking as WVU left the Bulldogs in the past and looked to the future:

"The sky is the limit."

* * *

Trouble is, the sky often falls on West Virginia.

Consider the events taking place on the day of the Sugar Bowl. Many WVU fans in Atlanta for the game were actually stuck in their hotel rooms because of tornadoes in the area. So confined, they found themselves watching coverage of the mining disaster, one of the few unfortunate ways that West Virginia receives national attention other than Mountaineer athletics. The uncertainty at Sago Mine tempered fans' celebrations after the game, until news spread two days later that the miners had all been found alive. This was amazing, the most pleasant surprise that could come from a situation that seemed so grim.

Late on January 3, just minutes before midnight, multiple news sources reported that 12 of the 13 miners had been found alive. Governor Manchin, who had left Atlanta on game day and missed his alma mater's win, was outside Sago Baptist Church, celebrating the news and reveling in the moment with the friends and family members of the miners. Word soon followed that the survivors had been brought out and were on their way to the hospital.

"Miracles do happen," Manchin said.

Time magazine had reported seeing Sago resident Lynette Roby around 1:30 a.m. waiting on the side of the road to get a glimpse of the miners as they were taken off to the hospital. She never saw that, but it didn't change the way she was feeling. "We're just completely overjoyed," she told the magazine.

But hours later, just before three o'clock on the morning of January 4, Roby interrupted a live shot of CNN's Anderson Cooper. Now, almost 75 minutes after speaking with *Time*, she had terrible news. With her two children at her side, Roby told Cooper that Ben Hatfield, the CEO and president of International Coal Group, which operated the mine, said 12 of the 13 miners were dead.

The initial report of the miners' safety was wrong and had never been confirmed, but it had been out there for three hours—three remarkable, blessed, and ultimately surreal hours. There was no explanation or justification, and all Hatfield could later say was that he regretted "allowing the jubilation to go on longer than it should have."

The explosion and then the cruel twist were the tragic bookends for what had been a storybook occasion for the Mountaineers. They had done something special for the Big East and for the program, but Rodriguez believed he'd done something far more meaningful for West Virginia and its people. He'd given them joy amid pain. True, it was, as he said, only football, but it was something the people could embrace at a time they needed something to hold onto.

"Hopefully the victory, because we have so much pride, will help people feel good about themselves," he said.

Two days later, it was snatched away.

* * *

Moments after the Sugar Bowl ended, the freshmen, sophomore, and junior players sat in the locker room and looked around at who was there and who'd be there for years to come. They thought and spoke openly about winning a national championship. They understood West Virginia football was in a position to do the sorts of things of which its fans had only dreamed.

But it just didn't happen. Theirs was a dream deferred.

From that point on, WVU was supposed to win the conference every year, string together BCS appearances, and perhaps even win a national championship. Instead, WVU didn't live up to the potential that everyone in that Georgia Dome locker room, and everyone in the state of West Virginia, could sense on the evening of January 2.

"There was that feeling of, like, 'We did this, but we never did that. We did this, but that should have happened,'" former kicker and punter Pat McAfee said years later.

There have been successes—big ones, even. But they've been overshadowed by everything else. The predominant themes have been about losing big games and wasting bigger opportunities, and coaching changes that evolved into ugly and bizarre stories because of unique and extenuating circumstances.

This in no way cheapens what WVU accomplished during those five years or even throughout history. The Mountaineers were 49–16 from 2006–10, played in five bowl games, and won three, including two BCS games. That's the second-highest win total across five years in school history. WVU won 51 games from 2005–09 and 50 from 2004–08. A school-record 14-game winning streak bridged the 2005–06 seasons. Only 11 college football programs had a better five-year record in that same period.

Twelve WVU players from the 2006–10 teams were drafted into the NFL. Four players were academic All-Americans. In 2006, the Mountaineers played the most-watched Thursday night game in ESPN history. A year later, they played in the most-watched Friday night game in the network's history. Mozes's Rimington Trophy in 2006 was the school's first individual award. He and Slaton were the 10th and 11th consensus All-Americans in school history. Slaton was fourth in the voting for the 2006 Heisman Trophy, and White was sixth in 2007 and seventh in 2008. Among the best players WVU has ever enjoyed, they were arguably the best set of teammates.

Many great things have happened in the 119-year history of WVU football. There have been All-Americans and college and professional football hall of fame players. There have been conference and bowl champions. There have been unforgettable plays, games, and seasons.

There have been triumphs and defeats that have been difficult to believe.

It's a program that does more with less. It has the accomplishments of a place with far greater resources. It should never be ashamed of what it's achieved.

Yet for fans, players, and coaches who wanted and expected something unprecedented beginning in 2006, there has been a theme of disappointment. WVU football was supposed to give the state's people the sort of happiness that would forever silence detractors and put to an end the idea that the state couldn't have something great, that it couldn't overcome its social and economic problems.

WVU football had, and still has, that power. But during these years, it reinforced the age-old idea that people can't enjoy the highs because the lows will come. The ups are always followed by downs. With every success, there is a spooky feeling failure isn't far away. West Virginians' inability to enjoy the things they love is an unspeakable burden in this state, where the people love their WVU football, but where the Mountaineers have so often provided a pipeline for pessimism.

1
BEGINNINGS

College football was a fledgling sport late in the nineteenth century. Rutgers and Princeton played the first college game in 1869, but it took a long time for pioneers of the day, names such as Amos Alonzo Stagg and Walter Camp, to help get the game on other campuses.

It hit Morgantown for the first time on November 28, 1891, a full 22 years later. It was an experiment in curiosity, probably along the lines of what club cricket would be today. No one really knew what they were doing, but it looked fun, and if it could happen at other schools, then why not at WVU?

The Mountaineers, many of whom had never seen the game before practicing for the first time, lost their first game to Washington & Jefferson 72–0.

College athletics had none of the financial resources it has today. WVU was a whopping $160 in the hole after buying all the equipment needed to play that first game.

In his 2009 history of the WVU football program, John Antonik, the school's director of new media, revealed that the team used the proceeds from a performance of William Shakespeare's *Richard III* to pay back the debt.

Maybe you know *Richard III*. If not, surely you know the famous first line: "Now is the winter of our discontent." How's that for an omen?

And the play's ending? It's grievous. Let it be known that from the very beginning, football at West Virginia University was founded on a tragedy.

This is a fact. It's also worth remembering—or, perhaps, forgetting—when you think of this other fact: entering the 2012 regular season, the Mountaineers had played 119 years of college football. That's 1,203 games, and WVU had won 701 of them to build a healthy winning percentage. Yet no Football Bowl Subdivision team (that would be Division I for the majority of the audience) has ever won more games without winning a national championship.

Hang all the banners, retire any numbers, champion whatever achievement you want. That one will be there until it's scrubbed out in spectacular fashion.

That Washington & Jefferson game was the only one of the 1891 season. It was bad enough that the Mountaineers—or, as they were known then, the Snakers—took the following season off to get their act together before moving forward.

It worked. WVU lost to Washington & Jefferson again in 1893, but this time just 58–0. That was progress but also the beginning of a troublesome trend. WVU had won its first two games of the season. Washington & Jefferson was the third and final game and, of course, kept the Snakers from their first unbeaten season.

WVU football is a whole lot easier to understand when you study its past. The topics of today, the things that make WVU fans nervous and miserable, that prevent them from enjoying things to their fullest, are actually triggers that are generations old.

WVU won its first championship in 1898. A 6–0 win over Virginia gave the Mountaineers the title of "Champions of the South." That also sparked a celebration on campus that would include parades and bonfires, the first of many times blazes marked a big victory.

Remember when a certain amount of money was required to keep Rich Rodriguez as coach? In 1896, Thomas "Doggie" Trenchard became the school's first coach with a salary. That lured him from the

University of North Carolina, where he was 7-1-1 the year before. Trenchard scheduled 12 games for his first WVU team.

WVU had played all of 13 games in its entire existence before that.

The explanation? Trenchard was promised $100 per game. He made the most of it, too. WVU played Lafayette, the eventual national champion with an 11-0-1 record that season, three times. In three days. The Mountaineers lost 18–0 in Fairmont on October 15, 6–0 in Parkersburg on October 16, and 34–0 in Wheeling on October 17.

That was nothing. On November 26, WVU played to a scoreless tie against the Pittsburgh Athletic Club in Pittsburgh. Later that same day, WVU lost to Mahoning Cycle Club in Youngstown, Ohio.

The team finished 3-7-2 and was outscored 101–14 and shut out nine times. Plenty richer after that season, Trenchard left WVU—for Western University of Pennsylvania, also known as Pitt. It would be 52 years before WVU played another 12-game season.

The 1915 season was filled with the sorts of stories that would get a lot of ink today. "Hail, West Virginia," the university's fight song, was composed and written and ultimately played at a football game for the first time, and fans of WVU were excited about the things to come.

A lot had to do with the coach, Sol Metzger, who is maybe the most interesting coach the school has ever seen. He went to the esteemed boarding school Phillips-Andover Academy in Massachusetts and then to the University of Pennsylvania. There he studied architecture and was on the track and football teams.

Right out of school, Metzger was hired as the coach at Baylor. He worked there for a year and then in 1908 went back to Penn and won the national title with an 11-0-1 record. He quickly moved along to Oregon State in 1909 and was there for just a year, too, but took time off to satisfy a number of personal curiosities, including raising fruit.

Sideline jobs were more of a passion than a diversion. Metzger was a syndicated sports journalist who wrote stories and columns on competitive sports and outdoor activities. He wrote three books, including one on golf with Grantland Rice.

WVU hired Metzger in 1914, and he was the first WVU coach to travel widely for recruiting purposes. He was 5-4 that first season. A year later, he was 5-2-1, but that included the two strangest final scores in the program's history.

On October 23, WVU lost to Washington and Lee by an official score of 1-0. His team actually led 7–6, but Metzger was livid with the officiating. At the end of a series of calls that he deemed unfair, Metzger took his team off the field and went home. Washington and Lee was awarded the win via forfeit. How many times has WVU snatched defeat from the jaws of victory after that?

A week later, WVU beat Marshall 92–6, for the largest margin of victory in school history. That came with a sidebar, though. So confident was Metzger that he said before the game he'd eat his hat if Marshall scored (in 2007 against the University of South Florida, the Mountaineers would have been better off eating their Yankee hats).

The Thundering Herd did score, but with a sneaky play. Today they call it the Tower Play—and it's illegal. Marshall's quarterback threw a 15-yard touchdown pass to a running back who was sitting on the shoulders of an offensive tackle. This created the standard by which future opponents' villainous acts would be measured, whether they were committed by Kellen Winslow or Tremain Mack, Marvin Graves or Donovan McNabb, Vince Fuller or Michael Vick, Antonio Bryant or Larry Fitzgerald, Isaiah Pead or Mardy Gilyard, George Selvie or—well, you get the idea.

Antonik included this gem in his book, one he pulled from the school's 1915 yearbook:

> *Metzger, the Miracle Man, has filled West Virginia with confidence. He has, in two years, many times in the face of ill luck, developed the greatest team that ever drove eleven sets of leather spikes into the West Virginia soil. He has done promises of even greater things in the days to come. The stars of the past season included freshmen. What will they be as juniors? Heretofore, it has been said that if a football coach wished to meet his Waterloo, and lose all the prestige that he ever possessed, let him tackle the job at Morgantown.*

The sky was the limit, except Metzger didn't agree. He left WVU for another school. Does this sound familiar? It marked the beginning of WVU fans' inferiority complex and the pattern of coaches leaving the Mountaineers for other schools. Before Don Nehlen settled in for 21 years, WVU had 29 head coaches from 1891 to 1976, including a coaching change every year from 1894 to 1901. No one stayed for more than five consecutive seasons until Art "Pappy" Lewis served 10 years from 1950 to 1959. Lewis, who was admired locally and nationally and even made *Time* magazine, led WVU through its first extended "golden era," one that included big wins, bowl games, and players such as Fred Wyant, Bruce Bosley, Bobby Moss, Joe Marconi, Joe Nicely, Dick Longfellow, Chuck Howley, and, of course, Sam Huff.

That sort of continuous coaching turnover would cripple a program today. Good luck recruiting when opponents can point at a tradition of coaches running off, or being run off, after just a few seasons.

Metzger's exit wasn't a first, but it recalled what Trenchard had done years before. Metzger didn't leave for just another school. He left for Washington & Jefferson. That was the rival back then, so much so that the words of "Hail, West Virginia" include this line: "Others may be black or crimson, but for us it's Gold and Blue"—Washington & Jefferson's colors being, of course, black and crimson.

The athletic director at the time, George Pyle, came up with an interesting idea for how WVU would move on without Metzger. Again, this may sound a bit familiar: he let Metzger's assistants, Mont McIntire and Elgie Tobin, work as co-coaches.

It wasn't a disaster, though. The two achieved a harmony and went 5-2-2 and 6-3-1 with a very good roster that included the school's first two All-American players, Ira Errett Rodgers and Russ Bailey. Things were again looking good at WVU. Right on cue, the 1918 season was cancelled as World War I and influenza took their toll. Ninety-three years later, athletic director Oliver Luck decided he'd let Bill Stewart and Dana Holgorsen coach in tandem. The 2011 season wasn't cancelled, but it too was preceded by a historic conflict and an outbreak (of backstabbing) that made people sick.

A few years after the end of the Pappy Lewis era, Jim Carlen was named coach in 1966. The Mountaineers had their first coach who pushed for changes and things he thought would be better for the university. Chief among his many concerns was the state's highway system, which made traveling to or from Morgantown for games or recruiting a lot more difficult than he believed it should be.

Carlen also helped WVU get out of the Southern Conference, an exercise fans got to know quite well in 2011. WVU won the league two times with an overall record below .500 and another time with a 5-4-1 overall record. Carlen believed WVU needed a better schedule to get more exposure, larger crowds, and better recruits.

He also pushed for better pay for his assistants and sought better players for WVU. He tried to find ways to recruit more black players, offer more scholarships, and allow players to take a redshirt year and gain a competitive advantage later in their careers.

Had he insisted on a subscriber website for fans, free tickets for high school coaches, or the right for his players to sell back books and keep the money, Carlen would have foreshadowed Rodriguez by four decades.

And, like Rodriguez, Carlen didn't get the cooperation he desired. He coached the Peach Bowl victory against South Carolina in 1969 and a day later accepted an offer to coach Texas Tech.

His replacement was his assistant, Bobby Bowden. He was 42-26 in six seasons, but he was never accepted by the fans. They criticized and questioned him, sometimes with cause, and planted "For Sale" signs in his yard. Fraternities had fun hanging sheets out their windows that ridiculed Bowden. Morgantownians even hung him in effigy.

He led WVU to a 9-3 record in 1975 and a Peach Bowl win, but he left for Florida State after the season. His success there is a reminder of how WVU sometimes doesn't realize just how good things are, of how people are sometimes guilty of overzealous emotions and reactions, of how expectations are not always in line with possibilities, and of how patience is sometimes the best practice. Bowden was scorned before he departed.

He had his moments and his miseries, including one of those catastrophic games that have helped define the careers of many WVU coaches. WVU led Pitt 35–8 at halftime of the 1970 Backyard Brawl. The Mountaineers lost 36–35, and Bowden and his players still regret changing their offensive philosophy after halftime.

Bowden learned from his history, though, and was not condemned to repeat it.

"You never heard of me sitting on the ball again after that, did you?" Bowden said. "All you heard was people complaining about me running up the score. Well, you're dadgum right. I learned that in 1970 against Pittsburgh. I wasn't sitting on any score after that."

Nehlen had a few calamities as well, though at least he was around to experience them with fans who grew to appreciate him and his loyalty. Nehlen did what others before him did not. He resisted overtures from other schools and stuck with WVU.

Ask around about the moments that set WVU football on the upward path. You'll get answers that involve games and players, but one of the most significant, most underrated moments came at the end of the 1982 season. Nehlen declined an offer to coach South Carolina, which had let go of Carlen. This was even bigger than accepting the WVU job despite suggestions from those close to him, including his boss at the time, Michigan coach Bo Schembechler, who urged him not to go to WVU, to stick with the Wolverines a few more seasons to get a real job and not one he'd want to leave after a few seasons. That was the reputation the Mountaineer program had upon Nehlen's arrival. It was as deserved as it was accurate, but Nehlen changed it.

By 1988, Nehlen had the Mountaineers in the Fiesta Bowl, playing for the national title against Notre Dame. Yet before the WVU fans who had been waiting their lifetimes for this game could really get settled in, quarterback Major Harris, a Heisman Trophy finalist, dislocated his shoulder on the third play. He'd return later, but he couldn't throw the ball very far or effectively, and the Mountaineers were clearly doomed from that point forward.

After the 1993 regular season, WVU and Nebraska were the only unbeaten teams, but the Mountaineers were kept out of the national championship game. WVU was instead picked for the Cotton Bowl against Texas A&M.

After some discussions, WVU ended up in the Sugar Bowl, which had a more lucrative $4 million payout that was better for the university and the Big East, but it also came with a more formidable opponent, the Southeastern Conference champion Florida Gators.

The Mountaineers scored a touchdown to cap an 80-yard drive to start the game. Early in the second quarter with the score tied 7–7, co-quarterback Darren Studstill was in the game. In a play that became symbolic of the mismatch, Studstill scrambled and gained a few yards but was taken off his feet and driven into the ground by a humongous hit from linebacker Monty Grow.

Studstill was struck directly under the chin but tried to keep himself together. He threw an incomplete pass on second down. Before third down, he tried to adjust his chin strap but had it sideways, perpendicular from where it was supposed to be and somehow, comically, fastened above his facemask.

The Mountaineers needed a timeout to compose themselves. On the next snap, Grow blitzed Studstill and hit him on the release. Lawrence Wright intercepted the fluttering ball and returned it 52 yards for a touchdown.

The game, as well as WVU's argument to put in a claim for the national title, was over. The Mountaineers lost 41–7.

Nebraska then lost the Orange Bowl. To Bobby Bowden. The coach and Florida State had their first national championship while WVU had whiffed in its second opportunity for its first.

To start off the 1994 season, WVU got its game against Nebraska and lost, 31–0.

In 1996, WVU was 7-0 and ranked No. 12 while playing host to No. 25 Miami. Up 7–3 with just 29 seconds to go, all the Mountaineers needed to do to get a rare win against the Hurricanes was simply punt the football on a fourth-and-short.

Trouble was, WVU had already had five punts blocked in its first seven games. Miami cornerback Tremain Mack had already blocked seven punts in his career. He made it eight when he smacked the ball just as it left the punter's foot. The ball bounced up to one Miami player, who handed it to Nate Brooks, who ran in for the game-winning score. Most WVU fans will forever believe it was an illegal lateral.

Three years later, Virginia Tech was No. 3 when it came to Morgantown on its way to the national championship game against Bowden and Florida State. On November 6, though, WVU managed a 20–19 lead behind the emergency effort of quarterback Brad Lewis. In for an injured Marc Bulger, he threw an 18-yard touchdown pass to Khori Ivy with 1:15 remaining to give WVU the advantage.

Freshman quarterback Michael Vick rallied the Hokies, who had no timeouts. In one stellar display, Vick cut sharply to stay in bounds and raced up the sideline past defenders who were backing off the play, certain Vick would step out of bounds to stop the clock. Vick kept on going and picked up 24 yards to move to WVU's 36 with 23 seconds to go. One completion moved the ball to the 27, where Shayne Graham lined up and kicked a 44-yard field goal to win the game 22–20 as time expired.

Nehlen lasted one more season at WVU. He took the Mountaineers to unprecedented heights but coached a few shockers and heartbreakers that the team's fans would never, ever forget. It was a period when WVU proved it could—almost—reach the top of the college football world, getting just close enough to make those disappointments sting all the more.

2
TRANSITION

They sat there in silence, *a thick cloud of gloom filling the West Virginia locker room. Large, muscled men, heads buried in their hands, stunned by yet another impossible defeat on their home field.*

That's when Don Nehlen walked into the room. They thought nothing could shock them more than the way they had given away a 31–27 decision to Syracuse, leaving them at 4-4 for the season.

They couldn't imagine the way their coach would turn their world upside down by announcing he was resigning after the season's final game.

After 21 years, after 199 victories, the man who had carried the West Virginia program to national prominence with a pair of undefeated regular seasons and shots at a national championship was stepping aside.

"I just felt it was time for me to go down the pike," he was to say later.

He wasn't sure what to say to his players, not at this moment, not after a coaching mistake had cost his team the most important game it had played this year.

Conversely, they didn't know how to react, what to say, what to do.

Their season was crumbling before them. They openly were second-guessing the decision to throw a pass with a 27–24 lead and 4:17 remaining, a pass that was intercepted, leading to one final Syracuse drive and a touchdown pass from freshman quarterback R.J. Anderson to Malik Campbell from 13 yards out with 10 seconds to go.

One player, before Nehlen addressed the team, walked past the media and mumbled:

"Bull---- coaching, and you can write that."

Now, 10 minutes later, that player and his teammates were being informed the Don Nehlen era of coaching was over.

"The end of an era has come about," said offensive tackle Tanner Russell, a senior captain. "What he's done for this program, this city and this state will never be forgotten."

Indeed, Nehlen replaced Frank Cignetti after four losing seasons. He came after a head coaching stint at his alma mater, Bowling Green, and a learning period under Bo Schembechler as a Michigan assistant.

He came and stayed 21 years, only to be faced on the day he announced his retirement with one of his toughest defeats, toughest because he knew he had to shoulder much of the blame.

As he began addressing the media, his wife of 43 years, Merry Ann; his son, Dan, the equipment manager; his son-in-law Jeff Hostetler, a former player and Super Bowl hero; his daughter, his grandchildren, were all on hand as he had to first speak of the defeat.

"We should have won that football game. We should have won it. Coaching error. The ball should have never been thrown. We should never have given them the interception. Stupid. Absolute stupidity," he said.

That had to be hard to say moments before he revealed to the world what he had told athletic director Ed Pastilong two weeks earlier that he was retiring.

Nehlen is seven weeks shy of his 65th birthday.

"Three more games on the sideline like this one and I won't see 66," he said.

The work load has just become too much.

"I've had a great run here. It's a lot of fun but it's time for somebody else," Nehlen said. "This job is about 85 hours a week. It's seven days a week about 10 and a half months out of the year. We'll let some younger guy do it."

That was the game story in Morgantown's *Dominion Post* on November 5, 2000, and one that would win Bob Hertzel a first-place award for news writing from the Associated Press Sports Editors. It is a time capsule for the final few seasons Don Nehlen spent as WVU's coach.

It's one description of one postgame, but it covers so many topics from Nehlen's end. Defeat. Disappointment. Disenchantment. The Mountaineers weren't winning and weren't taking it very well.

They weren't alone, either.

Nehlen's retirement announcement came after a fan had hired a plane to fly around Mountaineer Field towing a banner that said "Nehlen Must Go." It echoed the actions of fans a generation earlier, the ones who helped drive Bobby Bowden away by hanging him in effigy.

People were turning against Nehlen. Following the 1993 season, Nehlen's final seven seasons were played all of nine games above .500—and that included nonconference games against Ball State, Louisiana Tech, Kent State, Western Michigan, Tulsa, Navy, Miami of Ohio, and Idaho.

The Mountaineers were under .500 twice, a game over once, and two games over twice. They were better than fourth place in the Big East just once, and that tie for second place in 1998 actually left them fourth in the standings. With Miami restored and Virginia Tech emerging, the situation wasn't likely to change.

The best record was 8-4 in 1996, with the nation's best defense, and in 1998, when Nehlen had quite possibly his most talented team. Jerry Porter, Charles Fisher, Marc Bulger, Gary Stills, Amos Zereoue,

Barrett Green, Corey McIntyre, Solomon Page, Anthony Becht, and John Thornton all played for those Mountaineers and then in the NFL.

Yet that season got away early when the Mountaineers opened with a home loss to top-ranked Ohio State. Nehlen would say again and again that the high hopes and the early letdown made certain WVU was never the same that season.

Nehlen liked to say that a special player had "it," whatever "it" was, but from that season a concern grew that Nehlen himself no longer had it. Recruiting probably wasn't much different than it had been through the years. There was more area to cover and there were more players to scout and more competition from more quality college programs, but it wasn't more important. It was more publicized, though, and if Nehlen wasn't landing players, people knew about it. If WVU wasn't occupying a slot somewhere near the top of the recruiting class rankings, then he wasn't doing his job very well, was he? It was a new measure by which coaches were judged.

An older gauge was age, and that was working against Nehlen, too. That was something he couldn't control, but it was used against him in concert with other arguments about his recruiting performance or his conservative offense. Coaches creeping up into their 60s were becoming more and more rare, and the increasing, year-round demands placed upon college coaches were, at times, too much for an aging man.

Nothing has changed so many years later. Of the 120 Football Bowl Subdivision schools, only 17 of their coaches were in their 60s when the 2011 season started—10 years after the youthful Rodriguez replaced the aging Nehlen. Only 11 would be 65 or older during the season.

Many of these were marquee names, too, such as Joe Paterno, Frank Beamer, and Steve Spurrier. Others were oddities who had retired and returned, such as Bill Snyder at Kansas State, Chris Ault at Nevada, and 77-year-old Howard Schnellenberger, once a winner at Miami who was rebuilding Florida Atlantic

Colleges have adjusted what they require from their coaches, too, and there's been an emphasis on the energetic, compelling coaches who are starved for success. In other words, young coaches.

Since Nehlen's resignation, only Beamer, Bob Stoops, Mack Brown, Kirk Ferentz, and Troy University's Larry Blakeney stuck with their schools. Every other school has made at least one change, including WVU, which has now made three changes and was one of the 23 to make a change before the 2011 season.

In 2001, Rich Rodriguez was exactly what the Mountaineers were looking for in Nehlen's successor. He was a West Virginian and a WVU graduate. He'd lived and understood the relationship between the school and the state, and he knew what it would mean to bring a winner to both. And he was young and had grown up in the game while studying the new model of a head coach.

"I can't imagine a better place to live than West Virginia, and I know about it firsthand," he once said. "When I tell recruits about the friendly people in this state, about the great education you can get at the university, about the way your neighbors and your friends become like family, and about the way Mountaineers love their football team, I'm telling them about me and my life. When they hear me speaking from experience like that, I think it carries a little more weight."

Rodriguez was from Grant Town, in Marion County, and a four-sport prep star at North Marion. He was an all-state player in basketball and football and helped the Huskies win the state football title in 1980.

He grew up, like so many others, coming to WVU games, first at the old Mountaineer Field when he was in just eighth or ninth grade. He dreamed about wearing the blue jersey and running out of the tunnel for tens of thousands of screaming fans.

"I can't remember who we played, but I remember West Virginia won, and the atmosphere of walking up to the stadium through the campus and all the people in the stands," he said. "That was impressive to a young athlete. I decided after that day that I wanted to try to reach the level of Division I sports. Although I wasn't sure which sport it would be, football or basketball, I knew that was my goal."

He chose to walk on and play football at WVU, and he toiled with the Mountaineers for three seasons. He'd ultimately get his scholarship and play in the defensive backfield as a safety. In 1984, he made 37 tackles, 27 solo, and he enjoyed no greater moment than his interception against Penn State late in a 17–14 victory.

The Mountaineers and Nittany Lions had played every year since 1947, and WVU had won just three times—and not since 1955, the last win in a three-game winning streak. Rodriguez had his career highlight in one of the most memorable ways available to a player of his skill level at his position.

"There was a tremendous atmosphere in the stadium that night, and I was starting and then the fact we won—amazing," he said. "I will never forget the energy and how it carried over across town following the game."

This was to Rodriguez what the busted play and run around the corner against Penn State was to Major Harris, what running over Brandon Meriweather was to Quincy Wilson, what Ron Wolfley's fake punt touchdown was against Boston College, what knocking down Louisville's two-point conversion pass in the third overtime was to Eric Wicks, what the acrobatic touchdown catch against Pitt was for John Pennington.

Maybe this wouldn't keep Rodriguez in the minds of fans through the years he was away from WVU, but it was what they thought of when they were reminded of his name.

Rodriguez worked under Nehlen as a student assistant in 1985–86 and then took a job running special teams and coaching defensive backs at Salem College. In 1987, the same person who would become one of college football's most creative and most accomplished offensive coaches was promoted to be Salem's defensive coordinator. A year later, Rodriguez, all of 24 years of age, was named the head coach.

He was the youngest head coach in all of college football. Not long after, he was the youngest unemployed head coach in college football.

"I went 2-8 my first year and got the program dropped," Rodriguez said of the administration's decision to do away with football after the 1988 season. "I was thinking there probably aren't a whole lot of programs who are going to hire a guy who got his program terminated."

Rodriguez was just a few weeks from marrying his college sweetheart, Rita, a former WVU cheerleader who stood by her coach when things got tough for the first time. Rodriguez returned to WVU as a volunteer assistant, hardly the most lucrative position and a test not only for his financial future, but also his football future. He remembered thinking, "If I want to stay in coaching after all this, then I'm a lifer."

Glenville State hired Rodriguez as its head coach in 1990 and went 1-7-1. When he celebrated his 100th career victory in 2007, he recalled that Glenville State was where he did his greatest coaching job.

"We only had about 30 guys on the team and half of them didn't play in high school," he said. "And I was the biggest guy in the room."

Rodriguez would never allow for limitations. He only coached to win. He hated losing and detested the concept of moral victories. He took over a Pioneers program that hadn't won the West Virginia Conference since 1959, and he simply proclaimed that Glenville State was going to win the WVC. Soon.

It touched off a celebration that made Rodriguez proud, that made him laugh.

"They were so uncoordinated they couldn't even high-five each other," he said. "I thought, 'This might not be as easy as I think it's going to be.'"

The team got a standing ovation the first time it got a first down. When the band played the fight song after the first touchdown, it sounded terrible. Players had to tell a cringing Rodriguez that the band wasn't used to playing the song.

"At least the expectations aren't high," he thought.

The Pioneers won the conference in 1993 and played for the NAIA national championship. Three more conference titles would follow. People were paying attention to this system that spread out the offense and caused the defense to adjust accordingly, and then attacked with quarterbacks who threw the ball like crazy.

Sometimes the quarterback could run on a draw, but that was either a busted play or desperation. The Pioneers would throw it 50 or 60 times a game.

Rodriguez's Glenville State exploits caught the eye of another WVU connection. Tommy Bowden, Bobby Bowden's son and a former receiver for the Mountaineers, hired Rodriguez to be his offensive coordinator at Tulane.

Rodriguez inherited Shaun King as his quarterback in 1997, and this is where Rodriguez really built his offense around the abilities of his quarterback for the first time. King passed for 6,072 yards and 62 touchdowns and rushed for 1,144 yards and 16 touchdowns in his two seasons under Rodriguez. He finished 10th in the Heisman Trophy voting in 1998, when he became the first NCAA player to pass for 300 yards and rush for 100 in the same game. The Tampa Bay Buccaneers drafted him in the second round in 1999.

"[Rodriguez] gave me a chance to showcase my skills," King said.

The Green Wave finished undefeated, and Bowden was hired away by Clemson. Despite the success of the offense and the 11-0 regular-season record, the administration allowed Rodriguez to follow Bowden to Death Valley. Rodriguez wasn't even afforded the chance to coach Tulane in the bowl game, apparently because the people who mattered weren't fans of the way Rodriguez handled and presented himself on the field.

The Green Wave hired Chris Scelfo, the offensive line coach and assistant head coach at Georgia, and he led the team to a Liberty Bowl win against BYU and a final ranking of No. 7 in both the AP and coaches' polls. While Rodriguez went on to fame and fortune at BCS programs, Tulane went 37-57 and forced out Scelfo after the 2006 season. He had two winning records and one bowl appearance and never finished better than fifth in Conference USA.

Imagine if Tulane had kept Rodriguez, and he started plucking players from Louisiana and Mississippi and Oklahoma and Texas and kept winning in a mediocre conference. That decision was the first of two forks in the road for Rodriguez that ultimately delivered him to WVU.

The second came a year later. Clemson was 6-6 in 1999, but it sure looked like the offense, despite the transition in the first year with Rodriguez in control, wasn't the culprit. The Tigers scored 30 or more points seven times and averaged more than 400 yards of offense for just the third time ever.

They had a game changer and a ticket seller in quarterback Woodrow Dantzler. He was a talent and the kind of player who did the kind of things that made athletic directors across the country sit on the edge of their office chairs and wonder about Rodriguez.

In 1999, Dantzler passed for 1,506 yards and rushed for 588--as the backup who played only 28 of the team's 48 quarters. He was on the short side at just 5 feet, 11 inches tall, but he was thick at 200 pounds and possessed speed that distinguished him at quarterback.

With Dantzler, Rodriguez could return to the laboratory, like he had at Glenville State, and experiment with ways to baffle a defense. In 2001, Dantzler became the NCAA's first player to pass for 2,000 yards and run for 1,000 in a season.

"It was nothing but fun to be in that offense," Dantzler said. "I always had so many chances to be versatile."

He clinched a game in the fourth quarter against North Carolina with a 56-yard touchdown run and a graceful navigation of the tight space between the sideline and angry defenders trying to pursue him. Later that season, he broke a 52-year-old school record when he had 435 yards of offense—16-for-23 passing for 252 yards and 22 carries for 183 yards—against Maryland.

Dantzler averaged 209 yards of offense in his limited appearances in 1999, which was the second-best total in school history, and was No. 31 nationally in passing efficiency. Dantzler was actually eighth in the Atlantic Coast Conference in rushing in 1999, better than even Michael Vick.

No longer was a running play by the quarterback a trick play sprung by Rodriguez. Dantzler and Rodriguez had two ways to beat you, and college football was taking note.

Texas Tech wanted Rodriguez badly after the 1999 regular season. He was there twice in late November, and, as far as all the experts were concerned, he was the obvious and imminent pick. Texas Tech's athletic director and chancellor came out and said Rodriguez was the leading candidate. Even Rodriguez figured it was just a matter of time.

On Monday, November 29, 1999, Rodriguez was interviewed by the *Lubbock (Texas) Avalanche-Journal* and revealed an uncanny awareness of a state law stating university jobs must be open for 10 days before a hiring can be announced. "I don't think the job can be offered until next Wednesday," he said.

The next Monday, Rodriguez removed his name from consideration. The Red Raiders hired Oklahoma's offensive coordinator, Mike Leach, who assembled a staff that included a young assistant he'd known at other stops named Dana Holgorsen.

Rodriguez never really concealed the reason he got out of the running for that job. Sooner or later, he knew the WVU job would be open.

"He struggled with that decision so bad," Rita remembered in John Antonik's 2009 book. "He always wanted to come back here. We knew if he went to Texas Tech there was no way that would happen because of the contract and a large buyout. He passed on that job hoping things would work out here."

It was a gamble, but Rodriguez was a gambler and, as he often did, he got his wish when Nehlen announced his resignation. Clemson was playing host to Florida State that night in what was then known as the "Bowden Bowl," between coaches Bobby and Tommy. WVU had played and lost to Syracuse earlier in the day and Nehlen's announcement made its way throughout college football.

"Now the rumors will start," Rodriguez thought.

The courtship was quick. The list of other candidates was relatively short, though it did include another Bowden. Terry, who had played running back for the Mountaineers, had resigned his head coach position at Auburn during the 1998 season amid a list of issues that nevertheless wouldn't prevent him and his pedigree from making a serious case for the WVU job.

The pick was Rodriguez, though, and he was introduced on November 26. Immediately, he embarked on doing and saying all the right things. His Mountaineers would pick up a lot of yards and score a lot of points. His Mountaineers would "spot the ball" and use a frenetic pace to stun and tire their opponents. His Mountaineers would move with an urgency that seemed as though their hair was on fire. His Mountaineers would come from all over the country but especially the most fertile recruiting areas out there.

Rodriguez gave WVU credibility while allowing the school to maintain its prideful prerequisites. He was the innovative offensive coach who was respected throughout the industry and coveted by a variety of teams. Yet the Mountaineers had him. He'd waited for them and they'd come calling. He'd worked for that call, and all that effort and all the results left WVU with almost no other choice.

"He comes from very humble roots," Terry Bowden said. "He wasn't born with a silver whistle in his mouth. He had to go out there and learn his trade. West Virginia, in his time there, was not necessarily running the West Coast offense. He had to go out and study that. I think he's a self-made man."

Rodriguez had more than the strong connection to the school and the state. He was about as close as the school could come to the antithesis of what Nehlen had become in his later years. WVU would have a modern identity on offense, and an aggressive, confident one to replace Nehlen's conservative approach. Rodriguez was young, eager, and ready to put in the 85-hour weeks, seven days a week for 10 1/2 months of the year.

Rodriguez aimed WVU toward the top, too. He wanted improvements to the stadium and the team facilities that could help the Mountaineers catch up to the Hurricanes and the Hokies in perception and recruiting. If WVU were to win the games on the field, it had to be competitive off the field, too.

Above all else, the most important thing he would say was that he wanted to be at WVU. So many years and so many dramas later, it's easy to forget what a commodity Rodriguez was and how significant it was for WVU to acquire his services. Rodriguez did everything, at first, to express his gratitude. People wonder now if it was a lie, or just another line to get the right people behind him, but at the time, it was what made him WVU's coach.

"I think in this profession, you are fortunate when other schools call you and seek you out," he said in 2001. "Over the last couple of years, that window of opportunity was open for me. And I think most coaches always keep an eye on the place where they grew up, where they went to school. That's certainly been the case with me, so the timing of the opening at West Virginia was perfect last fall. But I didn't come back just because it was home. I wanted to be sure I was going to a place where I felt we could win big."

3
SWIMMING

Through the years, West Virginia fans had come to expect a long and dreary wait between the seemingly annual bowl game loss—that is, if the team made a bowl—and the start of the next season. With the change in coaches came a change in the pace of the offseason.

The Mountaineers won their last bowl game for Nehlen against a stacked Mississippi team and then began the anticipation for Rich Rodriguez to draw back the curtain and reveal his offense. Winter conditioning, spring practice, and the summertime zoomed by in 2001. Rodriguez could do no wrong. He joked that the press conference that introduced him as head coach was the first to have a tailgate. Fans swooned over his recruiting and his aggressive approach to the weight room. They flocked to his speaking opportunities throughout the state, and they bought what he was selling.

This flashy offense generated visions of receivers running all over the field and defenders catching their breath, but it also came with a catchy marketing label that people ate up the first time they heard it.

"Spot the Ball" took control of fans who had grown tired of the conservative, between-the-tackles power offense of Nehlen. The shotgun offense sounded cool. The possibility of a running quarterback turned back the clock to the days of Major Harris. The prospect of a no-huddle offense that would pressure and fatigue the defense made this seem like an offense that could only be stopped by the end zone.

Rodriguez made it sound so simple, so obvious that everyone could relate and revel in it. The roots of his offense were so basic, yet so brilliant.

"I was just like a fan," Rodriguez said the day he was named head coach. "You watch a game and your team does nothing the whole first half or the whole game until they get in their two-minute offense. Then they get up and down the field and you think, 'Why don't they do that the whole game?'"

Any fan who had thought that now had a new hero. This was the common sense, common man's approach to offense, and yet no one they knew ever did it, or considered it, until Rodriguez arrived and vowed to play that way. Rodriguez also promised a system that could adapt to the defense and then conquer it. Ideally, his teams would be balanced in terms of a run-pass ratio, so long as the Mountaineers could force that balance by effectively mixing up the play calls and keeping the defense spinning.

Yet if Rodriguez could pass it 50 times because the defense created that possibility, he'd do it. He felt he could do the same with the run, too, and it was that part of the playbook that was growing, that he was proud of as a coach. He didn't want to be seen as a coach with one strength. He wanted to present dual personalities to frighten opponents, to continue to evolve to prove his mental prowess. All coaches have an ego. Rodriguez was only different because his was so big so soon.

Maybe it was necessary. He overhauled his coaching staff and only one assistant, Bill Stewart, came back. He made sure he'd share an office with coaches who shared his vision and his philosophy.

Rodriguez was forcing parts of his roster together to make his offense function, and a bunch of them didn't fit. He wanted slimmer, quicker linemen than what Nehlen's staff had recruited. The quarterback situation was a mess and the players Rodriguez actually recruited were not there yet.

Other parts, other players, he just didn't have time for them. Many left, some by choice and some because they felt they had no choice. Rodriguez was narrowing down the roster and making room for the athletes he needed by bouncing the players who wouldn't be and didn't want to be a part of his change.

He inherited a team that had hovered around average in the Big East in preceding years. In so many ways, he had to change things and make the changes by imposing his strong and sometimes abrasive personality. If you didn't like it—and sometimes, because he didn't like you—you were free to go. If you could take it, you were fit to be a part of what came next.

It wasn't entirely popular among the fans, many of whom weren't happy with what they had heard about Rodriguez and his assistants and how they did their jobs. There were whispers that important people weren't too happy with things, like the way practices went and the language that was used within.

Rodriguez knew he had a temper, and he confessed to the *Charleston Gazette,* "When I'm ticked, I'm really ticked. And it seems like I get ticked a lot on the field." Oh, he had a cute little quip for that, one that made people laugh and forget. He'd retell a story about how players taken aback by his personality would remark, "You're not the same guy who recruited me. You were so nice then." When the laughter stopped, the fact remained that some players just didn't like the way he treated them.

Mostly, though, there was this obstacle to overcome: WVU hadn't seen a coaching change in so long that it was difficult to accept all the differences between the past and the present. There was a new edge and it was attained through what then seemed like unconventional methods. Maybe players were treated more like property than people, but the cruel reality was that this was the way the game was played. Compassion was pushed aside to make room for competition.

"We used to use the analogy if you took 100 guys and went to the pool, some guys are going to jump in the water and some guys are going to put their toes in the water and test it before they decide to get in or get out, and some guys are going to say, 'Hey, I ain't swimming,'" said former tight end coach and recruiting coordinator Herb Hand. "That first year, we had a lot of guys decide not to swim."

The plan was compromised when the 2001 season began, first by the enormous expectations of fans who so desperately wanted success, but also by the roster created by the transition. It was nearly impossible to be a good team in 2001.

And the Mountaineers were not. Not even close. WVU did craft some notoriety, though. A 3-8 record was the worst since Frank Cignetti went 2-9 in 1978. There were only two other seasons in school history (0-8-2 in 1960, 2-8 in 1950) where the Mountaineers finished more than four games below .500.

Rodriguez did deliver on some of the exciting promises, though. He threw it 40 times in his first game, out of necessity. WVU lost at Boston College, 34–10, and committed five turnovers. Just 22 passes were completed. Three were intercepted. The Mountaineers lost two fumbles and committed nine penalties; they were happy just to get that one out of the way.

The next week was probably a better indication of the struggles that would come. WVU won and had 350 yards of offense and no turnovers, but beat a really bad Ohio University team only 20–3. Those Bobcats finished 1-10 and were shut out twice.

The Mountaineers got over .500 the next week, though they wouldn't reach that mark again for more than a year. WVU beat Kent State and its dazzling dual-threat quarterback Josh Cribbs, who became just the second-ever opponent to pass and rush for more than 100 yards in a game against WVU. He later became an all-pro kick returner for the NFL's Cleveland Browns.

Then came the return to reality. The Mountaineers lost four in a row for the first time since 1986, against 25th-ranked Maryland, No. 6 Virginia Tech, Notre Dame, and No. 1 Miami. In 16 quarters, WVU managed only five touchdowns and was outscored 146–47. The Mountaineers committed 17 turnovers and created only six.

The rush defense was terrible; teams didn't have to pass against WVU to be successful, and passes weren't necessary when teams led by as much as they often did—this was probably the biggest reason the Mountaineers finished No. 1 against the pass. In those four games, five individual opponents ran for more than 100 yards—and two more had 92 and 76 yards. The Mountaineers allowed 962 yards and 14 touchdowns on the ground those four games while WVU's entire offense totaled 1,138 yards.

Then came the totally unexpected treat of the season, the 80–7 victory against Rutgers. WVU had 627 yards of offense, including 462 on the ground, and averaged 10 yards per snap. Quincy Wilson, the fourth-string running back, played late and managed 129 yards and a 60-yard touchdown. This was fun.

"I sensed something different after Miami," Rodriguez said to MSNSportsNet.com after the game. "As soon as the game was over, there was something different, a different attitude."

In no way could anyone have predicted the massacre of Rutgers. Running backs Avon Cobourne and Cassel Smith both scored two touchdowns in the first quarter, and a field goal made it 31–0. The Mountaineers realized sportsmanship might be in order. WVU's attempt to stop scoring in the second quarter was met with Rutgers' inability to comply, and WVU scored four touchdowns in a little more than four minutes.

Rutgers committed two of its eight turnovers at that stage of the game. WVU safety Shawn Hackett outscored the Scarlet Knights by himself by returning a fumble and an interception for touchdowns. The second one made it 58–0, and Hackett celebrated by throwing the football into the stands. That earned a 15-yard penalty. The celebration continued and drew another flag.

No worries. Todd James, who was the kickoff specialist, jogged out onto the field for placekicker Brenden Rauh and drilled a 50-yard extra point.

The really weird part? Rodriguez was positively pleased. "I don't think I heard him scream more than three times today," safety Rick Sherrod said on the team website afterward. "Other than that, he just kept quiet. That was my first time not hearing him scream that much since he came here—the first day he came here."

Ultimately, it was just one day, a wonderful day, but in no way was the start of something new. The Mountaineers lost their final three games, including a 17–14 loss at home against Temple. WVU had won 10 in a row against the lowly Owls. It was the rock-bottom moment of the year, and the fans knew it, too. Only 37,120 attended. The volume of the voices growing against Rodriguez was heightened.

There was a telling lack of discipline in that game. Three personal foul penalties occurred in the stretch of six plays in the first quarter. Three more would follow before the end of the game. By the end of the season, WVU was No. 102 of 115 Division I teams in penalty yards per game. The offense came up with nothing on five of its first six trips into the red zone, and that included a pair of misses on short field-goal attempts.

Then again, that showed how thin WVU really was. Rauh was hurt in a practice a few days before the game, and James was forced into the main role. An injury to a kicker was the difference between victory and defeat against a team like Temple, a program so bad it had been informed earlier that year it would be kicked out of the Big East come 2004.

A loss to Pitt ended the season, but started the offseason. WVU fans quickly learned that the offseason would no longer be a quiet, settled period under Rodriguez. Despite the record and quality of play and discipline, despite the grumbling from inside and on the outside, and despite the player turnover, Rodriguez asked for and received a contract extension after the 2001 season and just before national signing day.

Any hints that other schools might put in recruits' ears about WVU getting rid of Rodriguez were brushed away. The extension would keep Rodriguez at WVU for the entire time a player in the 2002 recruiting class was in Morgantown.

Even with his signature on new and extended contracts, Rodriguez would avoid ever making the same commitment. What WVU did, whether it realized it or not, was capitulate for the first time and at the first opportunity.

The following December, Rodriguez was contacted by people he called "friends" of the University of Alabama. Soon thereafter, he revealed the University of Kentucky had also contacted him about moving along to the Southeastern Conference. The difference that time was that Rodriguez had all the leverage after a 9-3 regular-season record in 2002. WVU was a far, far better team in the second season, mostly because players had experience and identities. Avon Cobourne, Lance Nimmo, James "Dirty" Davis, Ben Collins, Angel Estrada, and a wealth of seniors gave the team a voice.

"Those guys were the ones saying, 'We're not having this again. Get in the pool,'" Hand said.

It worked, and there were hardly any ripples. Rasheed Marshall was now the unquestioned quarterback, and it made a difference. The year before, Brad Lewis had that unenviable task, and loud and large portions of the fans grew to rather dislike him.

They booed him often, even though he wasn't fit to run the Rodriguez offense, and cheered when he broke his collarbone in his final game with his parents in attendance. I had a friend who fashioned something of a homemade jersey, taking a plain, white T-shirt and inking Lewis's No. 14 on the front and "Boo this man!" on the back. He was cheered more than Lewis.

The negativity affected Lewis, too. Remember, he started that season as a bit of a hero, revered for leading a comeback to a near-victory against Virginia Tech in 1999 and for playing out of his mind in the Music City Bowl in 2000. He was a pretty good athlete and a very good competitor, but he was ill-suited to the changes Rodriguez was making. After the 2001 season, I saw Lewis out in Morgantown and mentioned the invitation the Chicago Bears had extended to Lewis to attend a tryout camp. I added that one of my friends was a Bears fan, to which Lewis replied, in a revealing manner, "Is he pissed?"

Lewis deserved better than that, but he was a victim of the expectations.

Marshall, who was sidelined much of the 2001 season with a broken wrist, flourished with Rodriguez and could pose the dual threats the system required. The losses in 2002 were more acceptable than the year before. The first came at No. 25 Wisconsin, 34–17, though WVU acquitted itself well enough by winning the second half

14–0. The 48–17 loss at Maryland was bad, but the score of the 40–23 home loss to top-ranked Miami was misleading, as the game had been tied 23–23 in the third quarter.

The Mountaineers recovered by beating Temple, Boston College, and then No. 13 Virginia Tech and No. 17 Pitt on the road. The reward was a spot in the Associated Press poll at No. 15 and a date with Virginia in the Continental Tire Bowl. Against Virginia and its quarterback, Atlantic Coast Conference player of the year Matt Schaub, WVU lost 48–22 and was never really in the contest.

Rodriguez had all sorts of things in his corner, but nothing larger than momentum and his status as an up-and-coming coach. This worried administrators in the university and athletic department. Every time a school fired a coach, WVU had to think and fret. Rodriguez had the leverage, and he'd hold onto it for as long as he was on campus.

WVU started the 2003 season 1-3, and the groans about the head coach returned after the 9-4 record in 2002 had brushed them aside. To make matters worse, the Mountaineers next traveled to No. 2 Miami for a Thursday night game. They played well, and while they gave up yards to the Hurricanes, they didn't allow many touchdowns.

With two minutes remaining and the Mountaineers trailing by six, Marshall flicked a screen pass left to running back Wilson. The play appeared doomed as Miami's speed outplayed the design of the screen and totally nullified the blocking scheme. But Wilson shook one defender in the backfield and then sped away from a leaping tackler before cutting left and away from another leaper. A blocker took two defenders out of the play on the sideline, and Wilson ran toward the end zone with only safety Brandon Meriweather in the way.

Wilson lowered his shoulder and blasted Meriweather, sending the future first-round draft pick flying five yards backward. Wilson then hurdled Meriweather and crossed the goal line in perhaps the most memorable play the Mountaineers have ever produced. WVU took a one-point lead.

The defense forced a fourth-and-13 right away on the next drive. WVU blitzed Miami quarterback Brock Berlin, who floated a ball into the middle of the field. What looked like a panicked pass was instead snared with one hand by tight end Kellen Winslow. The play gained 18 yards. Three plays later, Miami was at WVU's 6. Jon Peattie kicked his fifth field goal of the game to win it for the Hurricanes.

Final score? Another 22–20 defeat.

Wilson said a day rarely starts and ends without someone either asking him about the play or engaging him in a conversation about it. Some people think his touchdown won the game, but Wilson said those people aren't WVU fans.

The WVU fans know better, not just because the memory remains, but because that was an event that conditioned them to expect, if not accept, the worst.

"It's one of those things where, if you talk about the other shoe dropping, that's what you mean," Wilson said.

* * *

Rodriguez and the increasingly veteran Mountaineers recovered from the 22–20 loss to Miami that ruined Wilson's magical run. The team managed to take the anger of the loss and turn it into a winning streak in the final seven games of the regular season, a winning streak the length of which WVU hadn't experienced since the start of the 1996 season, the one that was ended by Tremain Mack's blocked punt.

"What surprised me?" Rodriguez said when asked to look back. "I think the fact our young guys stayed so resilient when adversity struck us early. With an older, more veteran team, you hope to have the experience and patience to work through some early struggles, but you're never sure how younger players will handle it. That really made me proud."

The subsequent bowl loss to Maryland extended the streak of postseason misery and reinforced the control the Terrapins had extended over the Mountaineers, but it couldn't ruin the anticipation for the upcoming season. WVU was old enough to pull itself together in 2003 but young and talented enough to present delightful possibilities for 2004.

That 2004 season was the season everyone had envisioned back in 2001, the one they had kept straining to see during the low moments on and off the field the previous three seasons. It was the year fans anticipated so feverishly in 2002 and 2003, when it looked like Rodriguez really knew what he was doing.

"I feel that we've worked hard to install the foundation and our house is in order, so we're ready to become that type of perennially successful program," Rodriguez said.

The preseason hype was, quite frankly, shocking. Not only was it unprecedented at WVU, but also it put the Mountaineers up with the elite. From the top of the Associated Press poll, WVU was behind only Southern Cal, Oklahoma, Georgia, Louisiana State, Florida State, Miami, Texas, Michigan, and Ohio State. Start a conversation about the top 10 college football programs, of this or any other time, and try not to include a bunch of those teams. That was the group WVU had been seeking to join; now it had.

One of those schools was no longer WVU's immediate problem. Miami was gone from the Big East and off WVU's schedule. WVU went from 12 games to 11 and was playing Division I-AA James Madison instead of the Hurricanes. Little things like that, when combined with the late-season breakthrough from 2003, made the Mountaineers a trendy pick.

Athlon Magazine, one of the summer's most-anticipated preseason publications, put WVU at No. 5. Marshall heard about it, but he was so obsessed with preparing for his senior season that he pushed all the hype aside. He wanted to make the most of every moment leading up to the start of the season, whether in practice, the film room, the weight room, or just in the quiet times in his apartment.

The magazine disrupted his plans.

"I was nervous about the guys accepting that and not really putting out, so to speak, and then it kind of panned out that way, almost like the work ethic kind of tailed off a little bit," he remembered. "I just didn't feel the same sense of focus after that that we had when we were making that climb to get to where we were. I didn't feel we had the same fight after that.

"Now, did we work? Yeah. Were guys out there giving the effort during the summer workouts? Yeah. But at the same time, at the end of the day I felt like there were some moments where guys kind of felt like we were being handed things."

That angered Marshall. He was the team's leader. Fans were proud to wear shirts that said "Rasheed: The Only Marshall That Matters." It was a totem of their love for their quarterback and disdain for the Thundering Herd down in Huntington. He was a worthy target for their affection. He'd been around to know the lows and appreciate the highs, but he knew the pitfalls, too. He tried to ignore publications and to avoid all the accolades. He devoted all his attention to his preparations. He wanted to make sure he started sharp and stayed sharp.

When he didn't see everyone following the example he and others set, he got mad.

"There were so many things during that summer that—I don't really know another way to say it—pissed me off," he said.

WVU took extreme pride in its offseason workouts. Its summer conditioning program gave the Mountaineers an edge to survive and prosper during camp. Mike Barwis, the team's strength and conditioning coordinator, was a magician in inspiring and improving players in the weight room. Marshall knew it. He wondered that summer why others did not.

"There were times that summer I had to go to Mike personally and basically call some guys out," Marshall said. "It was my job to do that. I didn't like seeing stupid things and guys coming up with excuses to miss workouts—and they weren't even really excuses. They were bald-faced lies that I knew about. Things were building and I was fed up with it.

"Stuff like that gets under my skin; there was no reason guys shouldn't be out there working like every other guy on the team, knowing it was going to be a tough day and they wanted no part of it. What was that going to mean for the rest of the season?"

* * *

The preseason coaches' poll came out July 31, 2004, and ranked West Virginia No. 11. On August 15, the Associated Press put the Mountaineers at No. 10 in the preseason poll. Never before had they been ranked as high before the start of the season.

The town was on edge. The time between the 1988 and 1993 regular seasons went by quickly compared to the time between 1994 and 2004. Morgantown was readying for anything.

And in that town at that time, that came with a literal interpretation. Before the start of the 2004 season, the town's fire chief, David Fetty, was asked what might happen if the Mountaineers won a national title.

These were the conversations people were having. Their Mountaineers could win it all, and the fans were capable of anything.

"My initial reaction is, 'I'd like to see it,' because I would know we won a national championship," Fetty said. "It's my greatest desire to see what would happen because I would know we won a national championship."

Yes, "we." The town and the people are like that with their relationship with their school and their football team. When WVU won, the state and all its people, the school and all its fans, graduates, employees, and students won, too. And when WVU loses, everyone loses, too. So numerous have been the defeats and the disappointments, though, that the celebration loomed as too large to prevent, too necessary to prevent.

"We know that by the nature of our community with our university that there is going to be a certain amount of parties and celebrating," Fetty said. "As long as it's within reason and under control, we're OK with that."

No one was OK with what would follow.

Rodriguez insisted that year's team wasn't good enough to play average football and win. Some teams were so talented they could have a bad game and still get by with big plays or big-time players despite lousy execution.

"We're not good enough to do that yet," he said.

That dynamic defined the 2004 team. Very talented, very aware of it, but also very affected by it. The start of the 2004 season included a jinx-breaking overtime win against Maryland and its expatriate quarterback, former Mountaineer Scott McBrien. WVU had a laugher the week afterward against JMU but then went to Blacksburg,

Virginia, ranked No. 6 and lost to unranked Virginia Tech.

The offense was 0-for-13 on third down, never got into the red zone, and had the ball almost 12 fewer minutes than the Hokies, mostly because the Mountaineers couldn't tackle running back Mike Imoh and quarterback Bryan Randall. WVU had just 10 first downs and gave Virginia Tech five of its 21 first downs on penalties. Marshall struggled—9-for-18 for 81 yards and a meaningless interception on the team's final play—though he received little help.

John Pennington, who a year earlier made a fantastic and acrobatic diving touchdown reception against Pitt that swung the game in WVU's favor, had perhaps the most reliable hands on the team. Down 6–0 late in the second quarter, he was in the slot opposite teammate Eddie Jackson.

Again and again in practice that week, Rodriguez had his offense repeat this play. Jackson would clear the middle and take a safety with him. Pennington would slip into the space vacated by the departing safety and the dropping linebackers.

Marshall threw the ball and followed through with his throwing hand left in the air. He repeated the throw just as they practiced it. The ball was on the spot, in a place where the Hokies couldn't get it and Pennington could. It would be first-and-goal near the goal line and the Mountaineers could take a 7–6 halftime lead.

"It was a little wet because of the rain, but the throw went to a good spot and he went down to get it and it hit him right in the chest," Marshall said. "I can still see it, standing behind center, watching him go down for the ball."

Pennington dropped the pass.

"John wasn't the fastest guy in the world. Everyone knows that. He wasn't the most gifted, he wasn't the most athletic, but he had a pair of hands that if he got them on the ball, he'd catch it," Marshall said. "I guarantee you if we go back in time now and we're back in that situation and we get another shot, he catches it."

The consolation was a short field-goal attempt to cut the deficit in half. That's when disaster struck—Virginia Tech's special teams prowess combined with WVU's inevitable misfortune. The field goal was blocked and returned by Vince Fuller 74 yards for a touchdown.

The Mountaineers snapped the ball six times in the third quarter and only had possession for 7:39 after halftime.

"Outsiders might make it seem like if John catches that ball, West Virginia wins the game and since he didn't catch it that's the reason we lost, but that's not how it goes," Marshall said. "There were a ton of other things that went wrong."

In the next three games, WVU seemed to gather itself. The Mountaineers built leads of 17–0, 14–0, and 14–0, but only won 31–19, 27–6, and 35–30. The Rutgers game, the last of those three, was an embarrassment on multiple levels. WVU couldn't put the Scarlet Knights away, and Rodriguez would later say his team did nothing more than escape.

Receiver Chris Henry didn't start the game, a punishment for an unspecified rules violation, and he wouldn't finish it either. Two unsportsmanlike conduct penalties in the same drive triggered his ejection and nearly triggered a sideline melee.

Henry caught a touchdown pass and was flagged and tossed for bouncing the ball off the defender's facemask. Rodriguez grabbed Henry around the collar and lit into his receiver, but Henry wasn't having it and broke free. Mike Barwis had to force Henry from the field, but the fans had a target and started screaming all sorts of things at him and throwing plastic bottles his way. Henry gestured before he disappeared and the crowd only grew louder.

This sort of behavior was nothing new, either. Henry and others, most notably running back Kay-Jay Harris, developed a needless habit of celebrating a big play by standing upright, arms folded across their chests, and cocking their heads to the side in an arrogant display.

Harris had since tabled the celebration, but Henry had not and he earned extended looks from the officials. Marshall called the move "stupid." He talked to Henry about it. Sometimes Henry listened. Most of the time, he did not. Rodriguez rued the way it derailed his offense. Not only did it cost his team 15 yards and pause the action, but it gave everyone unnecessary apprehension. Every time Henry made a play, whenever he used his 6-foot-4 frame to gracefully overcome a defensive back, whenever he fooled opponents with his speed and had offered an extra gear when the person covering him could not, whenever he made something so difficult look so easy, Rodriguez couldn't enjoy it. He had to stop and look for a penalty flag.

Henry was a personification of the frustrations of WVU fans that season. He was a marvelous talent, but one that could not be fully enjoyed.

Even worse, a reputation became attached to all of this. The officials warned Rodriguez during the game about the way both teams were acting. Afterward, the Rutgers fans derided the Mountaineers as they left the field, accusing them of a flagrant lack of class and calling them "thugs."

Rodriguez would contest that, but he had to suspend Henry. His best player wouldn't start the following week against Temple. He wouldn't play the entire first half. He might not play the entire game or at all the rest of the season, Rodriguez allowed.

The undefined punishment seemed loose and flexible, almost as though it hinged on what happened next to the Mountaineers. "Well, let's just say that Rodriguez didn't exactly throw the book at Henry and that was probably a good thing, because Henry just may have caught it, jumped to attention and posed with his arms folded, which was how the whole mess started," Bob Hertzel opined in the *Dominion Post* the day after Henry was semisuspended.

Who knew if the Mountaineers could hold themselves together or when the next episode would occur? To what lengths would Rodriguez go to keep discipline and performance in order? WVU was now under the microscope, but for all the wrong reasons.

This was a team with a lot of egos and a sense of entitlement, a feeling that there couldn't possibly be consequences attached to their actions, be it bad performance or bad behavior. Not for them.

"It ruined us," Marshall said. "If it was reading the newspapers or hearing things about where guys were going to go in the draft, whatever the case may be, it tore us apart. When it came down to a tight situation where we needed to be together or we needed guys to step up and fight, it became a 'me, me, me' thing, almost like, 'Ah, I'm not really worried about this too much. I've got something else,' where some guys just didn't have a full commitment."

The following week, WVU played like it was carrying that added weight. Temple trailed 21–14 at the half, and Rodriguez ended Henry's suspension in the middle of the third quarter. On his second play, he caught a 40-yard touchdown pass and, remarkably, flicked the ball behind his back and into an astonished defender.

An official insisted he was the intended target and told Rodriguez as much, but that didn't matter. Rodriguez had ordered Henry to hand the ball directly to an official after every play. The point remained. WVU was willing to proceed and to win with Henry and his misdeeds.

Despite the negativity, WVU was 8-1 and, because Virginia Tech was no longer in the Big East, unbeaten in conference play. The national title was out of reach, but the conference title and a BCS appearance were not. WVU needed only to beat Boston College, which had lost six straight in Morgantown, and Pitt, which had allowed 52 points to WVU the year before.

The Mountaineers, almost as if they knew those facts well enough to rely upon them, lost both games. Boston College returned two punts for touchdowns in its bid for its first victory in Morgantown since 1990. WVU trailed by 17 points at the half and then lost a fumble on the kickoff to start the second half. The home fans booed at a volume not heard in a long, long time at the end of the game.

In the finale, WVU played without a suspended Henry and blew a 10–0 lead. The Panthers stole the BCS bid when Syracuse upset Boston College, which could have taken the BCS berth with it out the door to the ACC. Pitt represented the Big East poorly, turning in an embarrassing Fiesta Bowl performance against Urban Meyer's Utah team.

The Eagles were the last of the three teams to leave the conference. It looked like WVU was ready to position itself in their absence, but Cincinnati, Louisville, and South Florida were set to arrive and to provide new obstacles.

By the time WVU got to the bowl game, Henry had struck again. In an interview with the *Charleston Gazette*, he said, "I think I need a real quarterback to play with so I can really show my stuff."

It should be noted that Henry's "fake" quarterback was named the Big East's Offensive Player of the Year. Marshall, who had a fan pour a beer on him as he drove home after a season-opening loss to Wisconsin a year before, had done enough as a player to not watch Henry's comments go unpunished.

Rodriguez, perhaps competitively attached to Henry, possibly hoping he could keep his stud receiver for another year so the 2005 team wouldn't be so thin on offense, did nothing.

The relationship between quarterback and receiver was featured in coverage leading up to the Gator Bowl loss to Florida State. Henry then used the postgame as the stage to announce he was leaving WVU for the NFL. This was a shy, introverted kid who was awkward when he was forced to speak with reporters. He rarely spoke in public venues, yet after a loss in a bowl game he was willing to tell everyone he was going pro a year early.

Adam "Pacman" Jones, who had his share of issues on campus but actually developed into a productive teammate and offered no publicized problems after his involvement in a pool hall brawl his freshman year, also left early for the NFL.

The 2004 team was undeniably full of talent. WVU had 12 all-conference players, five players invited to senior all-star games, and two NFL draft picks, but still battled itself to an 8-4 record. Five months earlier, when the Mountaineers opened preseason camp, that conclusion would have been unthinkable.

4
SURPRISE

In the media guides before Rich Rodriguez's second, third, and fourth seasons, he was asked in a Q&A what surprised him most about the preceding season. That question didn't make the 2005 media guide. No one needed to explain the disappointment of 2004, least of all Rodriguez.

In all, WVU would lose 27 lettermen from that team. Gone were the top two tacklers and the leaders in sacks, tackles for a loss, interceptions, and fumble recoveries. On offense, WVU would be without quarterback Rasheed Marshall and his backup, as well as the team's top two rushers, top four receivers, top punt and kickoff returner, and top three scorers, including the kicker.

The 2005 team couldn't be found in any preseason poll. The Mountaineers got one vote in the preseason Associated Press poll and 12 in the coaches' poll. They were third in the Big East coaches' preseason poll. The depth chart in the summer before the 2005 season didn't inspire much hope—though even if it had, the fans would have been hesitant to buy in. They'd just been burned a season before by more proven talent.

That 2005 media guide did mention one thing worth noting.

Rodriguez admitted the Mountaineers had "a lot more question marks this year than at any time during the past four."

"Obviously," he said, "we have to get our young guys ready to play at a high level. That's a bigger challenge than in past years."

And that's what made the 2005 season so special. With all WVU lost from 2004, and with the way it had struggled to deal with high expectations, it sure looked like it would be a long, long time before a chance to get it right would come around again.

Certainly 2005, with the young and unproven players on offense, wouldn't be that team. It was going to take some time to identify the quarterback and the running backs to make the spread offense work, and then they'd need more time to learn the system and develop within it. Another good look at the national title was years away.

In the end, the experts were all wrong about West Virginia's 2005 team. Unrated in the polls and underrated in the conference predictions, those Mountaineers nevertheless believed in themselves and all the things they could, and eventually would, achieve.

There was no alternative.

One thing that must never be taken away from Rodriguez is his ability, his seven-figure skill, to connect with and inspire his players. Even in the lowest and ugliest moments following his exit for the University of Michigan in December 2007, his suddenly former players wouldn't bury him. Not publicly, at least.

He probably deserved a good pelting from his scorned players. It would have been therapeutic, but it would have been inconsistent. They just wouldn't let him have it. They rationalized his decision by talking about what it meant for his career and for his family. He'd done too much for the players and they weren't about to be ungrateful, no matter that he'd turned his back on them. Some came from bad neighborhoods and fractured families. A few had character or academic concerns. Some were overlooked or just below-average players. With Rodriguez, they'd grown and become and achieved the sorts of things they'd been raised to believe weren't realistic.

It's difficult to understand and probably impossible to explain unless you experienced that relationship. Some might call Rodriguez manipulative, but they must also know how great a compliment that really is.

That 2005 team is proof. Simply stated, it wasn't supposed to be that good. Not 11-1 and Sugar Bowl–champion good. This is college football. You can't lose Ben Lynch and Jason Hardee, Scott Gyorko and Adam Lenhortt, Pacman Jones and Lawrence Audena on defense and just reconvene the next season. You don't lose Marshall and Henry and everything they did, despite their relationship, and say goodbye to Tim Brown, Jeff Berk, and Mike Watson on the offensive line and just replace them with young players and say the talent will trump all the obstacles inexperience affords.

Yet Rodriguez and the Mountaineers did all that and said all that, not because they had no other choice, but because they allowed for no other choice. What some identified as weaknesses, WVU used as strengths. If someone said the Mountaineers couldn't do this and wouldn't be that, they instead worked to do this and be that.

Patrick White had looks from Southeastern Conference schools, but as a receiver or a cornerback. LSU preferred Jamarcus Russell, who was already on campus, to White. Say what you will, but Russell was the No. 1 pick in the 2007 NFL Draft. Rodriguez told White he would play quarterback for the Mountaineers, and that was enough for White to not only sign with WVU, but to decline a professional baseball contract and a $400,000 signing bonus as a fourth-round pick by the Anaheim Angels. Offensive line coach Rick Trickett, who recruited White out of Daphne, Alabama, predicted White would help WVU win a national championship.

Running back Steve Slaton was on an average high school team in Levittown, Pennsylvania, and had enough success and attention to warrant a scholarship offer from the University of Maryland. The Terrapins rescinded the offer after getting commitments from players they valued more than Slaton. Wisconsin and Boston College would talk to Slaton, but only about using him as a cornerback.

Receivers Darius Reynaud and Brandon Myles were Prop 48 players who had to sit out their true freshman years and stay away from football. Center Dan Mozes was lightly recruited but became a freshman all-American guard before becoming the team's center in 2005.

Rodriguez refused to let his Mountaineers consider, let alone believe, they couldn't be the best. This is what Owen Schmitt liked so much about Morgantown and why one meant so much to the other in their four years together.

Schmitt had grown up in Wisconsin in the tiny, rural town of Gilman, with his grandparents and his mother. His grandfather was a legendary head coach at Gilman High for 35 years and won a state title with a 12-0 record in 1986. His greatest achievement, as far as WVU fans are concerned, was letting his grandson get close to the game at a young age.

Owen was a water boy, a "fat, chubby, little kid with glasses," as Schmitt described himself, who watched the game from up close and then became very comfortable with danger. It was he who would run out onto the field to retrieve the tee after kickoffs.

Schmitt and his mother moved to Fairfax, Virginia, when he was in eighth grade. He became a very good high school player, but not good enough to end up in a big program with a free ride. He settled on the University of Wisconsin–River Falls. It was a Division III school. Owen Schmitt, all 6 feet, 2 inches and 250 pounds of him, was not a Division III player.

He wouldn't accept it. Schmitt played in an option offense in 2003, and the team threw the ball all of 71 times in nine games. He rushed for 1,063 yards and five touchdowns and couldn't shake the feeling he was capable of doing so much more.

He made calls and reached out, hoping to get someone's attention, but nothing was working. The University of Maryland gave it some thought and really did like Schmitt—just enough to tell him to stay at River Falls and become a three-time Division III All-American. Schmitt kept thinking about WVU and of joining some of his high school friends who had gone there. One day that December, Schmitt and his mom showed up at the team's headquarters and delivered a highlight tape.

Rodriguez liked everything he saw and let Schmitt join as a walk-on. Rodriguez had nothing to lose. Maybe Schmitt would make it. If he did, it would be because he proved himself worthy. Certainly a player with that kind of will was someone Rodriguez and his players would accept. And if Schmitt didn't make it, so what? He was a walk-on. Even Schmitt figured if it didn't work out and he wasn't on scholarship in 2005, he'd just head back to River Falls.

Schmitt never stopped acting like a Division III player. Every block, every carry, every smashed facemask, every hurdle was performed as though he was that talented Division III kid trying to prove himself to someone, to anyone who had doubted him.

He was the scout team's player of the week twice during the year he sat out, which may not sound like a lot for a 12-game season, until you remember he was a fullback. Schmitt then attached himself to chiseled linebacker Marc Magro and earned the team's Iron Mountaineer Award as the top performer in the winter workout program.

He wasn't going back to River Falls. The scholarship was his. Patrick White and Steve Slaton would gain more yards, score more touchdowns, get the largest headlines, and best embody what the Mountaineers would do those next three seasons. No one better embodied how the Mountaineers did it than Schmitt.

"Honestly," Schmitt said, "I think it was the coaching we had. I always thought it was going to work for us, no matter what."

There are things you can't learn about a team unless you're part of it. Life as a transfer, who has to sit out a year and watch home games in warm-ups and road games from home, is completely different than being on the team's active and traveling roster. Schmitt finally joined the team during spring practice in March 2005 and immediately learned the way things were done.

"The first meeting, Coach Rod gave us a piece of paper," Schmitt remembered. "He said, 'Who do you think are going to be the best teams in the country next year? No. 1, No. 2, No. 3?'"

The players gave it some thought. Southern Cal had Matt Leinart and Reggie Bush. Texas had Vince Young. Tennessee and LSU were loaded in the SEC, as were Michigan and Ohio State in the Big Ten. Some of the Mountaineers knew Virginia Tech and thought the

Hokies would be very good. Even Louisville in the Big East would get a No. 1 vote in the Associated Press preseason poll.

"It was a trick question," Schmitt said. "Coach Rod wanted us all to think WVU was going to be No. 1 the next year. Nothing else mattered."

The players were quiet, kind of surprised by the coach's tactic, kind of ashamed they hadn't been thinking that way all along. They chuckled and shrugged and started from scratch. It was at that moment when the Mountaineers started to do what they would do that season.

"That was something where once we all gave it a second to think it over, it made sense," Schmitt said.

The country wasn't as easily convinced. *Sports Illustrated*, which a year later would identify the Mountaineers as a title contender, predicted a spot in the Motor City Bowl in 2005. It listed the Big East's top 10 players in its season preview and omitted WVU's altogether.

The *Blue Ribbon Yearbook* started its preview on the Mountaineers by saying, "West Virginia, like the Big East itself, will sport a new look in 2005. But while the conference is completing its makeover, the Mountaineers are just beginning the process. Coach Rich Rodriguez enters his fifth season in Morgantown with a radically different team from the one that has captured Big East co-championships each of the last two seasons."

At least NationalChamps.net got WVU in its preseason top 50. At No. 49, one better than Wake Forest.

Rodriguez knew he was dealing with more unknowns than ever before. There was a difference between having a number of promising quarterbacks and in having an established and reliable starter. There was something reassuring about having a few talented running backs, but he would have felt better knowing who the best was. The preseason was just different for the Mountaineers. They didn't have the swagger or the hype they had the season before, and Rodriguez found himself making odd statements, like bragging, "We'll be deeper at tight end than ever before."

He still managed to spin it and sell it to his players. He had that gift. Years later, when he was at Michigan and rubbing people the wrong way with his recruiting practices, then-Purdue coach Joe Tiller called Rodriguez "a guy in a wizard hat selling snake oil." In 2005, it was exactly what the Mountaineers needed. Rodriguez would take what many were presenting as obstacles and present them to his players as opportunities.

"There are so many freshmen and sophomores in the two-deep that they can look to their left and to their right and know their time is now," he said before preseason practice. "The challenge to us as coaches is to teach these guys quickly the right way to do things. For the players, it should be a lot of fun, because our guys love to compete."

The fun, the competition, would start right away for those freshmen and sophomores. WVU opened with a nationally televised road game in Big East play against Syracuse in the Carrier Dome. WVU's offense wasn't up to the occasion, but the defense saved the day against an Orange offense, playing its first game in a new system under a new coordinator for new head coach Greg Robinson.

WVU's defense wasn't sure what to expect, but it held Syracuse to only 103 yards, turned away all 15 third-down conversion attempts, and forced punts 11 times. Quarterback Perry Patterson was 15-for-31 for 85 yards and threw two interceptions, struggling often against a new formation the Mountaineers introduced that game. WVU played with a sixth defensive back on some obvious passing downs and called it the Swat Team, something Jeff Casteel's defense would come to lean on a whole lot in the future.

Safety Eric Wicks returned an interception for a touchdown to tie the score 7–7 in the second quarter. Defensive lineman Ernest Hunter sacked Patterson in the end zone in the fourth quarter for a safety and a 12–7 lead before freshman Pat McAfee kicked his second field goal for a 15–7 victory.

This was a game WVU wouldn't have won the year before for sure, and probably not in the other three seasons Rodriguez had been in charge. It didn't make any sense and it made everyone feel pretty good, but not so good as to ignore the obvious.

All the worries about the offense were realized. Adam Bednarik would start and play most of the game, but he shared time with

White. Bednarik was actually serviceable, completing 14 of his 21 pass attempts, though for just 104 yards. He somehow ended up as the leading rusher with 72 yards on 12 carries.

That wasn't good news for the running backs, particularly Jason Colson. A patient veteran who'd waited his turn, Colson lost all three of his fumbles against his hometown team, which had never offered him a scholarship. His 11 carries for 26 yards created an opening for freshman Jason Gwaltney.

Gwaltney was easily the most celebrated recruit under Rodriguez, and arguably of all time at WVU. The Mountaineers, and in particular assistant coach and recruiting whiz Herb Hand, had beaten Southern Cal and Ohio State for Gwaltney's services. A burly and surprisingly agile 6-foot-1, 240-pound back, Gwaltney had rushed for 2,882 yards and 45 touchdowns and scored 282 points at North Babylon High, on New York's Long Island.

As a senior.

In an unbelievable prep career, he'd set the Long Island and Suffolk County records with 7,800 rushing yards and 135 touchdowns. Twenty-seven of those TDs came on runs covering at least 50 yards. In one game, Gwaltney rushed for 435 yards and nine touchdowns.

Rodriguez and WVU had reached for the top-shelf recruits in his first four years and won a share of some significant battles, but none as meaningful as the one waged for Gwaltney. It was an arrival of sorts for the Mountaineers, to not only have the nerve to target a five-star prospect like Gwaltney, but to go up against the game's elite programs and then to secure that player come national signing day.

WVU relished the moment. Chuck McGill was the sports editor at the campus newspaper, the *Daily Athenaeum*, at the time. He, like so many others, thought he knew how the pursuit of Gwaltney would go. WVU would hang in there and maybe even stick around until the end, but the blue chip player would ultimately pick the more known, reliable, and productive program and sign with the Trojans or the Buckeyes.

So sure was McGill that he promised to eat a jar of mayonnaise if Gwaltney signed with the Mountaineers. Rodriguez arrived at national signing day with a smile on his face and a jar of mayo hidden in the podium.

"I still remember the morning of signing day, waiting on the letter of intent to come across the fax machine, even up until the last minute, and being on pins and needles," Hand said. "It was a huge, huge deal because we beat some of the national programs for a change."

Despite his talent and achievements, Gwaltney couldn't distinguish himself from an otherwise undistinguished group of running backs in the preseason. Colson was the starter. Pernell Williams was a backup. Gwaltney was in the plans, though he became *the* plan when Colson couldn't hang onto the ball.

Gwaltney carried the ball six times and gained just 19 yards against Syracuse. His longest rush covered four yards. Once he was stopped on third-and-1. That Rodriguez went to him, though, was a sign of things to come—the Mountaineers asked a freshman to lead that day.

Gwaltney's time as a star wouldn't last long, though. The Mountaineers started 4-0, but in those next three games the freshman carried just 28 times for 98 yards. In the week leading up to the showdown with No. 3 Virginia Tech, he didn't show up for all the practices and study halls and began to fall out of favor.

The team released a statement two days before the game in which Gwaltney was labeled as merely homesick and not disgruntled, while Rodriguez criticized the nature of rumors and the effect they have on players and their family and friends who read them in the newspaper. Gwaltney played against the Hokies and gained 12 yards on five carries in a 34–17 loss. He had the best day of his career in the following game against Rutgers with 57 yards on six carries, but that was his final game with the Mountaineers.

He sprained his right knee against the Scarlet Knights and was supposed to miss four weeks, but Gwaltney didn't follow the rehabilitation plan. His attendance in the training room and in class diminished. When he was in class, professors and even teammates were further shocked when he'd sit by himself, put on his headphones, and disappear into his hooded sweatshirt.

Rodriguez could no longer defend the freshman. He didn't indict him either, though, and instead tried to redirect some of the blame to the recruiting websites as he explained why Gwaltney was having a hard time adjusting to a lower profile at a higher level. A regular weekly press conference in the middle of a really successful season was heavy on Gwaltney inquiries.

"In building them up, all they are doing is projecting success on the field," Rodriguez said in the *Dominion Post*. "But having success on the field relates to all that other stuff. Recruiting sites don't take that into consideration.

"Can that guy make adjustments? What's his maturity level? Obviously, if you are eligible, you made the academic requirements and should be able to handle that."

By the end of the year, Gwaltney was no longer with the team. And it didn't matter. The chemistry issues that spoiled the 2004 team were locked out in 2005. There were stories about some players policing the team in the locker room and making sure every player, regardless of class rank, would not become someone or create something bigger than the team and what it was doing. What could have torn the team apart was instead set aside and left to work out alone.

"I think at some point everybody got together and realized, 'Hey, we've got something special here. Let's put our problems aside and let's try to win football games,'" Schmitt said.

Egos were not allowed. If you could play, you would, and never was that more clear than with the rise of Slaton and White. Slaton came off the bench against the Hokies and had 90 yards on 11 carries. Colson wasn't playing. Gwaltney couldn't be trusted. Williams fumbled to set up a Virginia Tech touchdown. Slaton, who had carried just eight times during the 4-0 start, took over.

A week later, he carried 25 times for 139 yards and scored the first of his school-record 50 rushing touchdowns. Then came the season-changing game against Louisville that shifted the fortunes of the 2005 team and the program. The Cardinals were the preseason pick to win the conference and led 24–7 in the fourth quarter before WVU pulled off the unfathomable comeback and triumphed in three overtimes.

Slaton carried 31 times for 188 yards and five touchdowns, and he caught three passes for 20 yards and a touchdown. After the coaches watched the film, they were shocked to discover two things. First, Slaton had played all 91 snaps, and second, he was never once guilty of a "loaf," a term the staff used to label lazy plays.

The win left the Mountaineers in an extremely fortuitous position. Not only had the Cardinals now lost two Big East games to trail WVU by two games in the standings, but WVU finally had its unquestioned running back and quarterback. The Mountaineers averaged 328 yards and four touchdowns rushing the next four games against Connecticut, Cincinnati, Pitt, and South Florida, with White, Slaton, and Schmitt leading the way. They recorded only 383 yards and four touchdowns passing, total, during the same stretch.

The hidden secret to that team's success was that while the Mountaineers were surging in the final four games, they were still figuring themselves out and continuing to get better. Colson carried 11 times against UConn and Williams, 10. Williams got another 10 carries a game later against the Bearcats. No quarterback, running back, or fullback but White, Slaton, and Schmitt ran the ball in the final two games.

Then came the prep time for the Sugar Bowl. WVU won the Big East and the BCS bid when Connecticut beat USF on November 26. The Mountaineers won in Tampa, Florida, on December 3 to end the regular season. The bowl game was January 2. The Mountaineers practiced 15 times before the bowl game, the same number of times they regularly work out in spring practice and about half the practices they fit into preseason camp. The end of the regular season was not the end of their development. White and Slaton learned more and more of the offense, as did the players around them. When to press a block, when to slice inside, how to cut a defender, how to crack back against a linebacker; all the ins and outs were taught and learned again and again.

"Rich Rod was probably the meanest human you'd ever met in practice," kicker Pat McAfee remembered, "but we had great practices."

By the time the game arrived, the Mountaineers were itching to play instead of practice. They erupted, and the fast start left the majority-Georgia crowd dizzy. The Mountaineers weren't intimidated. They were ready.

"They executed beautifully," Georgia coach Mark Richt said afterward. "If I wasn't coaching against them, I would have enjoyed watching it."

The ending, with Phil Brady taking the fake punt and scrambling for the stunning first down to clinch the game, gave the school its most satisfying win ever. The team had restored its postseason image and given the Big East something to tout, but it had also done something for the people who hadn't counted them out. The Mountaineers inflated the deflated, and for a state reeling from the unfolding mining accident in Sago, the victory was especially poignant.

Rodriguez's father had worked in the mines in Marion County. He had a brother and uncles who would join the coal business, too. Rodriguez knew the explosion and the mining tragedy in Upshur County that day was immeasurably larger than football, but Rodriguez also knew he and the football team had provided a pleasant respite. If they could do that, if they had that ability to occupy, entertain, and inspire people, they could also do so much more. Slaton started it off, saying in the postgame press conference that the Mountaineers could win the national title the following season. They were going to make believers out of everyone, no matter what it took.

Herb Hand didn't get to bed until about four o'clock in the morning after the game. He was on a plane a few hours later, headed for Daytona, Florida, to see a receiver WVU really wanted to sign. Latarrius Thomas left his house early that morning for school and stopped short before the door closed behind him.

Hand was in front of his house, sitting on the hood of his rental car.

"Coach," Thomas said, "I just saw you on TV. What are you doing here?"

"I could be anywhere in the world right now," Hand said, "but this is where I want to be."

Somehow, Thomas resisted and ended up signing with Louisville, but the season was a success for Rodriguez. When it started, he'd tricked the Mountaineers into believing they could be No. 1. At the end, he'd coached them into professing the same.

"It was just crazy," Schmitt said. "It was our first big game and we were all so young, and we were supposed to get our butts whipped by Georgia. Then we go out, guns blazing like we did, and win on the fake punt, and it was just incredible. I think right after that game it was like, 'Oh, man, look what we did and look what we have.' We saw we had a chance to do something pretty special."

5

EXPECTATIONS

Here was that optimistic feeling again, sooner than most anyone expected, and everyone agreed the best was yet to come. As excited as everyone was about that 2005 season and the Sugar Bowl win, the highest level of anticipation was reserved for 2006.

For this football program and its history of stunning disappointments, abandoned expectations, and failures as the frontrunner, that was extraordinarily bold.

"The things this team can achieve are unthinkable," guard Jeremy Sheffey told the *Dominion Post* before the season. "We could go as far as the national championship. I really believe that. But at the same time we are staying focused."

That last part wasn't easy. Virtually everyone in the 55 counties and all the alumni bases that crowd the East Coast and dot the rest of the county wanted the same thing. They wanted greatness, and they wanted it for themselves as much as for their Mountaineers.

"I grew up in West Virginia, and I think the biggest thing I've seen is how the people attach themselves to you," said Quincy Wilson, a running back from 1999 to 2003. Wilson was from Weirton, in the northern part of the state, and he was a high school legend who set the state's career rushing record. "I came here as a freshman, and I was by no means the best player, but I got the biggest applause just because I was from West Virginia.

"The people from all over the state have a great pride for West Virginia, whether it's football or basketball, or just the school in general. When you get into these times, where we've had such a great run from, I'd say, 2003 to now, we've been to Final Fours and BCS games, this is what the people have always wanted. This is their pro team and these are their heroes."

Such external pressures and expectations can conspire against a team. It had happened in the past, but it was different in 2006. Veterans patrolled the locker room and policed attitudes and mentalities. Stars and leaders sounded and acted humble. These Mountaineers weren't going to be shaped by the thoughts of others.

WVU had been playing football for 111 seasons before getting unprecedented preseason hype in 2004. The expectations were rewritten just two years later. The Mountaineers were No. 5 in the preseason media poll and No. 7 in the coaches' poll. Owen Schmitt stood with Pat White and Steve Slaton on a regional cover of the *Sports Illustrated* season preview. The theme: The Battle for No. 1.

In addition, what the Mountaineers did in the Sugar Bowl changed everything for the Big East, too.

"Over the last 27 years of the Big East, there have been some real watershed events," commissioner Mike Tranghese said at the conference's media day. "I think the WVU-Georgia game was one of those. That's how important it is. For our league to be able to succeed and develop, we needed to get this cloud of doom and gloom off our backs. All of a sudden, people look at us differently. Our bowl and television partners look at us differently."

By the start of the 2006 season, the hopeful feeling was familiar; the fans had reached a point where they found it easy to expect to reach the greatest of goals. This didn't feel like a one-year thing, the sort of season that comes along once every few years when all the conditions line up properly. This was the beginning stage of a program turning itself into a powerhouse.

Season ticket sales jumped from 32,400 in 2005 to 37,900 in 2006. Perhaps the most anticipated game of the regular season in all of college football would be a Thursday-night showcase between WVU and Louisville. Both figured to be top-10 or maybe top-five teams by the time of the early November matchup. And the players were determined that the 2006 season was going to be different than 2004. The Mountaineers wouldn't be the ones to beat the Mountaineers.

"We've been through that, when we had high expectations and failed," Dan Mozes said in an ESPN.com article that summer. "Some guys thought more about the next level than about the team. That's not going to be a problem with this team."

The problem of identifying the team's cornerstone players was gone, too. Slaton would start the 2006 season as the star offensive weapon.

Pat White would be the unquestioned starting quarterback. With Brandon Myles and Darius Reynaud, the Mountaineers finally had two good receivers who had been in the system a while.

As Mozes had said, the sky was the limit.

* * *

The legacy molded by the 2006 team can be debated.

The Mountaineers won 11 games, just the sixth time they had ever reached a double-figure win total, and the first time it ever occurred in back-to-back seasons. They won a second straight bowl game for the first time since the Hall of Fame and Bluebonnet Bowls in 1983 and 1984, the latter which preceded WVU's horrendous bowl losing streak.

Steve Slaton and Dan Mozes were consensus All-Americans, the first time teammates had ever done that at West Virginia. Mozes was the first West Virginia player to win a national individual award by claiming the Rimington Trophy as the nation's best center. Slaton, Mozes, Ryan Stanchek, Patrick White, Owen Schmitt, Reed Williams, and Pat McAfee were on their way to all-timer status. Even Butch Jones, an assistant coach on the offensive side for a second season, rode the success at WVU to a head coaching job at Central Michigan at the end of the season.

The Mountaineers set records for performance and for viewership, and generally entertained fans and even foes along the way, but their failures were perhaps surprising and disappointing, a feeling that irks those Mountaineers to this day.

"If people have got a problem with going 11-2, then it's on them," Schmitt said. "There are, what, 120 schools? To be 11-2 and not be satisfied ... obviously, nobody is satisfied unless you're undefeated and win the national championship, including players. It's not like we didn't feel that way either.

"But when you look back, sure, at first you're disappointed, but you know what? We won a lot of games, we played some great football, and we finished the year on a high note and brought good vibes for the next year."

True, all of it, but 2006 was never supposed to be the catapult for 2007. It was supposed to be the year the Mountaineers wrapped their hands around that crystal trophy. They'd spoken openly about it, first after the Sugar Bowl and then, with caution and respect, in the time that followed the celebration and preceded the start of the 2006 season.

And why not? WVU had Slaton and White. The other team did not. That was a pretty good reason to believe.

Those two would perform some ridiculous feats in 2006. Nothing was more laughable than what they foisted upon Pitt at Heinz Field. Slaton had 215 yards and two scores rushing and added 130 yards and two more scores receiving. White was perhaps better, especially during a first half in which Slaton was held to just seven yards on the ground. White rushed for 220 yards and two touchdowns and also passed for 204 yards and two touchdowns.

Such phenomenal performances were hardly commonplace in college football, yet it seemed as though it was reasonable to expect as much from White and Slaton.

So why were so many left with a tepid feeling about that team? Maybe the biggest goal was too big of a goal; despite all of the team's accomplishments, the Mountaineers also lost their two most important games of the season, didn't win the Big East outright, and had to go back to the Gator Bowl one more time. The Mountaineers were very good, but they knew they could have been great.

It didn't just feel uneven. It looked uneven, too. Try this on for size: WVU was ranked No. 2 nationally in rushing offense ... and No. 109 in passing defense. As much as the former propped up the Mountaineers and made them who they were in victory, the latter dragged them down and led to defeat.

The 2006 season, the one what was supposed to be the beginning of something magical after the Sugar Bowl victory, was in fact the beginning of the end. The 2006 season instead gave every indication the Mountaineers had a finite period of time to work with, and the clock was ticking with a tempo that matched the team's pace on offense.

"We watched all the games together on Saturdays, because we usually played on Thursday or some other day, and that's when all the big games were on," McAfee said. "So we'd watch together and we'd think, 'Man, we'd beat the hell out of these guys.' We had that self-confidence, and we knew we should do something really, really special. I think we did something special, but obviously not up to what we could have done."

WVU handled everything exceptionally well to start the 2006 season. The team scored a touchdown on its first possession of the first six games and trailed just one time in one game, and for all of 1:47 against Syracuse, in the first seven games of the regular season.

The Mountaineers seemed to be playing a different game, too, almost like games within the game. When it was "just" 28–14 late in a game on the road against Mississippi State and its cowbell-ringing fans, the Mountaineers scored two touchdowns in the final 3:02, including a 50-yard punt return that made the score look much better, but did not make cornerback Vaughn Rivers feel any better.

"Nobody feels like we're No. 4 right now," he said, overlooking the four-touchdown win in SEC country.

But in fact the Mountaineers didn't look much like the No. 4 team that day. They committed 11 penalties for 132 yards and gave the Bulldogs seven first downs with flags. On one drive, Mississippi State ran 11 plays and moved 38 yards in 5:27, but its offense was credited with minus-two yards. WVU committed two personal fouls and a holding penalty to chip in 40 yards. In another case, WVU converted a third down in the fourth quarter, only to have the play called back by a holding penalty. The offense converted the much longer third down on the next snap, only to see another holding penalty nix that gain, too.

"If we catch a top team and play like that, we lose. Simple as that," safety Eric Wicks said outside the visiting team's locker room.

The Mountaineers dropped a spot in the polls and took it personally. Syracuse scored a touchdown on the first drive of the next game, but WVU scored on its next three drives, beginning with White's 69-yard run on the offense's third play. It was a simple counter play, but one with a twist. The Mountaineers could remember running it only one other time all season. It would be called two more times, and White would score two more times, basically because he could.

WVU led Connecticut 30–11 in the fourth quarter a week later, but Slaton had been bottled up with only 59 yards on 16 carries. With the blockbuster game against Louisville up next, perhaps he'd come out of the game with six minutes to go, even as the ESPN graphic touted Slaton's Heisman Trophy candidacy and UConn's defensive achievement in containing him that night.

Slaton instead stayed in the game. He gained 10 yards to surpass 1,000 for the season. He fumbled on the next carry and WVU was backed up 15 yards by a personal foul after that, but Slaton took the next carry a career-high 56 yards for a touchdown. He was over 100 yards for the game and done for the night.

After the game, Rodriguez met his team in the locker room. He knew what the players were thinking—Louisville. He lifted the lid off the moratorium he'd placed on the Mountaineers long ago.

"Finally," he said, "you know who's next."

The players roared. Fifth-ranked Louisville was still 13 days away, but now it was the next game. "Now you guys can bring it up and talk about it," Rodriguez said to the media in the postgame.

Louisville head coach Bobby Petrino made his players off limits for the out-of-town media. When he spoke, he leaned on clichés and recycled rhetoric and stayed miles away from saying anything even bordering on controversial. Rodriguez, meanwhile, was less constrained.

"I think it's just individual philosophy," Rodriguez said that week. "I don't have a thought or lean one way or another on that, but I've never been like that."

As if to provide proof, Rodriguez concocted a reckless, needless act of self-promotion three days before the game. The University of North Carolina was getting rid of its coach, John Bunting, and made the decision known in late October.

Eight days later, Rodriguez was doing his bit on the weekly Big East coaches' teleconference when a writer from a paper in North Carolina popped in to ask a question. He asked Rodriguez about the job and mentioned to Rodriguez that his name was already being linked to the job, seeing that he'd been successful in the Atlantic Coast Conference as an assistant at Clemson.

The reporter knew it was a touchy subject and that he possessed absolutely awful timing, so much so that he prefaced his question by stating, "Coach, I'm sure it's the last thing you want to hear right now with the big game coming up ..."

You could visualize the reporter closing his eyes and holding his breath, hopeful Rodriguez wouldn't flip out and offer a lecture rather than a reply. Rodriguez then opened his mouth and opened the window to provide a view of how he conducted the business of contract negotiations at WVU.

"Anytime any coaches on our staff, or myself, get mentioned, it's very flattering," Rodriguez said. "It's not something I've ever viewed as a distraction. I've always said this is a great place to coach. You take this job as if it's the last job you'll ever have, and I think I've always taken that approach and I'm taking it now."

Fair enough. It wasn't a refusal to comment, even if it wasn't an outright denial of any interest, and it almost seemed like an apologetic way to avoid the question and not shame the reporter, who was just doing his job. No danger in that.

"I don't think you ever say never to something, particularly right now," he said.

OK, what the hell was that supposed to mean?

"Particularly right now," as in, while riding a 14-game winning streak and building a powerhouse BCS program currently ranked No. 3 in the country? Or while still bent out of shape about the previous contract renewal that didn't deliver everything desired?

Whatever the case, this was neither an accident nor a mental lapse. This was the coach of maybe the most tantalizing program in the country on a conference call with the national media. Everyone involved was preparing for the nation's game of the year. Rodriguez would send out a statement later in the day and urge everyone not to misinterpret his comments, though he never retracted them or even sought to clarify them. What was said wasn't the issue, he contended. The problem, as he presented it, was how his comments were digested.

He tried to pull things back to normal. Soon enough the attention went back to the game, which Rodriguez agreed was "as big as it can be at this point." The folks in town were taking preventative measures. The game would be played in Louisville, but the Morgantown Police Department was in what it called "special event mode." The same police force dedicated to a home game was available for this one and would be spread around town instead of isolated in and around the stadium.

The Sunnyside neighborhood was on lockdown. Sofas and loveseats were moved off of front porches. Parking was prohibited on one stretch of Grant Avenue from 5 p.m. to 7 a.m., basically because the police and fire departments didn't want people's cars set on fire after a win or a loss.

That's when you know it's a big game in Morgantown.

It was the Mountaineers who were burned, though. They played fairly even through the first half, and WVU's defense did well to force three field goals and trail just 16–14 entering the locker room. Then Slaton, who became a fumbler in the NFL but had heretofore never been known as one in college, suddenly became unable to hold onto the ball.

He ran 20 yards on the first play of the second half and then gained 12 on the second, but at the end of the run he was hit hard on the left elbow. The funny bone sent a numbing charge through his arm and hand, and he lost the ball. Louisville recovered, but on its first offensive play, Vaughn Rivers bailed Slaton out and forced a Louisville fumble at the end of a 27-yard pass play. Slaton then went back out and fumbled again on the very next play, basically because he hadn't regained strength and feeling in his arm. The ball was scooped up by a Louisville linebacker and returned 13 yards for a touchdown.

"[Slaton] shouldn't have been out there," Rodriguez said.

That was a ridiculous revelation. Slaton hardly ever fumbled. Coaches and teammates couldn't even remember him putting the ball on the ground in practice, not even in those drills where defenders gang up and try to strip the ball.

A simple glance from the press box or the stands or even on television showed Slaton was not right after the first hit. He winced and shook his arm and made a fist, but he also trotted back out onto the field, apparently never having been checked out on the sideline.

Some of that is on him, to be sure, because he didn't exactly go out of his way to find a trainer and submit himself to a quick screening. There wasn't much time in the flurry of turnovers, either. Still, angered by the first fumble, Slaton tried to play through the hindrance and saddle the adrenaline. The Cardinals were smart, though, and wanted to rip the ball out of his grasp.

The Mountaineers, who had trailed just once, and only briefly, the entire season, were now down 24–14 and starting to look worried. There was a loss of three yards, a penalty for an illegal shift, and then a loss of six. On fourth down, punter Scott Kozlowski came in under orders to punt to the left side of the field.

The punt went right, and it was returned 40 yards for a touchdown. The Cardinals, who were ranked No. 99 in punt returns, were suddenly up 30–14 and on their way to the 44–34 victory.

Losses happen. Players fumble. Punters shank one every so often. The loss and the mistakes hurt, but what stung most was how it all happened. Slaton had fumbled just twice all season and never lost one. Kozlowski was, by the numbers, one of the best punters in the country. WVU was No. 5 nationally in net punting and had allowed just 10 yards on punt returns all season. The punt was even returned by someone who wasn't supposed to return the punt on that play.

As shocking as it was, it was also predictable. "Come on," people said afterward, "this is what always happens when WVU plays with a whole lot on the line."

WVU had actually played a fine brand of football, with the exception of the fateful three minutes and 43 seconds just described. Consider this: Slaton had 156 yards and a touchdown on just 18 carries and added 74 yards on three receptions; White ran 23 times for 125 yards and four touchdowns, but also completed 13 of 20 pass attempts for 222 yards and no interceptions. In all, the offense produced 540 yards.

Yet the Mountaineers lost. They hadn't scored 30 or more points and lost since 1999, a streak of 41 straight games. Go figure. It was weird, but try as the players and the coaches did to say they hadn't played Mountaineer football, they actually had—it just wasn't quite good enough. The offense was what people had come to expect, save the turnovers, and the defense offered no surprises.

Louisville took advantage of WVU's suspect pass defense. Brian Brohm, in his third game back from an injury that was supposed to keep him out longer than it had, passed for 354 yards on just 19 completions. Six different teammates caught a pass. Two had six catches for more than 100 yards. Two had 40-yard receptions, and another added a 32-yard gain.

It was a bad night, from front to back, for the defense.

"We must have blown a basic blitz every time we tried it," defensive coordinator Jeff Casteel said. "I think we called it eight or nine times and we didn't run it right once."

This was the first time an opponent had passed for more than 300 yards since 2004, but it was no stunner, either. The signs were there earlier in the season, when East Carolina's James Pinkney passed for all but 29 of the team's 276 yards one week, and then a trio of Mississippi State quarterbacks managed 250 yards a week later.

WVU was very good against the run, and the offense scored a lot of points. Together, that forced the other team's offense to pass a lot and to pick up yards and scores that were sometimes meaningless. The Cardinals were a different threat, though. They *liked* to throw the ball, and they really liked their odds against the Mountaineers. Louisville called an aggressive game on offense, running passes on 13 of the first 25 first downs of the game, when the outcome was still in question. Brohm was 8-for-11 for 177 yards with gains of 22, 25, 26, 36, and 40 yards.

WVU knew the Cardinals would throw on first down, and they even expected to see play action, yet players were either surprised or hesitant, or both, and could only admire what Louisville had done.

"They attacked us," safety Quinton Andrews said afterward. "They weren't sitting back and giving us a chance to make plays. And to be honest with you, they played it pretty smart. Us being a better run defense, if they run it on first down, it might put them in a hole and then they'd have to throw their way out of it. Rather than do that, they threw it on first down and put us in a hole."

Those Mountaineers would end up surrendering 31 pass plays covering 25 yards or more that season, but 10 were in the final four regular-season games after the Louisville loss. It was bad enough that freshmen Guesly Dervil and Boogie Allen were asked to play late in the season, with Dervil getting a start against Cincinnati right after the Louisville game and Allen getting a lot of snaps and responding with an interception against the Bearcats.

There were no fixes, though. In those final four games, WVU would play the teams ranked second, third, fourth, and fifth in the Big East in passing offense. Against WVU, Pitt, Cincinnati, and Rutgers had season-high passing totals, and South Florida had its second-best day. Cincinnati was 23-for-41 for 310 yards and had three touchdowns and three interceptions. Pitt was 28-for-37 for 341 yards and had two touchdowns and no interceptions. South Florida was 22-for-30 for 279 yards and had one touchdown and two interceptions, and Rutgers, which was ranked No. 96 nationally in pass offense, was 19-for-26 for 278 yards, with one touchdown and no interceptions.

The Mountaineers handled the Cincinnati defense mostly because WVU was too fast and too talented. The Bearcats were No. 17 in the country against the run but fell victim to some gadget plays. Early on, WVU ran a series of freeze plays by the offensive line that unplugged the front seven's aggression. Then Slaton scored a 65-yard touchdown on a reverse in the second quarter as he flowed one way after the defense had started to flow to the other. In the end, WVU had 313 yards on the ground, about four times what Cincinnati was surrendering on average, and all seemed to be back to normal. Also, Rutgers beat Louisville two days earlier to open up the Big East race once again.

"Maybe [the Louisville loss] took away a goal or two," Rodriguez had said after that game, "but it's not the end of the season."

Now WVU had recovered and was in position to, at worst, share the Big East title and still possibly get into the BCS.

Slaton and White conspired to embarrass the Panthers in the next game, as they became just the third Division I teammates to rush for 200 yards each in a game. Slaton was the first Mountaineer to rush for 100 yards—or 200—and also have 100 yards receiving. White was the eighth college player to pass and rush for 200 in a game, and he tied Marc Bulger's school record with 424 yards of offense. White also went over 1,000 rushing yards for the season in that game, something no WVU quarterback had done before him.

"I can't remember any better performance by a quarterback," Rodriguez said in the postgame.

Two days later, Rutgers suffered its first loss of the season to Cincinnati, bringing WVU and Louisville into a three-way competition with Rutgers for the league title. Had Rutgers won and come to Morgantown two games later against a one-loss WVU team, WVU could have taken the Big East, again in a three-way competition, but by virtue of owning the second tiebreaker with the highest BCS ranking.

Cincinnati's upset complicated matters, but the Mountaineers really screwed things up against South Florida. The Mountaineers lost at home on a day when White and Slaton combined to run for 60 yards. Sixty!

There had been whispers of a certain disharmony behind meeting room doors, that some ideas on offense were suggested with the best intentions yet were dismissed without much consideration. Rodriguez was even bent out of shape by assistant coaches taking bottled water from a mini refrigerator outside his office, so much so that he put a piece of paper on it soon thereafter with a message to make it clear the water in that refrigerator was for the head coach only.

Sure enough, the Mountaineers looked like they were battling themselves against the Bulls. On a fourth down early in the first quarter, the Mountaineers decided to go for the first down. Rodriguez didn't want to run a normal play, despite the insistence of others who wanted to avoid a risky gimmick. Rodriguez opted for a fake field goal. The holder, Travis McClintic, was to run left and, if he needed, to pitch the ball to the kicker, Pat McAfee. McClintic was tackled instead. Some who were standing on the game film camera platform say a headset came flying from the coaching box.

"We had the look we wanted and the numbers we wanted, but we didn't execute it," said tight ends coach Herb Hand. "It was one of those days, one of those games. It reminded me of the Temple game from the first year."

WVU gained no traction with its running game and was matched speed-for-speed by South Florida's entire defense. The Bulls had agile defensive ends who could read and attack the zone read. They spied on the quarterback on the read play and crashed inside to blow the play up again and again. The Bulls' linebackers were fast and secure tacklers. The cornerbacks were good enough to handle WVU's shaky passing threat, which freed up one or two safeties to step forward to stop the run.

The Mountaineers let it happen by continually using three and four receivers. There were discussions to put a tight end in the game and get more control at the line of scrimmage, but there was no adjustment. In 2003, when Quincy Wilson was running for 1,380 yards and 12 touchdowns, WVU used two tight-end sets more than any other set. Nine times the Mountaineers started two tight ends, and they had that ability with Tory Johnson, Ryan Thomas, and Josh Bailey.

The 2006 team was different.

"If you're going to put a tight end on the field, who are you going to take off the field?" Hand reasoned. "Are you going to take Owen

Schmitt off the field? Are you going to take Darius Reynaud off the field? It was a matter of who do you take off the field and does it really create that much of an advantage?"

What seemed inconceivable that day would be understood later. The Bulls did more than win a game. They presented a plan to stop the WVU offense.

Opponents took notice of the Bulls' successful defensive game plan, but beyond that was WVU's curious inability, or refusal, to change or adjust. Again and again, the offense ran the same stuff and didn't do enough to counter the defense. This was the beginning of a theme. It might have been the beginning of the end, too.

Among Mountaineer players, coaches, and fans, there was much frustration and anger. The Big East title was gone and the BCS bid was all but unattainable. Rodriguez was asked if this felt like the 2004 season; he brusquely stated 2004 was not a bust and any such assertion was "ridiculous."

"Are we at the point now where if we're not in a BCS bowl it's a bad year at West Virginia?" he asked. "I don't know, but I guess we're finding out."

6
FLIRTING

Rich Rodriguez had to ask himself some serious questions at the end of the 2006 season. Was a season without a BCS game a failure? Had the expectations of his fans warped that much? Could he change the expectations? Could he satisfy the expectations? Could the school do what he deemed necessary to take the next step? How far was he willing to go to make his point?

Rodriguez did what a lot of other coaches in the profession do. He wanted to be the best. He wanted the best for his job and his school. Sometimes he had to abandon his best intentions and do some things he didn't want to do. He discovered leverage, and he exploited it. In truth, it wasn't an unusual tactic in college athletics, even if it was a novelty at WVU.

Then again, business was like that at WVU. Coaching situations were never static. They were becoming noisy and jagged and annual and perpetual. Who knows how this particular situation got started, but the most valuable lesson to come out of the episode was that no one could be trusted.

Before the Mountaineers' final game, word surfaced that the University of Alabama was courting Rodriguez. What happened at the end of the 2006 season wasn't a surprise, but it again proved there couldn't be anything normal when a WVU coach comes to consider his future at the school.

The most unusual and revealing part of Rodriguez's flirtation with Alabama in 2006—remember, you have to qualify it because the Crimson Tide had some level of interest in 2002—is that Rodriguez had to deal with the rumors about his association with Alabama during the final week of the regular season.

During his regular press conference on the Tuesday before the finale against Rutgers, where a win, combined with a Connecticut victory against Louisville, would get WVU a share of the Big East title and the BCS bid, a healthy amount of time was devoted to the rumblings that Alabama was again interested in Rodriguez, and perhaps vice versa.

It wasn't too much earlier that WVU and its fans were confident they wouldn't be taken down that low country road again. Mike Shula led the Crimson Tide to a 10-2 record in 2005, which quieted the crowd growing against him. A year later, though, the Tide's regular-season record was 6-6 with a 2-6 mark in the Southeastern Conference. Meanwhile, Rodriguez was rolling and doing it in a style with which the SEC could identify, never mind the seven-year, $8.65 million contract he'd signed with WVU six months earlier. So when Alabama fired Shula on November 26, the Mountain State took a deep breath and buckled up again.

Rodriguez dismissed the possibility as a rumor and blamed the proliferation of the Internet. He even accepted that it all came with the territory. He said he hadn't spoken with anybody from any other school, insisted he was focused only on Rutgers and recruiting, and promised he wasn't distracted. He did, however, stop short of saying he wasn't interested in the job, which would have been entirely appropriate. He never really mentioned those "friends" of the Alabama program who'd reached out before and, technically, they weren't what someone in Rodriguez's position might describe as people from another school; for instance, actual program representatives. Nick Saban, Steve Spurrier, Bobby Petrino, and Jim Leavitt all said they weren't interested. Rodriguez would not.

Then it was discovered that Chuck Neinas, a headhunter for colleges searching for a head coach and something of a mysterious figure, had contacted Rodriguez just to learn about his contract. Neinas, who would later become the interim commissioner of the Big 12 when it agreed to invite WVU, had been hired by Alabama to assist in the search, but he was also working in the same capacity for the University of Miami. That didn't help anyone feel any better about anything.

Predictably, there was a report Rodriguez had agreed to a deal and would wait until after the Rutgers game to accept the offer formally. The story gained momentum, and the papers covering Alabama were sending reporters to Morgantown to be at the Rutgers game and in town, just in case something happened.

And then something happened, something rather seismic. The night before the game, and just a day after another report surfaced saying Rodriguez would take the Alabama job, then-ESPN.com columnist Pat Forde appeared on a radio program. Forde speculated that if Alabama could offer a seven-year contract for $3 million or so a year then, sure, he thought Rodriguez might accept.

That possibility made its way to West Virginia MetroNews, which calls itself "the voice of West Virginia" and is often taken to be "the voice of West Virginia University." There is a difference and one that is often overlooked or ignored because of certain arrangements. No matter how often or how well MetroNews tries to explain things, its operation and its allegiances can be confused because of its close relationship with the athletic department, one that has existed since 1940. MetroNews is the truck that delivers WVU's coverage of its sporting events to its fans. It has the microphones and satellite systems and recording equipment and also some of the personalities whom WVU uses. Tony Caridi, for example, is a MetroNews employee and the regular host of MetroNews' signature sports program, *Statewide Sportsline*. He is also the play-by-play voice for the football and men's basketball teams and a host for magazine shows on the university's Mountaineer Sports Network. He often writes opinion pieces on the university's MSNSportsNet website and emcees WVU functions. There are other dynamics like that, other people who work for

MetroNews and for MSN. Caridi is merely the most visible and easiest to explain and understand.

Anyway, MetroNews published a story stating Rodriguez was ready to accept an offer from Alabama. So strong is the MetroNews brand, so close is its glove to the university's hand, that people predictably panicked. The MetroNews story cited sources within the athletic department, and it suggested Rodriguez was rounding up assistants to take with him, but it also interpreted Forde's "revelation" as a sign the hiring was imminent.

Forde was surprised. Back on the radio, he called MetroNews "morons with a comprehension problem," and wondered why, if he was reporting this news, that it wasn't on ESPN.com.

The Mountaineers, meanwhile, were at Lakeview Golf Resort & Spa, sequestered the night before the game, as they always were. *Statewide Sportsline* hit the air at 6:06 p.m. and that Friday night's episode detailed the story about Rodriguez and Alabama. Word of the MetroNews story got around, and for the first time it was coming from within West Virginia. Thus far, the state's media outlets had tried to extract a story, but had been told again and again, either by Rodriguez or athletic director Ed Pastilong, or sources close to the primary actors, that there was not yet one to be told. The MetroNews report spread fast and breached the walls that were supposed to isolate the team at Lakeview.

Rodriguez called *Statewide Sportsline* and lashed out. "This is not responsible journalism. It's crazy," he said on air to the hosts, one of whom was Greg Hunter, who—though he wasn't alone—had done much of the reporting and writing for the MetroNews story.

Rodriguez said his wife had called him in tears. Recruits were calling coaches. Players were asking questions. Rodriguez, who had stubbornly but proudly, and probably wisely, refused to offer any insight on any job his name was connected to, felt he had no other choice but to break protocol. Rodriguez was angry, assertive, provoked. He didn't hold back, either, and let it be known he'd been wronged by the report and that what it had done to the curious players, recruits, and spouses was a tragedy.

He'd later take his rage to the top of the MetroNews company, but to him, the people behind it, not the people who'd penned it, were the chief culprits.

"The athletic department source needs to be taken to task," Rodriguez said on the air. "If someone is making that up, they need to be taken to task."

The next day MetroNews took a moment out of pregame programming to address the story because of the relationship it shared with MSN. The story had been retracted and taken down from the website, and MetroNews apologized for its inaccuracies. Rodriguez won.

Still, this was no longer so much about the nature of the story as it was about the source. It became an extension of the battles that were happening behind the scenes at WVU. Rodriguez was still bent out of shape at the way the previous contract renegotiation went down and how he believed WVU hadn't been prompt in the way it did business with Rodriguez's agent.

Any excitement over the thrilling triple-overtime victory against Rutgers, and the heroic effort of Jarrett Brown in place of the injured Pat White, was all but extinguished in the postgame. One of the Alabama reporters on hand asked Rodriguez about the news. Rodriguez threatened to end the press conference—which would have triggered a melee among the local and traveling writers—and he was serious.

The Mountaineers accepted a Gator Bowl invitation the following day, but Rodriguez's battle soon went public. The *Charleston Gazette* had a story in its Monday editions saying Neinas had contacted Rodriguez again on Sunday. The story went into detail about Rodriguez's fear that WVU wouldn't follow through on pledges for facility improvements and increases to assistant coaching salaries. Rodriguez also was said to be bitter about the previous contract taking six months to finalize and the lack of progress with the academic center the school contractually promised to helped fund and build.

The story was anonymously sourced. Neinas was good about answering his phone and talking to reporters about the type of work he does, yet his reputation is that he never, ever says anything about specifics. Thus, the general suspicion was that the story came from somewhere within the football office. It seemed curiously specific, particularly as people remembered nothing coming from within WVU for a long, long time. WVU was used to only being bombarded by the reports and assumptions from elsewhere. Administrators weren't skeptical so much as they were convinced. And steamed.

After all, just three days earlier Rodriguez stated on the radio, "I plan on being the coach at West Virginia the rest of my career if they'll have me. That's what I plan on. I don't plan to talk to anybody this week or next week. I plan on doing everything I can for West Virginia football."

Now it all made sense: "if they'll have me." As in, "if they do the things I asked for and they promised. And if not, I can be seated across from an athletic director from a hiring university real fast."

Sure enough, Rodriguez was in New York that Tuesday for the National Football Foundation College Football Hall of Fame Dinner. He met with Alabama's athletic director, Mal Moore, for about an hour. Earlier in the day, Moore had called Pastilong and left a message stating he would meet with Rodriguez. Pastilong would only say someone who identified himself as Moore had called to leave a message, but he wasn't sure if it was Moore. Word got back to Rodriguez's camp that Pastilong believed it was a prank call, a story that actually made it into Pastilong's deposition in the lawsuit against Rodriguez some 16 months later.

Pastilong and Rodriguez spoke before the meeting, and Pastilong said he was aware of Alabama's appointment. Later in the day, the two spoke again and discussed the facility renovations, specifically the academic center. Pastilong said Rodriguez had been involved in discussions about the academic center since July, when they started talking about designs. Pastilong flatly denied there was a lack of commitment and said WVU was behind the growth of the football program. He was out there, public and proactive. He had to be.

The only paper that Rodriguez spoke to for the next day's editions was the *Charleston Gazette*. The paper that stated it couldn't get Pastilong or President David C. Hardesty on the phone? The *Charleston Gazette*. This couldn't be a coincidence. It looked as though lines were being drawn and actors were taking sides. A day later, Rodriguez was in Charleston to watch a WVU basketball game and stressed he wasn't waging a battle against WVU and wasn't in it for personal gain. He simply wanted to know WVU was behind his vision. At the same game, Hardesty told the *Gazette*, "I'm not going to negotiate in the papers."

A day later, Rodriguez appeared to be gone. The *Pittsburgh Post-Gazette* and the *Birmingham News* both reported on their websites that Rodriguez had agreed to terms with the Crimson Tide. "The Grant Town guy with the down-home, West Virginia euphemisms, the Mountaineers' alum with the wit about jumping off the Westover Bridge, the patent-holder and purveyor of the modern spread offense, the coach with the ball cap, steel sideline demeanor and red-and-green wristbands waving in plays just before the snap—you can color him gone. Gone in a Crimson Tide," read the *Post-Gazette*, as written by Chuck Finder, who wasn't in the habit of making guesses or swinging wildly hoping to hit the truth.

Herb Hand had the hard job of working as WVU's recruiting coordinator at this most uncertain, most important time. The days after the end of the regular season and before bowl preparations are part of a critical contact period, where coaches can visit players and try to keep them committed or get them to join the class. A lot of recruiting battles are won and lost there, and a lot of recruiting classes are made or broken there. Hand was in Arizona visiting the home of a junior college linebacker named Morris Wooten. He sat with Wooten and his mother, talking about what it seemed like everyone else was talking about at the time.

"He's supposed to come to Morgantown the next day for an official visit and here it comes across the ticker on ESPN that Rich was named the head coach at Alabama," Hand said. "The kid and his mom look at me. 'Coach, what's going on?' I was honest. 'I don't know. I have no idea what's going on, but I'll find out.'"

Alabama had the big stadium and the new facilities, and it was Moore, a former player and coach, who had overseen these major projects. He could be trusted to support Rodriguez and to pay him nicely. The reported figure was $13 million across six years, as well as a pledge to pay the $2 million buyout at WVU.

Rodriguez arrived at the football facility the next day and was in his office for around three hours, first with his wife, Rita, then Pastilong, and finally with his two children. He exited and walked into the team meeting room across the hall from his office. The players had been waiting there, summoned earlier for an announcement, entirely clueless and helpless. Rodriguez's face was flushed. He had tears in his eyes and looked like an emotionally spent man.

He entered the meeting. Outside the room, where the media was gathered to witness something, nothing but silence was heard for a few minutes. And then a cheer. And a second. Rodriguez marched out, not looking much better than he had a few minutes earlier. The sounds from the team room indicated he was staying but, again, you couldn't trust anyone. Rodriguez walked by a crowd of reporters and said simply, "I'm staying," and disappeared until a press conference that was to begin some two hours later.

Rodriguez downplayed the reports from overnight that said he was off to Alabama. He expressed shock and disappointment and made it sound like he hadn't made up his mind until he left his office. Rodriguez was ultimately overwhelmed and swayed by the support that flowed in from influential backers, who helped WVU convince Rodriguez it could give him everything to win it all. The school had again extended and sweetened his contract and included in it a pool of money to split up among his assistants to provide them raises, as well as assurances that renovations to the academic center and the team's locker room would be financed and completed on a schedule.

Rodriguez said all the right things, noting that the details of the contract would prove he was committed to WVU "for a very, very long time" and that WVU was committed to him for just as long. Now Rodriguez was relieved, happy, quick to flash a goofy grin and a thumbs-up for the cameras. Wooten was on campus the next day and committed, though he'd later flip and head to Arizona State.

"I have a rule of thumb now that until there's a press conference and someone puts a hat on his head, he's not hired," Hand said. "After that deal went the way it did, I felt like Rich was going to be at West Virginia for a long time."

Rodriguez had never been a larger figure in West Virginia than he was at that very moment, but he was rather disliked in Alabama. Rodriguez knew it. "I'm not real popular there right now," he said in the press conference.

And why's that? Finis St. John, then the chairman of the University of Alabama System Board of Trustees, had an answer in the *Birmingham News* the next day: "We're sorry he changed his mind."

What Rodriguez rued as falsehoods presented as fact was seen very differently at Alabama. The school believed it had its coach. "There was a written document that dealt with all aspects of him becoming the head football coach of the University of Alabama that was agreed to by his representatives and representatives of the University of Alabama. It was reduced to writing Friday morning," trustee John McMahon Jr. told the *Birmingham News*.

Something wasn't right. Seeing as Rodriguez had, in word and in deed, left the door open for coaching opportunities elsewhere in the past, there was no need to believe that would change, no reason to feel at ease about the security offered by his newest contract.

Whether the reports of his dealings with Alabama were true or premature, there were still questions about Rodriguez and his loyalty, as well as the school's allegiance to him and all he had done. Fans were reminded of the days when a WVU coach wouldn't stay long after securing some success. West Virginia's people had enough issues and insecurities dealing with the way outsiders treated them. When they had to question one of their own, it made them sick.

And what if it didn't work out? What would happen if he poked WVU again the next winter? What more could WVU to do appease his persistent demands? What if he felt WVU couldn't, or wouldn't, extend any further? What if he felt WVU again wasn't living up to its word? Where would it leave WVU? Did it have enough to offer more, or had the university just had enough?

WVU played in the Gator Bowl, as it had two times before with Rodriguez. It only drove home the feeling that a season that was supposed to be so different felt so familiar. How familiar? WVU had beaten Georgia 38–35 in the Sugar Bowl; WVU beat Georgia Tech 38–35 in the Gator Bowl.

Slaton played sparingly because of a hamstring injury, but Pat White, who was suffering from a leg injury of his own, refused to let the Mountaineers lose. Despite falling behind by 18 points, WVU stormed back into the lead, played much better defense in the second half, and finally turned its Gator Bowl fortunes around. After the bowl, two of the team's most valued assistants, Hand and offensive line coach Rick Trickett, left. You had to wonder what was happening behind the scenes.

Rodriguez had come to WVU at the perfect time for the program. He was a young, successful coordinator who wanted to take his alma mater with him to the top. There was no one else like that out there for West Virginia. There wasn't a replacement waiting for the call. There wasn't a list of coaches lining up to take the WVU job as they might do for an opening at Alabama or, say, Michigan.

"The main reason I'm staying is because of the reasons to stay," he said, "not the reasons to go."

Fifty-three weeks after Rodriguez made that statement, a painfully familiar, yet far worse drama would unfold.

7
YANKEES

The fears imagined in the wake of the 2006 season were realized in 2007. That window that opened following the Sugar Bowl win began to close. As far as golden eras go, this one at WVU was as fantastic as it was brief. There were irresistible players and moments and undeniable successes, but also stunning lows, devastating disappointments, and a clock that was ticking terribly fast, even if no one wanted to acknowledge it.

The 2007 season began with great promise once again. Just as with 2006, in 2007 West Virginians thought surely this would be *the year*. The Mountaineers were No. 3 in the preseason polls, again an all-time high for the preseason. Pat White, Steve Slaton, and Owen Schmitt were back and could feel good behind veterans Ryan Stanchek, Greg Isdaner, and Jake Figner on the offensive line. White's experience and expected growth in the offense would open up the passing game, and with slippery Darius Reynaud and reliable Dorrell Jalloh catching passes, there was hope that the run-stopping, Cover Zero defense (i.e., zero high safeties in the defensive formation, thus allowing more defenders to set up close to the line of scrimmage) East Carolina and South Florida had employed, and that others had mimicked, could be conquered.

Then there was this little freshman running back, an Internet sensation with a library of eye-popping highlight reels on YouTube and a personal background that tugged at the emotions of the stoniest observer—Noel Devine.

The highest hope, though, was on defense. Simply put, the Mountaineer defense wasn't likely to be such a weak point as it was the year before. That was great news, particularly with the weapons returning on offense.

"The '07 year, I thought we were going to have really good depth, which we'd lacked a little bit," defensive coordinator Jeff Casteel said. "We had some veterans and we had some young guys who'd played in some big games for us before and I thought they'd gain confidence as the year went on. I thought the Maryland game that year was the game for those guys when they went out and really played a complete game. From there, they really just kind of took off together and played well together."

The secondary, which had been picked on and picked apart so much in 2006, had more experience and talent than before. But if WVU was to be good on defense, it had to begin with the defensive line. The idea was to stop the run and then control the pass. If the three defensive linemen could compromise blocking and either make plays or let linebackers or defensive backs sneak in to stop the run or harass the quarterback, then the odds were much better at winning the more predictable passing downs.

And WVU was going to be good on the line. Johnny Dingle returned as a defensive end, and Keilen Dykes was the nose guard. The defensive tackle position was tricky, but there was a thought that freshman Chris Neild could handle his business at nose and maybe let Dykes move over to tackle. If not, Dykes could stay at nose, and tackle could go to redshirt freshman Scooter Berry, who had come to WVU in January of 2006, seemingly as a sidekick to his half-brother, Jason Gwaltney.

The linebackers were all new in name, but they'd been watching and waiting. It had been years since a trio would play quite as well collectively as Marc Magro, Reed Williams, and Mortty Ivy did in

2007. They were fast, tough, smart, and agile, and they allowed the line and the secondary to worry only about themselves.

The cornerbacks, Larry Williams and Antonio Lewis, weren't superstars. They had their scary moments, but they were mostly solid and anonymous. Their names didn't come up much during the games, but that wasn't a bad thing. Vaughn Rivers could play a little, too, usually in reserve as a cornerback or moonlighting as a safety on passing downs.

The keys, though, were the safeties. WVU had a bunch of them for a change.

"The 2006 team, we were really a safety short and we had to play a Sam [strong-side] linebacker at one of our safety spots every down," Casteel said of the 6-foot-3, 230-pound John Holmes, who was a better fit as a linebacker with pass rushing, run-stopping abilities than he was as the bandit safety. "The next year, he was a third-down player and he did a great job for us."

Eric Wicks had seen just about everything from an offense. Quinton Andrews could be hard to handle as a person, but as a player, when he was invested in the game, he reminded folks that he was that kid who was a freshman All-American. Andrews and Wicks were interchangeable at the spur and bandit safety spots, and veteran Ridwan Malik added further flexibility.

WVU's base 3-3-5 defense used three safeties, though, and the third was the key to it all. Ryan Mundy came to campus in the offseason as a postgraduate transfer from the University of Michigan, soured not by the experience in Ann Arbor but by the team's failure to beat Ohio State the year before and get to the national championship game. He'd spent four years with the Wolverines, but he was a medical redshirt in 2005. He had remained interested in playing football but also in pursuing his education in a field not offered at Michigan.

An NCAA rule allowed him to transfer to a school that offered the postgraduate topic he wanted to study and be immediately eligible to play his fourth season in his fifth year. He was a Pittsburgh guy like Rivers, Wicks, and Ivy. He clicked right away and was perceived as a player who could help everyone get to that national championship game that had evaded him the year before.

"He solidified us," Casteel said. "He was really smart and really fit in well with the kids right from the start of camp. By the time the second or third game came along, he'd already solidified himself as a leader. He was a blessing for us."

There was no debating WVU's potential in the preseason, no reason to believe the Mountaineers couldn't focus on their annual goals of winning the Big East, playing in the BCS, and stalking the national title. Slaton was healthy and healed from offseason wrist surgery. White was only going to be better. Rodriguez, who sometimes humbly hedged when he talked up his players and deferred out of respect to the rest of the country, stated White and Slaton were "the most explosive performers in the country."

As expected, the Louisville game was circled. It would have to wait, this time until the ninth game of the season. The Cardinals were No. 10 in the preseason media poll and No. 11 in the coaches' poll, never mind losing coach Bobby Petrino to the Atlanta Falcons and running back Michael Bush to the NFL. Quarterback Brian Brohm was back, and the Heisman Trophy candidate was enough to spook WVU fans.

The Cardinals started 2-0, destroying people under their new coach, Steve Kragthorpe. Murray State fell 73–10 and Middle Tennessee State followed with a 58–42 loss. Meanwhile, WVU had little trouble of its own. It beat Western Michigan in the opener 62–24 and then beat Marshall 48–23 (despite Marshall holding a 13–6 halftime lead).

Devine was slowly coming out of the shadows behind Slaton. His first carry against Western Michigan was a one-yard gain; he received a standing ovation. Against the Thundering Herd, he carried just five times, but gained 76 yards and scored on 12- and 10-yard touchdown runs.

"He's got a gift," Rodriguez said afterward. Stanchek called Devine an "absolute stud" and said Devine reminded him of Slaton when he was younger. Slaton agreed and confessed Devine had more talent than he did when he was a freshman.

There was no denying Devine, or the idea he belonged in the offense. Aware of how Slaton loitered on the sideline while the running game struggled in 2005, Rodriguez vowed to get Devine in the game sooner, and not just in the second half—as had been the case in the first two games.

A week later the Mountaineers played at Maryland, and Slaton tried to rub it in against the team that had snubbed him and denied him his scholarship, much as he had in the 2006 matchup. He scored three times and totaled 137 yards on the ground in a game WVU won 31–14, but Devine stole the show. He carried just five times but finished with one less yard than Slaton. He averaged almost 30 yards per carry and showed off his marvelous ability, as his chiseled legs and enormous arms pumped like red-hot pistons and carried him through tackles and away from defenders.

Early on, Devine's college experience was a change for him. In high school, when he'd gained more than 6,800 yards and scored 92 touchdowns, he ran behind an average offensive line. Listen to him tell the stories or watch the highlights online and you can tell a lot of his runs were improvised, the product of keen vision and split-second decision making when a missed block left him with no other choice than to run for his own gain. With the Mountaineers, there was a plan in place, and the veterans up front nailed it every play. All Devine had to do was see the spot, run to it, and accelerate through it.

That was easy. Opponents took it hard. The Terrapins were frustrated by the slippery and surprisingly strong Devine, who ripped through arm tackles. One defender tugged him toward the ground by his facemask, only to let go and then have to shove Devine out of bounds. The most startling part of Devine's early days was how often the sideline made the tackle. Defenders couldn't do it quite as easily.

Two days after WVU moved to 3-0, Louisville, then ranked ninth, lost to Kentucky.

WVU made it to 4-0 with no trouble, and Rodriguez was bristling at suggestions his offense was susceptible to a Cover Zero defense. Western Michigan and Marshall had tried it, and WVU had no issue with it. The counterpoint was that better opponents had better personnel, and that personnel made the plan work.

It was East Carolina in 2005 that really brought the Cover Zero strategy to the attention of defensive coordinators readying for the Mountaineers. The Pirates had a reliable secondary, cornerbacks who could be trusted to handle WVU's receivers by themselves, and really good safeties who could run and tackle in space and handle whatever mismatches WVU tried to present. One or both safeties could be asked to step closer to the line of scrimmage and play the run. If it was a pass, then the safeties could adapt and cover while the cornerbacks would have to survive on an island, covering their receivers man-to-man without safety help.

In 2005, WVU had 127 yards on 46 carries against ECU, none of which were by Slaton and only three of which went to White. In 2006, WVU ran the ball 42 times for just 153 yards, and White couldn't pass effectively enough to open the defense or force the safeties back enough to compromise the plan.

A few weeks later, USF, with better athletes at the same critical positions, played the same plan. The Bulls had their own unique touches but had more success in a victory that kept WVU out of the BCS.

In 2007, the Pirates came to Morgantown. The Mountaineers were brilliant, amassing 588 yards of offense, 397 on the ground. It was a 48–0 game, and ECU had just 93 yards of offense before picking up a meaningless 67 yards and a touchdown on its final possession. Rodriguez couldn't have been more pleased with himself or his offense. This was as good as his team had looked in years, and he didn't deny it.

"In the spread offense, you have to make the defense defend you all 53 1/2 yards," he said afterward. "Today we did that pretty well."

That was an understatement. It was 10–0 early on, and then WVU did the sort of thing great teams do. A 13-play drive covered 83 yards and saw seven different Mountaineers catch or carry the ball. It might have been eight, but a pass from White to seldom-used Eddie Davis on the first play fell incomplete. The mere idea the pass would go to a player as anonymous as Davis was bizarre, but the point was made.

The Mountaineers challenged the defense to guard against everyone and everything. There were passes, options, reverses, and dives. On one play, White faked inside to Schmitt but kept the ball and pitched to Slaton for a big gain. Two plays later, White faked to Schmitt again and pitched to Slaton again, but Slaton looked to throw the ball before tucking it in and getting 12 more yards. A few moments later, White gave the ball to Schmitt and faked the pitch to Slaton.

The Pirates were spinning and it only got worse. White looked to run on a draw, but then he stopped just short of the line of scrimmage and threw the ball left to Slaton. How on earth do you stop that? ECU was hopeless, and never was that more apparent than on the next snap. The handoff went to Devine, who went outside and faked a reverse to Reynaud. Defenders followed Reynaud across the field and pushed him out of bounds as if he still had the ball. Other defenders managed to tackle Devine for a loss, which was almost miraculous considering the confusion among the Pirates. Mercifully, the drive ended on the next play when White carried for the first time and scored on a 13-yard run.

The game was over. The Pirates were finished. They had to play a base defense with very basic variations the rest of the way. WVU had posed a threat ECU couldn't ignore. With the safeties back and the running game humming, White completed 18 of 20 pass attempts for 181 yards and two scores.

The Cover Zero had been solved. The Mountaineers were so diverse, so unpredictable, so damned dangerous that there was no way they'd be stopped when a defense attempted to dictate the play with that aggressive approach Rodriguez had grown to detest. Those fears about the frustrated coach again puckering up in a big game were vanquished. Just adapt that ECU game plan to the next opponent, and then the next, and then the next, and there could be no problems.

West Virginia's confidence soared. Louisville would lose the same day to lowly Syracuse and fall to 2-2. WVU was on top of the world.

Word never reached the USF campus, though. Perhaps there was some communication gap, because the Mountaineers weren't very attuned to what was happening in Tampa, either. USF was, quietly, playing very well. The Bulls were 3-0 and had won in overtime on the road against a ranked Auburn team. A week later, they were ranked for the first time ever and crushed North Carolina before the now-curious hometown fans. That set the stage for the first sellout in program history with WVU coming to town, an achievement for which Rodriguez took some of the credit.

"I've talked to our team about how when a highly ranked team goes on the road to play somewhere, they're going to sell out the stadium," Rodriguez said the week of the USF game. "I think it's like the Yankees. Every time they go somewhere, they're going to get a big crowd. Every time we go somewhere, we're going to help them sell out."

Now you had material for the bulletin board. It was needless, and, astonishingly, it didn't stop there.

When WVU's team buses arrived at Tampa's Raymond James Stadium the night of the game, the majority of the players were seen wearing and bringing attention to New York Yankees caps. Despite all the research and interviews and conversations for this book, I didn't produce a ranking of the most egregious or arrogant statements or acts by WVU football players and coaches. Honestly, there isn't a need for one, because that act may be impossible to top.

Word of the Yankee caps got back to the Bulls with speed that would have made Devine blush. This was a stunning departure from the Mountaineers, who had preached and practiced being grateful and gracious about all the accolades that came their way. Players regularly wore black T-shirts with "SH, SH" printed on them—"Stay Humble, Stay Hungry." That was the team's motto. The Mountaineers were conditioned to succeed and to deal with all that came with it. The coach begged his players to work for it, to accept it, and to enjoy it, but to also make sure they were never satisfied.

Yet in the biggest game of the season, in their first opportunity to underscore their rise to prominence, the Mountaineers stepped totally and irresponsibly out of character.

Even more audaciously, the baseball caps weren't intended to solely remind the Bulls they only had a big crowd because the Mountaineers had graced them with their presence. The script "NY" on the caps conveyed a message—no, an insult.

"It stood for 'Not Yet,'" quarterback Jarrett Brown revealed. "We were ranked high, and they were saying it was their biggest game they were going to play and they wanted to set their mark with that game. We were like, 'Not yet.'"

The defending Gator Bowl champions felt pretty good about their position on top, but was this any different than crossing one's arms and cocking the head, or forming a W with one's hands to mark a big play or big score?

In truth, this was worse. And it came from the top. Years later, a player would confide that Rodriguez "was the one pushing that and got everyone behind it."

Predictably, it backfired. The Mountaineers were preparing for a WWE pay-per-view bout. The Bulls just wanted to win a football game. Their coach, Jim Leavitt, shrunk from the occasion during the week and offered tame sound bites toward the buildup. Louisville's Bobby Petrino had done the same a year before, and perhaps there was a lesson to be learned there. USF's greatest achievement was saving its sentiments for after the game.

Within the game, the Bulls were again tremendous on defense. This hinted that the personnel moves Rodriguez had made to his coaching staff in the offseason were ineffective. Rodriguez had needed to replace three coaches before 2007: Butch Jones was named the head coach at Central Michigan; offensive line coach Rick Trickett left for Florida State, not for money or for power, but just for a new job; and Herb Hand split for Tulsa. Hand didn't exactly want to go, though he was interested in adding to his résumé and expanding his responsibilities. He and Rodriguez spoke about Hand perhaps moving to either the wide receiver or offensive line coaching positions, but there would be a consequence to that that ultimately helped Hand make up his mind.

"I felt like maybe I had hit a little bit of a glass ceiling at West Virginia," Hand said. "I had probably gone as far as I could go in that program. I was plugged in as the recruiting coordinator, which was one of the big things that Rich and I talked about. My role as the recruiting coordinator was very important and he wasn't sure if me coaching the offensive line or the wide receivers would allow me to continue in the role as recruiting coordinator."

So Hand left for Tulsa, where he was hired as the offensive line coach and offensive coordinator before being renamed co-coordinator when head coach Todd Graham hired a young assistant named Gus Malzahn, who would later help Auburn's offense to the 2010 national title.

Rodriguez hired Tony Dews from UNLV to coach the receivers and then hired a pair of assistants from, of all places, USF. Greg Frey would coach the offensive line and, ideally, contribute some knowledge about the game plan or the personnel that had worked to defeat WVU in 2006. Rod Smith was named quarterbacks coach, which bumped Bill Stewart to coaching tight ends, a demotion disguised by giving Stewart the title of associate head coach.

Was it purely a ploy to beat USF? Not really. In fact, Frey was hired after Ron West had agreed to leave Clemson to join WVU but then changed his mind. Smith had played quarterback for Rodriguez at Glenville State and was a graduate assistant at Clemson and then at WVU.

The hats and the hires were rendered useless within the game. Smith's prized pupil—Pat White—was sidelined in the second quarter when he took a helmet to the thigh and never returned. Frey's line was fried by the Bulls. Center Mike Dent was so concerned about the defensive line crashing through the middle that he misfired on a few snaps, some in big spots. Right guard Eric Rodemoyer was singled out again and again. Those two were the only linemen new to the regular rotation that season.

Nothing else went right, either. The Mountaineers threw on seven of their first 11 downs, no doubt aimed at pushing the safeties back. Then came consecutive drives when WVU turned the ball over on downs, a Slaton fumble, an interception that skipped off Slaton and was returned for a touchdown, and then another Slaton fumble.

It was 14–0 in the second quarter, and any chance WVU had to get the emotion it somehow never started with disappeared. White scrambled for 18 yards on a fourth-and-5, but the tackle to take him down took him out of the game. When the score was 21–6 and a long run from Devine moved the ball into the red zone, Brown made an awful decision and his pass was intercepted in the end zone. WVU got moving again on the next possession, but Brown was intercepted again. He did connect with Reynaud on a nine-yard touchdown to make it 21–13 with 5:45 to go, and a sack by Dingle set up a fourth-and-23, but WVU came away with nothing on its final drive.

Losing White was immeasurable in its effect. WVU ran the ball 48 times for 188 yards—and that includes a bad snap that dropped the offense back 17 yards. Devine had only four carries for 43 yards, and one went for 37, while Schmitt had only five carries for 22 yards. WVU had the ball for nine more minutes than USF and finished with 163 more yards of offense, but the turnovers, the 5-for-17 effort on third down, and the inability to score touchdowns instead of kick field goals or commit turnovers was lethal.

The Bulls took plenty of joy discussing it.

"For the second year in a row," defensive tackle Richard Clebert told the *Lakeland Ledger* after the game, "Steve Slaton was a nobody, Pat White was a nobody."

Certainly the offense that clicked so convincingly a week earlier against ECU was caught off guard by the Bulls and either the aggression or adjustments in their plan. But Wally Burnham, the pleasantly grizzled, then-65-year-old USF defensive coordinator, said the Bulls changed "not one ounce." He instead relied on his tried-and-true approach to stopping the option.

WVU liked say it presented a complex approach. Burnham said it was simple. "You can't do but so many things against an option team anyway," he told Jack Bogaczyk of the *Charleston Daily Mail*. "You've got to have someone for the dive, someone for the quarterback, someone for the pitch. You play with discipline. It's not rocket science. It's football. The option has been around a long time."

The Mountaineers boarded the bus absent one accessory, one the Bulls were again all too happy to discuss. Matt Grothe, the quarterback who'd survived a rough night against WVU's defense and did just enough to win the game—nothing more important than avoid a blitz and connect with Carlton Mitchell on a 55-yard touchdown in the second quarter—pointed out the Yankees hadn't won a World Series since 2000. Burnham was less tactful, though no less impactful.

"You tell West Virginia," he ordered the *Tampa Tribune*, "they can take those Yankee hats and stick them."

Years later, Brown would shake his head and chuckle at the memory. "Whoops."

8
BREAKS

The loss to South Florida left WVU humbled and haunted again by the impression it had squandered a shot at the national championship. Such opportunities just don't come around, not at a place like WVU, but the Mountaineers and those who played and coached and cared for them were made to accept that verdict. Rich Rodriguez thought differently, though, and what mattered most to him was that the loss came in the fifth game of the 2007 season. A year earlier, the Mountaineers lost in the eighth game against Louisville, and they didn't have enough time left to recover their standing in the polls. Sometimes success in college football isn't about how many losses you have as much as when those losses happen.

With more than a half of the 2007 schedule remaining, Rodriguez trusted there would be more surprises to come from a season that had already proved volatile for the top teams. Twelve ranked teams had already lost before the Mountaineers lost to the Bulls. Ten of those 12 losses came against unranked teams. No game was more shocking or indicative of the completely unpredictable season to come than when Football Championship Subdivision powerhouse Appalachian State beat No. 5 Michigan in the Big House on the opening weekend of the season—a loss that would set the stage for moves and machinations that would affect much of college football, including, or perhaps especially, West Virginia.

WVU lost to the Bulls on a Friday. Seven more ranked teams would fall the next day. The Mountaineers met Sunday, and Rodriguez didn't have to do more than point at those games to support his rehabilitative message. "It looks like it's going to be a crazy year anyway, so it's not over yet," he said.

When the polls came out, WVU was No. 12 in the coaches' poll. We'll use that poll as the framework for what's to follow because it's one of two "human" polls that the Bowl Championship Series used to concoct its ranking. It's also the poll that would later give the Mountaineers their first No. 1 ranking.

In perception, there wasn't a lot of space between WVU and the top of the poll. In reality? Only time could answer that question. The Big East wasn't a particularly difficult conference, so an 11-1 record was by no means impossible. Then again, that record wasn't a ticket to the national championship game.

Never mind the way another loss to USF again revealed that WVU's potent offense could be derailed. WVU was going to need help to win just the conference title because the Bulls had the head-to-head win.

Beyond that? Were you really going to entertain a thought that grand?

The Mountaineers were going to need much, much more help to reach the BCS championship game. In fact, they'd need 27 breaks to make sure they finished the regular season ranked either No. 1 or No. 2 in the BCS standings. So far, 2007 had been ridiculously unstable for top teams, and Rodriguez was hoping to harness that so his players could ride it as far as it would take them. But 27 breaks?

Now, seven of the breaks the Mountaineers could control. They had to win their final seven games of the regular season. This was their playoff, if you will. Lose a game and it was over. Win and live to play another day. It was the best the Mountaineers could ask for, and the only thing they would concern themselves with for the rest of the journey.

In the end, 26 of those 27 breaks did happen. A lot of them occurred with the sort of circumstances that gave WVU and its fans a fateful feeling that its surge to the BCS title game was supposed to happen, that it was a matter of destiny. The teams WVU needed to lose kept losing, and strange occurrences along the way seemed to either facilitate those outcomes or enhance the idea WVU was actually meant to make it back to the top. As the Mountaineers saw everything falling into place, they were amazed by Rodriguez's calm confidence and ability to see into the future.

"He looks like a fortune teller because it's exactly what's happened," kicker and punter Pat McAfee said. "But you know what? It was really hard to believe. As the weeks went on and things started to happen, we started to believe it more."

WVU's road to the cusp of the national championship game started where the breakthrough 2005 season started. The Mountaineers dominated Syracuse in the Carrier Dome. They played with the attitude of an angry team on the way to a 55–14 win.

Then came the first wave of breaks.

Top-ranked USC lost to Stanford, 24–23, to end a 35-game home winning streak and a 24-game home winning streak in Pacific-10 conference games. The Cardinal, a 41-point underdog, felled the mighty Trojans with a fourth-down touchdown pass in the final minute.

LSU, ranked No. 2, won at home to drop No. 7 Florida despite trailing by 10 points in the fourth quarter. On the game-winning touchdown drive, the Tigers converted two fourth downs.

Illinois, which before beating No. 21 Penn State a week earlier hadn't beaten a ranked team since 2001, did it again. The Illini won at home against No. 5 Wisconsin to go to 3-0 in the Big Ten for the first time since 1990.

Eighteenth-ranked South Carolina won at home against No. 8 Kentucky while defensive end Eric Norwood tied an NCAA record with two fumbles returned for touchdowns.

Tennessee upset No. 11 Georgia after the hometown newspaper featured a game-day story that quoted anonymous former players discussing the downfall of the program. Tennessee coach Phil Fulmer fumed about the story, which he called "an incredible cheap shot," after the game. "It hit a dang nerve and I don't appreciate it," he said. The Volunteers scored touchdowns on their first five drives to win at home, 35–14.

Seriously, how about that for a start? A powerhouse loses a stunner at home, where it never loses. A top-10 team wastes a two-score lead and lets the opponent convert two fourth downs on a do-or-die drive. A pretender that never beats ranked teams beats another ranked team. A defensive end returns two fumbles for touchdowns. A newspaper gives its target enough momentum to upset a Southeastern Conference power. All in just one week.

The polls came out a day later and WVU was back in the top 10 at No. 9. The Mountaineers were off the next week, but they kept getting help. Top-ranked LSU lost on the road to No. 18 Kentucky, 43–37, in three overtimes. Then No. 2 Cal lost at home to Oregon State, 31–28. The Golden Bears trailed 31–21 late, but scored a touchdown and then forced a punt. The offense drove from its 5-yard line to the Oregon State 12 with 14 seconds left. Cal could have tied with an easy field goal, but quarterback Kevin Riley scrambled and inexplicably ran the ball despite having no timeouts left. He was tackled and time ran out on the Bears.

Inactivity didn't hurt the Mountaineers a bit. They were No. 7 in the next poll and No. 9 in the debut BCS ranking. Four days later, the Big East was back in play after Rutgers beat USF, which had risen to No. 3 in the poll and No. 2 in the BCS. The Scarlet Knights, playing at home, played with shocking aggression, first using a fake punt to set up a field goal early on and then creating distance when Andrew DePaola, the third-string quarterback, threw a 15-yard touchdown pass on a fake field goal in the third quarter.

The chase was on again. WVU beat Mississippi State, 38–13, but regretted that it hadn't won more emphatically. After the first play of the second quarter, WVU already led 31–0. As the day dragged on, the Mountaineers were dragged down by their inability to do more.

"We were saying, 'It's not us playing Mississippi State anymore. It's us playing the computers,'" cornerback Vaughn Rivers said. "We need as many points as we can get and to do as good as we can do. It's not anything against Mississippi State, but it's something we have to do to move ourselves up in the polls."

All the Mountaineers really had to do was go home and watch games to see themselves on the move. Kentucky, No. 7 in the BCS and No. 13 in the poll, lost to Florida 45–37, the 21st straight time the Wildcats lost to the Gators.

The Mountaineers even benefited from bad things happening to teams ranked behind them. Cal, part of a competitive Pac-10 that season, lost its second game 30–11 against UCLA, ensuring that a one-loss Bears team wouldn't jump a one-loss WVU in the BCS. It was getting harder and harder to shake the feeling WVU was fated to get back on top again.

Rodriguez tried to steer clear of it, though. He even agreed to go see a movie with his wife and kids, a rare escape from the constant constraints of time and responsibility placed upon his life.

"I went to one 15 years ago and it was *The Crying Game*, and I ain't been back since and you can understand why," Rodriguez said.

Rodriguez capitulated on this one occasion. He went to see *Evan Almighty*. He snacked on some popcorn and chocolate-covered raisins and had a pretty normal, pretty good night. Sometime later, Rita was at her husband's side as the team's charter flight headed to New Jersey for the game against Rutgers.

"We get on the plane, and they said the movie for the flight was *Evan Almighty*," Rodriguez said. "Rita said, 'It's destiny! I know we're going to win!'"

The Mountaineers, now ranked No. 7 in the BCS and No. 6 in the coaches' poll, crushed Rutgers 31–3. Timing is everything in sports; WVU had already exercised impeccable timing with its wins and the way they corresponded with the losses of others. But the win against Rutgers, the way it came with no suspense, was ideal. The Scarlet Knights had enjoyed one of their biggest wins ever a week before against the USF team that had WVU's number. WVU seemed unimpressed, to say the least.

Things got even better. Connecticut beat the Bulls 22–15, and

USF suddenly had two Big East losses. The Mountaineers were again in control of the Big East championship race.

"I told them that destiny doesn't win championships," Rodriguez said. "Determination does. I'm not a believer in being destined to win a championship."

No matter what Rodriguez said, no matter where you looked, events enhanced the idea that WVU was in prime position, and not just for the Big East title. The Mountaineers were catching up in a hurry and other teams couldn't keep pace. The same week USF lost its second game, so too did USC and Virginia Tech. They were no longer a threat to jump a one-loss WVU. Oregon already had passed the Mountaineers and Missouri was getting closer, but one could feel their time was coming.

Oregon survived the next week but did WVU a favor. The Ducks were No. 4 in the poll and No. 5 in the BCS, and they defeated unbeaten Arizona State, which was No. 6 in the poll and No. 4 in the BCS. Then Florida State beat Boston College, which was undefeated and No. 2 in the poll and the BCS. The Eagles' previously unflappable quarterback, Matt Ryan, threw three interceptions, including a late killer that was returned for a touchdown in a 27–17 loss. The Mountaineers were idle again, but jumped one spot to No. 6 in the poll and remained No. 7 in the BCS.

The Louisville game came the next week. WVU had its first scare in a while but won 38–31 in a game that oddly mirrored the last time the two teams played at Mountaineer Field. John Holmes, the safety who had played out of position the year before, sacked Brian Brohm in the third quarter and forced a fumble that Eric Wicks returned 44 yards for a touchdown. WVU mounted a 31–14 advantage, another 17-point lead in Morgantown. On this occasion, the Cardinals rallied and tied the score. But in the waning minutes Pat White did something only Pat White could do. He dropped back and turned what was supposed to be a pass play to the right side into a 50-yard touchdown run down the left sideline with one minute, 36 seconds remaining.

Ohio State was the top-ranked team that week, but its Big Ten–record 20-game winning streak and school-record 28-game winning streak came to an end in a loss to that once-lowly Illinois team. WVU rose to No. 5 while and the BCS ranked the Mountaineers No. 6.

Then things got really crazy. Oregon, No. 2 in the poll and the BCS, lost to Arizona. Oregon also lost its quarterback, Dennis Dixon, in the first quarter. Dixon was probably the favorite for the Heisman Trophy before his season-ending knee injury.

Oklahoma, No. 3 in the poll and No. 4 in the BCS, lost to Texas Tech on the road. Oklahoma's redshirt freshman quarterback Sam Bradford, the nation's leader in passing efficiency despite his youth, was sidelined for the game in the first quarter.

If you hadn't believed in WVU's destiny by then, you had no choice but to consider it now.

WVU's quarterback was fine, fortunately. White ran for 155 yards and passed for 140 in a 28–23 win against Cincinnati. WVU thwarted an onside kick attempt following the Bearcats' final score. That set up a game against Connecticut the following week. The Huskies had two Big East losses. WVU had one. The winner would be the Big East champion and the league's representative in the BCS.

What was once a ridiculous thought to consider—that WVU could reach the top of the BCS standings—was now a real possibility, but the players and the coach wouldn't look at it that way. WVU was only worried about the Big East at that point, and with good reason. Despite everything that happened in their favor, the Mountaineers still needed help.

The day after beating the Bearcats, the Mountaineers found themselves ranked No. 3. LSU and Kansas, the teams ahead of them, would be favored in their next games. Then there were the one-loss teams. Missouri had a game against Kansas; if the Tigers won, they'd make a move, which was bad news for WVU, ahead of the Tigers by just one spot in the BCS. One-loss Ohio State was done with its regular season, which meant the Buckeyes couldn't lose and could conceivably jump the Mountaineers, what with the way voters regarded the Big Ten. Even Arizona State had a chance with a game against USC and an opportunity to make a major statement.

WVU wouldn't be denied, though. Arizona State lost to USC

on Thursday night. The next day LSU lost to Arkansas, 50–48, in another triple-overtime game. The Mountaineers were staying that night at Lakeview Golf Resort & Spa in Morgantown in preparation for Saturday's game. They watched as the Tigers fell and created the ultimate opening.

"Everyone was screaming and running up and down the halls," running back Steve Slaton said.

Missouri defeated Kansas to clinch a spot in the Big XII title game against Oklahoma. In Morgantown, the Mountaineers made an absolute mockery of the de facto Big East championship game. They embarrassed Connecticut, 66–21, and scored nine touchdowns. Nine! And they had actually trailed 7–0, their first deficit since the end of the USF game. As in their earlier home game against East Carolina, the Mountaineers displayed a brand of football that seemed unstoppable.

The Huskies had a plodding offense and lumbering defenders and neither could keep up with WVU's race-car-fast players. Consider this: UConn had scored 30, 34, 38, 38, 44, and 45 points in its first 11 games, but was somehow averaging just 28.5 points per game. The Huskies were even outgained offensively in five of their six Big East games before seeing WVU. It was a total mismatch. The Mountaineers knew it and showed it.

"We were trying to prove something," Rivers said. "There are still a lot of naysayers out there who just do not want to see West Virginia in the national championship game. This was for them."

WVU now was ranked No. 1 for the first time in school history; the BCS put the Mountaineers behind only Missouri. The suspense was over. There was no need to study rankings and schedules or ignore the fact that pulling off this comeback was entirely possible.

After everything that had to happen had actually happened, all that was left for WVU to do was win a home game against a four-touchdown underdog—number 27 of those 27 things that had to happen for WVU to reach the championship. All that was left was Pitt, a 4-7 team that had done nothing threatening under coach Dave Wannstedt, a team that had allowed 90 points in the previous two games against the teams led by Slaton and White.

There are no sure things in West Virginia, no sure things for the Mountaineers—but this was a sure thing. So much so that some idiot wrote this:

Much like how Ralphie knew he was getting that official Red Ryder, carbine-action, 200-shot, range model air rifle, West Virginia fans seem similarly sure what they'll get for Christmas when their Mountaineers play host to rival Pitt Saturday night.

Victory is assumed and a celebration is imminent, even though the Mountaineers seemed to shoot their own eyes out that one night in Tampa, Fla.

A spot in the Bowl Championship Series title game is one victory away, so what better time than now to share another Christmas story?

Twas the night before Pittsburgh,
when all through my mind,
Were visions of couch burnings,
both yours and mine.
Firemen were resting and acting quite lazy,
But they knew that things were about to get crazy.
The players were nestled,
Markell did his dreads,
While visions of Bourbon Street danced in their heads.
There were Quinton's gold teeth,
Larry's son in his lap,
While the quarterback made noises to sound like a cat.
When down in the end zone there arose such a noise,
They sprang from their homes and called all their boys.
To the field they flew, fast as Devine,
Making sure to pick up the offensive line.
The invaders had arrived at the stadium early,
These Panthers were looking noticeably surly.
There was a point to this late-night trip through the hills,
They were out on the field doing defensive drills.

With a dapper old coach who combed his mustache,
You knew in a moment it must be Wannstedt.
He'd made his name as a defensive master,
And he whistled and shouted for them to run faster!
"Watch Slaton! Watch Schmitt! Watch Reynaud and White!
Watch option! Watch bubble! Could be a rough night!
Let's stand at the goal line and build a big wall,
And keep them from their shot to play for it all!"
As they began to believe his bold rally cry,
There was a flash and a pop up high in the sky.
They reacted the same, with a quick double take,
What they saw made them stop in their cleats and quake.
On the top of the stadium a man made his stand,
As he calmly adjusted his Nike wristbands.
He said "My name's Rich, as you surely know."
Then ran down the bleachers with Mountaineers in tow.
They were dressed all in gold, from their heads to their feet,
And they looked like they'd win a 12-team track meet.
A bundle of plays he had in his book,
And there was no mistaking that confident look.
Pitt's eyes, how they widened!
Their hearts, how they pounded!
All for the biggest game since this brawl was founded.
One side had momentum, the other desperation,
This battle wouldn't wait for the eyes of the nation!
Caridi was roused from a much-needed sleep,
So were Hickman and Hertzel, the last with a bleep.
They brought their pens, paper and elaborate prose,
To witness this battle of bitter old foes.
It was dark and cold, your breath you could see,
But that didn't stop the kickoff of Pat McAfee.
The tackle, of course, came from an old Hawk named Emery,
And so started this game that would soon be a memory.
They spoke so few words as they went to work,
But score after score drove the visitors berserk.

BREAKS

The Mountaineers rolled, as was expected,
While the Panthers backed off, clearly dejected.
There was a Gatorade shower that gave poor Rich shivers,
While no one seemed happier than one Vaughn Rivers.
They exclaimed after singing about Almost Heaven
"We'll see you in New Orleans on January 7."

9
HURT

On the final day of November, the literal night before Pittsburgh, the date before the annual Backyard Brawl—the 100th edition of this bitter rivalry—would be played at Mountaineer Field and forever chiseled into the memories of WVU fans, Mario's Fishbowl in Morgantown was a crowded and crazy place to be. It always is the night before a home game, but this was different. This was unique. This really was almost heaven.

Beer flowed into frosted mugs and the fans' anticipation for the events to come spilled over. You could see it coming through the smoky haze inside the local landmark on Richwood Avenue. You could taste it in the hot garlic sauce that saturated the chicken wings. You could smell it with the fried food and burning nicotine. You could hear it over the jukebox blaring Hank Williams Jr. The Mountaineers—their Mountaineers—were playing for a spot in the BCS championship game. And that scared the hell out of them.

The week spent waiting for the game was the longest of their fanatical lives. The days at work or in the classroom were just brutal. Never-ending. Foggy. Scary. Were their long years of suffering about to end? Or would the misery be extended and reach an unconscionable level?

Nah. Not this time, they told themselves as they shopped for airfare and tickets to the national championship game, as they booked hotels and scouted the nightlife in New Orleans. They did other things to pass the time. They called friends and family. They read newspapers and websites. They checked their email. They scanned the message boards. And if you had a phone or a computer, if you listened to the radio or stopped by the water cooler to chat, you heard that poem, that damned poem, about "The Night Before Pittsburgh."

It was forwarded to entire contact lists, to all the people the sender knew from work or school or that one night they met at that one friend's Halloween party. Like a virus, that recipient spread it to the mechanic and the mailman and the barber and the butcher. On and on it went. It was posted again and again and again and again on message boards. It was read on the radio when someone saw it, thought it was awesome, and wanted to share it on the air, as if some jockey hadn't already read it the day before or the day before that. It was passed around at work as a way to make those hands on the clock spin just a little faster.

It eventually made people sick, including me. I wrote it not as a coronation of the Mountaineers, but as satire, as creativity, as a celebration for what, at that point, was really a remarkable accomplishment. WVU needed only to beat its overmatched rival to move on to the BCS championship game. Nine weeks earlier, you would have had better luck convincing the people of Morgantown that Prohibition was a good idea than convincing them WVU would play for that ugly Waterford crystal trophy. So many people sent that parody of Clement Clark Moore's yuletide classic to me or told me about it or urged me to read it and promote it or find and interview the author that I was left feeling like so many others.

If I heard it one more time ...

Ah, but certainly the people at the Fishbowl would be different. This was a celebration, and WVU football was their cause. Nothing could deflate their spirits that night.

Or was the heavy emotion in the air, impossible to ignore as soon as you entered the bar and complete strangers cheered another stranger's arrival, really just tension? Were they worried?

Nah. Not this time, they told themselves as they licked the sauce off their fingers, ordered another round, and answered Hank Jr.'s three questions: "Why do we drink? Why do we roll smoke? Why must you live out the songs that you wrote?" This was their "Family Tradition."

Late that night, after someone had stuffed a dollar bill into that old jukebox and ordered it to play "Country Roads" for the fifth or 10th or 20th time, someone grabbed a beer mug and stood near the counter at the front of the old Richwood Avenue Confectionary and asked for everyone's attention. She was going to read that poem, that damned poem. After all, the author was in the building.

I slipped away to the shelter of the bathroom when I heard the muffled "Twas the night before Pittsburgh ..."

The boos and jeers nearly blew open the door. I flinched and lurched as if I were cramped in one of those airplane bathrooms when the jet rocks through turbulence. By Friday night, the poem was infuriating. The game was a formality. For the love of Rod, don't jinx it. Bigger and better things were waiting in New Orleans ... and hey, hadn't the fans been deprived that holiday in the Big Easy two years earlier when the Sugar Bowl was moved to Atlanta?

Everything made sense now.

Morgantown was on edge, fueled by fear as it ran away from its worst worries to finally embrace the ecstasy that had evaded the town for so many years. Stop with the poem. Enough of the pomp and circumstance. Just hurry up and get to the game already. The fans had waited a lifetime just to arrive at that agonizingly long week leading up to December 1, 2007.

* * *

"It went by so fast," kicker and punter Pat McAfee said.

Nightmares are like that. They might be long and terrifying, but when you snap out of it, you feel like it was very brief. The game actually lasted three hours and 10 minutes, and WVU snapped the ball just 57 times—the lowest total of the season.

Make no mistake, 13–9 was a nightmare.

"A flat-out nightmare," Rich Rodriguez said with a fragile voice as he faced the media with red, glassy eyes, his shirt splashed with liquid from a water bottle that he himself had probably hurled in anger and disbelief. Love Rodriguez or hate him, wish him the best or the worst, hell, even have no feeling toward him now after all these years. You can't watch him soldier through that press conference and sprinkle awkward pauses and fidgets over the top of it all and not feel for a man dealing with incomparable devastation.

It's impossible to circle the one thing that caused WVU's devastating demise. You could say it was fate. After all, these were the Mountaineers. True, they'd been riding destiny for weeks, but who were they to think they were beyond the trend? What made them so certain that what had happened to so many others wouldn't happen to them? WVU was the 59th and final ranked team to lose to an unranked or lower-ranked team in the 2007 regular season, the 13th top-five team to lose to an unranked team, and the seventh team to lose when ranked No. 2 in the media poll.

WVU typically doesn't arrive at the end as much as it crashes. Was it really so unexpected? Is that what threw fans into such an infinite sadness? They felt guilty, as though they had conspired to compromise their team by daring to take something so meaningful for granted. What if they hadn't been so sure, so confident, about a victory against a team that was three games below .500 after it gave up 48 points in a loss to USF?

The letdown at the end may very well have come from the high before it. Pitt after UConn was equivalent to USF after East Carolina, just a stunning and inexplicable switch from a diverse and imperturbable offense to a dull and inconceivable one. The Mountaineers went from being too good for UConn to being too good for themselves.

In the week before the Pitt game, everyone was writing about Noel Devine. Rodriguez had been tweaking his two-back shotgun set, and instead of Pat White, Steve Slaton, and Owen Schmitt, he had featured White, Slaton, and Devine. When WVU used that set with Schmitt, defenses would trend toward his side or follow where he went. More often than not, he was the blocker for the runner. With Devine in Schmitt's spot, the defense had no cues and needed to be far more honest. It was a battle of speed then, and the Mountaineers liked their chances, especially with Schmitt able to stay in the game as a tight end.

Rodriguez, who'd been tinkering with the set for weeks and actually took it for a spin a week earlier against Cincinnati, let Devine loose against UConn. The little freshman carried 11 times for 118 yards and a touchdown, and it looked like the hottest offense in the nation had just added another rod to the fire. It was too hard to stop White and Slaton and keep your eyes on Schmitt and Darius Reynaud. Add Devine to that and, by all means, just try to figure out a way to contain the Mountaineers.

Rodriguez was fixated on speed. Who could blame him? Why not give that group another go and see what they could do? He started them against the Panthers.

WVU was capable of being so very good at so many things, but not all at once. Devine ended up with seven carries against the Panthers. Slaton, the returning consensus All-American, had nine. The numbers showed WVU was extraordinarily hard to beat when Slaton hit 100 yards, but it's hard to get 100 yards on nine carries. Schmitt started at tight end that game. He was the fullback by the third snap, meaning the White-Slaton-Devine combo had all of two snaps to get going before the offense switched gears. Schmitt ran for 12 yards on that third play. He touched the ball one more time the rest of the game and not once in the final three quarters.

The Mountaineers ran the ball 41 times and finished with 104 yards. Twenty-three of the runs went to either White or Jarrett Brown. That Brown played because White was again injured, this time with a dislocated thumb on his nonthrowing hand (which kept him out most of the game), cannot be overlooked.

The two quarterbacks only threw 16 passes, even though Pitt was selling out to stop the run and hoping safeties and linebackers could run routes with running backs and tight ends, and cornerbacks could run routes with receivers. If the Panthers could make tackles in space, even if they gave up a completion or some yardage, that was fine with them. At the end of the game, Pitt's players had missed only two tackles that cost them all of seven yards. They made no mistakes and gave WVU no options.

"Pat White had one move that he really loved when he carried the ball and that was a jab step outside and then cut it up inside," Pitt defensive coordinator Paul Rhoads said. "We prepared for it hard and we prepared to take the ball out of his hands. Whether he was outside or not, he was going to be giving. He was not going to be keeping."

WVU let the Panthers sit in that defense and dictate the game. Hardly any of the passing or running elements that worked so well in the victory against ECU and then later against Connecticut were given a chance against the Panthers. Just as against USF, those things were almost nonexistent.

Would it have mattered? Almost certainly, and as proof, look ahead one season. In 2008, Rhoads became Auburn's defensive coordinator. His Tigers defense came to Mountaineer Field that year; WVU coach Bill Stewart and offensive coordinator Jeff Mullen crafted a game plan that asked for drag routes and crossing routes that forced the Auburn defenders to try to run with WVU's receivers and running backs. White passed for 173 yards with three touchdowns coming on a deep slant, a corner route, and a crossing route. Rhoads was forced to change up a little to cover the pass, and the Tigers couldn't stop Devine, who had 207 yards and a touchdown.

The Panthers used very fundamental football, strict adherence to assignments, and wonderful one-on-one tackling to control the game, but WVU never effectively discouraged the basic defensive game plan. Even when the Mountaineers had chances to force the action, they declined.

The game started perfectly for WVU. Panthers quarterback Pat Bostic threw an interception on the second play. Within six snaps, the Mountaineers moved to the Pitt 2-yard line. It was fourth down and Mountaineer Field was rocking, begging for the offense to land an early punch with touchdown. Rodriguez, purveyor of an offense averaging 41.6 points per game and going against a team that averaged 23.7, decided to kick a field goal. He asked the special teams to take a five-yard delay of game penalty so McAfee would have a better angle from the left hash, but Pitt declined the penalty so McAfee would have something to think about on an otherwise easy kick.

A whole lot of the 60,100 in the stands that night, whether they were Pitt fans or WVU fans, wondered why the Mountaineers didn't make Pitt regret its decision by going for the touchdown instead. Even if it didn't work, Pitt would get the ball near its own end zone and the Mountaineers could be really aggressive with 98 or so yards behind them to defend. But Rodriguez, who moments earlier thought the short kick from the left hash wasn't a good call, decided to let McAfee go from that spot. The kicker missed, and Pitt got the ball at the 20.

The Panthers offense was about as simplified as it could be and about as effective as they could hope for. Rather than mix things up or ask a freshman quarterback with limited experience and ability to go out and win the game, they instead handed the ball to running back LeSean McCoy again and again. He whacked at the defense 38 times, like an ax splitting the base of the tree until it fell. These were forceful, measured strikes. The longest run covered 19 yards. Only one other run went for more than seven yards and that 12-yard gain was the first play of the game. Six times McCoy picked up a first down and twice he did it on third down, including a huge seven-yard run on third-and-6 late in the fourth quarter. In the end, McCoy had 148 yards and Pitt held the ball for 14 more snaps and an extra 15 minutes, 38 seconds. With McCoy chopping away at the base, Pitt pushed and ultimately toppled the Mountaineers.

WVU had opportunities. The Mountaineers led 7–3 at halftime despite White having left the game on a drive in the middle of the second quarter, but maybe he'd be back after the break. Maybe he got that thumb fixed and secured and would be good to go in the entire second half. Plus, WVU would get the ball first to start the second half. Vaughn Rivers caught the kickoff at the 13 and sprinted to an opening. Ten yards. Fifteen. Twenty. Thirty. This was more like it. This was …

Rivers got smacked and lost the ball. Pitt recovered at the WVU 48 and pounced. On fourth-and-1 at the 39, the Panthers went for it and got it. They let Bostic pass on third-and-9 and were rewarded with an 18-yard gain. Four plays later, Bostic sneaked over the goal line. It was 10–7 and the Mountaineers were in trouble. Their quarterback was on the sideline. Their offense was in traction. Their fans were in denial. The Mountaineers ran four plays on offense in the third quarter. Four.

It looked like it might get better after the Panthers took a 13–7 lead with 6:17 to go. The crowd, frozen by fear, was thawed by the thrill of Devine returning the kickoff 48 yards to the Pitt 33 and then by the sight of White jogging back into the game. The fans were standing and screaming, but White's first carry gained no yards. On third-and-5, he came up three yards short. Rather than let McAfee take aim at a third attempt, this time from 45 yards away, and make it a three-point game, Rodriguez instead decided to go for it. On a play with no imagination, Slaton was tackled a yard short.

The defense forced Pitt to punt on its next possession with three minutes to go. Rivers nearly broke free on the return, but he was stopped near midfield. White gained a yard, then completed a pass for 20 yards and ran for 12 to the Pitt 21. This was it. It was happening. White was back. Maybe he was cold on the first drive, perhaps he shouldn't have even been in the game then because Brown was loose and in rhythm and gave the Mountaineers a better shot, but now White was warm. Hot. He'd find a way.

Incomplete.

Incomplete.

Fumbled snap. Seven-yard loss. Timeout.

What do you call when it's fourth-and-17 and you need to convert to get to the national championship game? White looked to the end zone for Wes Lyons, who had all of seven catches that season.

Incomplete.

Wait! Penalty flag!

The crowd gasped and hoped and then sighed. The Panthers were guilty of unsportsmanlike conduct for their celebration. They moved backward, from the 28 to the 14, and couldn't have cared less. They handed the ball to McCoy three more times and then trotted out their punter as the clock ticked toward zero. No one could believe what they were watching, so much so that when punter Dave Brytus took the snap and started running backward and across his own goal line so that time would expire and he could step out of the back of the end zone, many fans jumped to their feet and shrieked, wondering if perhaps a miracle had happened. It was an elective safety. The final score became the name by which the game would forever be known: 13–9.

"Today," Pitt coach Dave Wannstedt said, "we ran faster."

Losing to Pitt with the BCS title game at stake was bad enough. Letting Wannstedt have the last laugh with that subtle, sly dig was even worse. Two Backyard Brawls earlier, ESPN's Erin Andrews collared Wannstedt as he tried to leave the field at halftime. White and Slaton and the rest of the gang were running wild throughout the first half. The offense had 310 yards already, and White had two touchdowns with his feet and one with his arm. Wannstedt, an able and accomplished defensive strategist in college and the NFL, told Andrews the Panthers just needed to run faster. The quote became a punch line at his expense for two years until Wannstedt punched back and opened up a deep cut.

Fifteen or 20 minutes after the game, Rodriguez escaped a morbid locker room and tried his hardest to get comfortable behind the podium at his press conference. He shifted and fidgeted. He paused for 10 seconds. Fifteen. Twenty? Who knows? Things had stopped making sense; time wasn't relevant.

"I apologize," he said.

Center Mike Dent—who had nearly broken into tears when he faced the media four days after the USF loss, who played so well since misfiring his snaps in that game against the Bulls, who tried so hard to shake the feeling he might somehow be responsible for the USF loss and for his team not reaching the BCS title game—was the first player out. He called it the "worst type of disappointment." Schmitt called it a disaster. Piercing descriptions flowed like tears in the room where the Mountaineers spoke to the media, where players and coaches tried to come to grips with what had happened.

What *had* happened?

"We picked the worst time to play our worst offensive game in years," Rodriguez said.

* * *

On the day after the biggest crash in school history—and arguably one of college football's all-time biggest failures—WVU was selected for the bowl that had been the scene of its biggest previous disappointment. The Mountaineers would return to the Fiesta Bowl for the first time since the end of the 1988 season, when Major Harris was hurt and they lost the national championship to Notre Dame.

How about that for symmetry?

How about some symbolism? The sun never once came out in Morgantown the day after 13–9. It rose in the east and set in the west, but it never showed its face on campus or in any of the surrounding neighborhoods. Maybe it knew better. You don't mess with your dad the morning after New Year's Eve or your sister after a breakup. You can't console your friend when he puts his dog to sleep or your neighbors when their son heads off to college. In Morgantown, in West Virginia, in homes where fans or students or graduates or employees lived, you couldn't hurry them through the mourning. Not even the sun would brighten things up that day. This was a terribly difficult time.

WVU fans are, by and large, prone to express the emotions generated by the plays and the outcomes of the games they cheer. They scream and chant and sing and taunt. They storm fields and courts and tear down goal posts and dance with players. They set stuff on fire and parade down High Street, some on foot, some by car, some hanging out of sunroofs or passenger windows, to celebrate a big win.

After the loss there was nothing, for a disturbingly long time. This hurt. For these people, the people who'd been so disappointed so many times before, this really, really hurt. And it would only get worse.

* * *

Rodriguez was crushed. He absolutely hated losing. He wasn't good with it. He wasn't used to it. This is the guy whose childhood friends remembered as the kind of competitor who would race them to the water fountain. He played four sports in high school because he couldn't play five. He refused to be stopped when his first head coaching job ended when the college did away with the football program.

So he had taught driver's ed and worked bus duty at North Marion High School to make some money and financially justify his decision to work as a volunteer coach at WVU. He'd run the two or three minutes from his bus duty post to the parking lot, hurry into his car, and then dare the traffic lights to turn from green to yellow or yellow to red as he snaked through the wavy roads that took him from the tiny town of Rachel to Interstate 79. He'd race north to Morgantown so he could get to the stadium and change clothes in time for practice. On his best days, he won the race and was on the field when the whistle blew to start practice. Nothing mattered more to Rodriguez than winning.

It was his most admirable quality and, in the end at WVU, his most destructive. At the core of the disagreements that eventually split WVU and Rodriguez was one fact with which everyone agreed: Rodriguez asked for a lot to get to the top and the school gave him a lot, but the school thought he wanted too much and Rodriguez thought the school never did enough.

To get so close to the goal both sides wanted and to come away empty meant Rodriguez had to deal not only with that pain, but also with the reality that the relationship with his superiors and facilitators wasn't going to change. If he was going to stay at WVU, it wasn't going to be entirely pleasant. If he was going to win at WVU, he was going to have to pick some fights.

In truth, the battles started far, far earlier. The dalliance the previous December with Alabama generated a new contract, a farce of a press conference, and quotes about how happy everyone would be for years to come. Yet Rodriguez didn't sign the contract until August 24, 2007, and only when the school's new president, Mike Garrison, got everyone together to make sure it was signed before the season started.

In between the press conference defusing the Alabama scare and the signature that erased Garrison's apprehension, Rodriguez and his people were concerned about the promises they thought they were guaranteed and thought they deserved, but feared they might not get, the things the university believed it only promised to look into.

After the Pitt loss, Rodriguez was reminded of all of those suspicions, either by himself or by his people, and observers saw a different man descend into the depths of that devastating loss. He'd asked for more control. He was never obliged. He wanted the program to try new ways to generate revenue to make sure it remained competitive. He was denied. His financial advisor had warned in November of looming openings at Texas A&M and Florida State. They were never discussed. Rodriguez knew it was going to be hard for him to remain at WVU and easier to justify a move to himself, if no one else.

Garrison and his chief of staff, Craig Walker, watched that painful postgame press conference on the television in their suite. Then, as they did after every game they attended, they went to speak with Rodriguez. They walked through the locker room to console and reassure the players and were told that Rodriguez was already in his office. Garrison and Walker went there, knocked on the door, and were greeted by Rodriguez's wife, Rita.

Garrison knew this wasn't going to be easy. He'd had the same talk with Rodriguez after the loss to USF, and this figured to be exponentially more difficult. He told Rita that he, Walker, and the entire university were still proud of Rodriguez and the team and what they'd accomplished, and that they wanted to tell that to Rodriguez in person. The coach's wife wouldn't allow the visitors inside the office to speak with her husband.

A day later, Garrison called Rodriguez and asked Rodriguez and his wife to accompany Garrison and his wife to the men's basketball home game the following Saturday. Garrison thought it was important for Rodriguez to be seen out in public and among his people, to show that life was again normal. It would demonstrate that if he could move on and be happy with what his team had achieved, then so too could everyone else. Neither Rodriguez nor his wife ever responded; the president didn't speak with his coach until they attended a Fiesta Bowl function on December 10.

"He seemed out of sorts, and I think most who observed him during that time felt that way," Garrison said. "He said that he was unhappy. I couldn't frankly understand what would make him unhappy at that point in time, but I told him, 'If you ever want to talk, let's set up a time to talk.'"

One day, when things got really tough, Rodriguez grabbed his phone and called Lloyd Carr, the Michigan coach who'd announced his plan to retire a few weeks earlier. Rodriguez aired out a line of complaints. There was a pause to this unprompted conversation until Carr finally addressed the obvious: "Are you interested in this job?" And so it began.

On Friday, December 14, Rodriguez was in Toledo, Ohio, to answer that question. He was caught red-handed, though, and by the time the wheels went up and the airplane took him back to Morgantown, the story was breaking. The media met him at the airport in Morgantown. Rodriguez and his people had organized this little operation but had no clue how to manage it, no expectation they might not get away with it. He scurried from the plane and all he would say to the people who were demanding and deserving of answers was that he had a practice to get to. Yes, the day he picked to start this adventure was also the day he'd picked a while earlier to begin the Fiesta Bowl practices. Rodriguez would deny meeting with Michigan, despite a line of sources and stories saying otherwise. All Rodriguez was guilty of, he said, was meeting with his financial advisor.

Early the next day, the team was supposed to meet the media and Rodriguez obliged, but he refused to talk about what he called "rumors or innuendo" and what reporters considered to be the only story that mattered that day.

"We'll talk about this team, this season, this bowl preparation, aspects of recruiting we're heavily involved in right now, and that's about it," he said. "All that other stuff, I don't want talk about."

He thought that would work, that what he said was final, that he didn't need to account for his actions. It was time to test the parameters of the prohibition. "Coach," a reporter asked, "in that connection, what are you telling recruits that read these stories?"

Rodriguez stared straight ahead, not amused, and said, "I'm not talking about anything other than this year's team, this year's season, this year's bowl prep. That's all I want to talk about."

Too bad, a second reporter decided. "Well, to be a jerk here, Coach, you did say 'rumors.' Is that what they are then? Rumors?"

Rodriguez smirked, apparently amazed the media had such gall. "You all have not understood what I just said. One more question and then this conference unfortunately is over. You all know this. If the questions persist outside of that, this will be over."

The bluff had been called, and by now everyone was aware Rodriguez wasn't going to walk away from a crowd of cameras and microphones and recorders. Another voice spoke up and sneaked around the blockade. "OK, for the Fiesta Bowl then, are you going to be coaching the football team at the Fiesta Bowl?"

Now Rodriguez laughed. "You're tricky," he said before the conversation continued in another direction and actually grew to include the game and the opponent. When it was over, Rodriguez returned to his own little world. The first step he took away from the media was his first step toward Michigan.

The practice that Saturday night was cancelled, and a series of urgent phone calls and meetings began. His agent was hammering out a deal with Michigan while Rodriguez was trying to find anyone who could convince him to stay. He finally met up with his athletic director, Ed Pastilong, and the two talked about what had gone wrong and what might make things right. However, their relationship was shaky at best, and there wasn't enough time for one to assure the other they could coexist.

Then there was Walker, who was an underrated factor. Rodriguez trusted Walker because he had worked in athletics in his past and had Garrison's ear when necessary, and Walker was invested in the outcome. After Rodriguez and Pastilong met, Walker was at the Coliseum in the afternoon for a basketball game. He spent the entire game isolated in an arena tunnel, on his phone speaking to the boosters who wanted to keep their coach. This continued the rest of the day.

Rodriguez even went to Garrison's house late that night for an emergency meeting arranged by both sides. The president of the university came to the door in his slippers and the two had a long but ultimately unproductive meeting—Garrison just couldn't tell Rodriguez the things Rodriguez wanted to be told. Garrison wanted

Rodriguez to stay, but there wasn't much Garrison thought WVU could do. He believed WVU was living up to its commitment, but he really believed more concessions would set a very bad standard.

"I did not think we should tolerate that as a university, that it could be a yearly event when he might go somewhere else," Garrison said. "I didn't think that was good for the university, I didn't think it was good for the team, and I didn't think it was good for the sport."

The uncertainty ended Sunday, but the drama did not. There was a team meeting at 1:30 p.m. at the team's headquarters. Rodriguez arrived an hour or so early and locked himself in his office once again.

"We knew this could be a yearly thing and it may happen every year," Vaughn Rivers said. "We didn't talk about it much until the meeting."

Rodriguez was holed up in his office for 50 minutes or so before he slipped into the team's large meeting room.

"This felt different," Rivers remembered.

The meetings in that room always started the same, no matter the occasion. Rodriguez always exited his office inside the Puskar Center, turned right and walked down a hallway and into the lobby at the team's headquarters, turned left and walked a few steps, and then turned left one last time and entered the room. That meeting room is equipped for film sessions and has three large retractable screens in the front of the room and two sections of 10 rows of theater-style seating separated by an aisle in the middle. There were three ways to enter in the back end of the room—a doorway on the left, a doorway in the middle, and a doorway on the right. Rodriguez always arrived by walking through the doorway on the left. Always, except this one time, this last time.

Everyone in that room that day was on edge because they were worried about what was about to happen. Everyone noticed Rodriguez didn't come through the door he always used. They were alert for something like that because Rodriguez had broken another practice previously that got everyone's attention.

"Coach Rodriguez was the strictest guy," said safety Eain Smith, who was a true freshman that season. "You had to be 10 minutes early to be ready for a meeting. So we're all sitting there, all the seats are filled, and he's two minutes late. And then he came in the middle door."

Had he come in from the left like he always did or from the right, he would have had to walk down an aisle on that side of the room and then cross in front of his players and coaches and the support staff to get to the podium in the middle of the room and in front of the audience. What players remembered was that by walking through the middle door in the back of the room, Rodriguez was able to take the aisle in the middle and walk straight to the podium. He never passed before the room. His head was tucked into his chest, and no one saw his face or got a clue about what he was thinking until he ended a heartbreaking silence.

"He wasn't himself, so we all knew something was wrong," Smith said. "Then he started crying. He totally broke down and told us he was going to Michigan."

It wasn't a long speech. The room was filled with the noise of interruptions and reactions. There was despair and devastation. There were questions and disbelief. And there was anger. Defensive lineman Julian Miller was a true freshman and he was sitting with the rest of the players on the line. Keilen Dykes, Scooter Berry, and Johnny Dingle all yelled at Rodriguez.

"I was scared," Miller said. "Being a young player and witnessing all of that, I didn't know what to think."

The outside world was clueless, too. Beyond the closed doors, where the media waited for some sort of sign, it was again calm and quiet, like it had been a year before when Rodriguez held a similar meeting to tell the team he wasn't going to Alabama. The silence that day was broken by a celebration.

There would be no cheering this time. The silence was shattered when a door flew open and slapped the wall. Players stormed out of the meeting. "This [expletive] sucks," said Dykes, who was one of many players who skipped a workout and simply went home that afternoon. A bunch of Mountaineers remained in the room, trying desperately to wrap their minds around a conclusion that hadn't been completely explained by the man who had demanded complete dedication. The entire team was in the meeting. Only three players agreed to speak with the media afterward. Rivers, Schmitt, and linebacker Marc Magro were at a loss for words, and given the uncertainty of the moment, they defended Rodriguez's motivations, whatever they were, and paraphrased what Rodriguez had told them: there were things in play that the common people just couldn't understand.

Rodriguez was back in his office for a long time until doors opened and a crowd of people filled the hallway outside his doors. Then someone yelled at the invited media and threatened to call security. Another person stomped outside and ordered a television crew to move. One of Rodriguez's graduate assistants, the very one who delivered to Pastilong the letter of resignation from Rodriguez dated January 3, then ran outside carrying car keys. He hopped into a white SUV and pulled it around to an alley on the far side of the building. The camera crew shrewdly followed and caught Rodriguez slinking out of the building for the last time, a blue sports coat on his back and an overnight bag slung over his shoulder. The entourage followed. The graduate assistant got out of the SUV, and Rodriguez got in. He drove away by himself, never once looking back at his alma mater. He left the parking lot with a left-hand turn onto Don Nehlen Drive and headed toward the airport, where he flew to Michigan.

The media was outside, watching this all take place, taking notes, dealing with the feeling they had all been down this road before but had never traveled so far, and wondering if it was really a surprise. They turned around on a cold December afternoon and tried to go back inside the Puskar Center.

The door had been locked.

A day later, Rodriguez was in Ann Arbor, Michigan, and once again charming and compelling behind the microphone as he was introduced as a Michigan Man charged with replacing Carr and returning the Wolverines to national prominence. It was extremely difficult for WVU fans to watch and make sense of this. He was their coach, after all. They had cheered him as a player and prayed the circumstances would allow him to come home to coach their team.

Some had even gotten over the fact he wasn't very loyal, which was enormously important in a state that appreciates loyalty from their own like they do coal as energy, Democrats in office, and pepperoni in their bread dough. Why, there he was, hours away from the place he once called home, wearing familiar colors but emblazoned with a capital M.

This nightmare, the one that started on December 1, seemed unending.

Many people changed the way they felt about Rodriguez the moment he was asked about his buyout. "Buyout" had become a bad word at WVU, stemming from when John Beilein bolted from WVU earlier that year and abandoned a pretty good men's basketball team, also to coach at Michigan. He also didn't think much of the buyout clause in his contract and then aligned himself with a ferocious attorney, Robert Fitzsimmons. They argued against the concept of liquidated damages and managed to cut $1 million off of the $2.5 million he had been contractually obligated to pay WVU. The parallels between Beilein and Rodriguez were impossible to ignore, so Rodriguez was asked about the $4 million buyout in his contract at WVU, a place where insult and injury know each other quite well.

"The lawyers," he said, "are working on it."

With those words came the emphatic end to the best time WVU had ever had playing football. And in typical and tortuous fashion, the curtain fell like a guillotine.

10
FIESTA

Ryan Mundy was a safety, but at that moment he could relate to what it must have been like to be Steve Slaton or Pat White on the football field. He had a narrow opening and a singular focus, and was unconcerned with the chaos around him. Nothing that was happening on the periphery mattered. Opponents were approaching from straight ahead and from angles off to the side, and they were all making menacing and exaggerated motions. Mundy was unfazed. He could see his destination and all the moves he'd have to make to get there unaffected.

Pitt's players and coaches were going absolutely berserk on the turf at Mountaineer Field, unabashedly celebrating their stunning victory in the 100th Backyard Brawl. All Mundy wanted to do was find the tunnel that took him from the corner of the field and toward the locker room, where he could be alone with his thoughts and oblivious to the party on the field and the devastation in the stands. Every step took him closer to where he so badly wanted to be, but no farther from an agonizing reality.

"This can't be happening again," he told himself, again and again, until he dropped down in front of his locker, shed his helmet and shoulder pads, and came to accept the truth. It was happening again.

A year earlier, he'd been with the Michigan Wolverines and part of what many were saying was one of the best defenses in the history of college football. They had their annual end-of-the-year rivalry game against Ohio State, but this one was like no other. The winner was going to the BCS National Championship Game at the expense of the loser. The Buckeyes won and picked apart that Michigan defense. The Buckeye quarterback, Troy Smith, passed for 300 yards to seal his Heisman Trophy campaign, while a receiver had 100 yards receiving, and a running back had 100 yards rushing. Michigan's offense was almost as good and scored 39 points, but ended up three points short.

"That was probably the worst game of my college career," Mundy said. "I was so disappointed in myself. It really hurt me."

Mundy had taken a medical redshirt for a shoulder injury as a junior in 2005 and graduated after that 2006 season, his fourth year at Michigan. He wanted to work toward his master's degree, but Michigan didn't offer the program he wanted to pursue. With a year of football eligibility remaining, he was allowed to transfer to a school that offered the master's program and would be permitted to play that one last season. He could have gone to any of a list of schools that had what he was looking for, but WVU provided more. It had the sports administration curriculum he wanted to study, plus it offered another look at the national championship he wanted even more. He couldn't let it end the way it had in 2006, with the opponent celebrating on the field and his heartbroken teammates shuffling toward the locker room. That visual remained in his mind, right next to the most powerful motivation he could find:

"I didn't perform my best," he said.

It was Mundy who pulled the WVU defense together in 2007 and made it into something special. It was he who picked the team up after the USF loss and let people know it wasn't over, that the Mountaineers were still contenders and there was still time left to prove it.

Now, for Mundy, the crushing disappointment of 2006 was happening again.

Mundy knew how the story for the 2007 Mountaineers could end if they were not careful. That Michigan juggernaut had allowed just

133 points in the first 11 games of the season, but the Ohio State loss stung and the Wolverines never got over it. They played Southern Cal in the Rose bowl and lost 32–18. The Trojans picked apart the secondary again with 391 yards passing and four touchdowns, but the way Mundy remembered things, Michigan lost to the Buckeyes twice. The Mountaineers couldn't lose to the Panthers twice.

"If I had any advice for this team, it'd be to stay focused on Oklahoma now," Mundy said.

Good luck with that. No one wanted to talk about the game. The game was secondary to the coaching search, maybe even behind the inevitable battle WVU would wage against Rich Rodriguez to get every penny of the $4 million buyout.

But the players just didn't bother themselves with that stuff. They knocked out their final media obligation in Morgantown a few days after Rodriguez left, and were alone with themselves and their practices and then the holiday break until they arrived in Arizona a week later. They were isolated and concerned only with playing and winning the game.

They took their cues from Bill Stewart, the assistant coach who had been stripped of his title as quarterbacks coach in the offseason and assigned the tight ends, though he had been placated with the title of associate head coach. WVU had named him the interim coach when Rodriguez left, but it really had no other choice. It seemed like a reward for surviving so many seasons with Rodriguez, and then not getting on the plane for Michigan with Rodriguez and the other coaches. Stewart was a caretaker, a housesitter, the neighbor you call to walk your dog when you get held up at work.

And Bill Stewart was the perfect man for the occasion. In words and in deeds, he was precisely what the situation prescribed and exactly who the Mountaineers needed. He was a true West Virginian, the one who was so folksy, so friendly that you were stunned to discover it was genuine and not generated. He was the one who would open up and give people a hug, and only let go when the other half felt better.

"When it gets too tough for others, it's just right for Billy Stewart," he said.

Who says that? Who cares? The Mountaineers had their guy and they loved it. They loved him. He made a difficult time a fun one. He made an overwhelming situation seem like one they would conquer. Oh, he talked a big game. He likened the Fiesta Bowl to a national championship game, saying those who were inside the sport and paid really close attention saw it that way, too. He thought his team was worthy of calling itself the best. He thought Oklahoma was playing better than anyone in the country. He didn't ignore the challenge, but he wouldn't run, either. He vowed WVU would empty the holsters.

"I promise you we'll show up," Stewart said. "This is not the Charge of the Light Brigade."

Nothing quite like comparing the Bowl Championship Series to the Battle of Balaclava. How many in the locker room were up to speed on the Crimean War? Again, who says that? And, again, who cares? The point was made, and all the players needed to take away from it was that Stewart wouldn't lead them into slaughter. He'd have them ready—not ready to play, but ready to win. The kids liked the guy and the way he treated them. With everything happening outside their little world, Stewart never panicked. With a job interview in the balance, he never campaigned for it. He worried only about what the Mountaineers needed to do that particular day so they'd be ready on January 2.

They had a really good practice in Morgantown late in their final week together, one day before they were to split up for the holiday recess. Stewart met with them, commended them on their attitude and chemistry and preparation, and gave them the next day off as a reward. He never admitted to them he actually needed the next day to get caught up on his Christmas shopping. When they did practice, he didn't berate the players and string together profanities. He coached them and treated them like he'd want someone to treat his son. He wouldn't scream at a kid for fumbling. He'd give him tips on how to avoid doing it again. He didn't yell at a cornerback who dropped an interception. He instructed the player to focus on the nose of the ball and follow it into his hands.

He made a complex game and a complicated time seem so simple. In meetings and lectures before the game, he stressed a strange little formula he'd put together: $B + T + H^2 = V$. Basically, if WVU blocked better, tackled better, hit harder, and hustled more, WVU would be victorious. When he did pull someone aside at practice in Scottsdale, Arizona, he'd put one arm around the player and extend the other to point toward the mountains in the background. He shared a story he'd heard first when he was an assistant at Arizona State from 1988 to 1989. Those were the Superstition Mountains, where a German immigrant named Jacob Waltz knew there to be a gold mine. Waltz kept the location a secret until he died, but it never stopped people from searching for something no one ever knew existed.

"He was saying the people were searching for fool's gold and that we weren't here for fool's gold," safety Eric Wicks said. "We're here for the real thing and we're going for gold in the game."

Stewart relaxed and reassured the Mountaineers by being himself, by blending in, by abandoning the idea he was a superior. He didn't like the idea that players couldn't approach him or joke with him just because he was the head coach. He didn't explode when Johnny Dingle called him "Coach Woody."

"You know *Toy Story?*" the defensive end asked. "You know Woody."

Stewart was just a guy with a whistle, a cheery disposition, and a bunch of funny things to say. Maybe it was because he hadn't been a head coach since 1996, or maybe it was just because of the way he was, but he never felt quite at ease with all the things that came with the job. He felt weird with state troopers escorting him around Arizona, so he did what everyone tends to do when they feel uncomfortable; he had some fun with it.

"You don't know this, but when I get back, I go into incarceration," he said one day when he was surrounded by the troopers. "Those guys just aren't leaving my side because when all this limelight came, they said, 'That's the kid right there, from the mountains of West Virginia. He stole turnips out of the neighbor's gardens.' I did. 'He threw snowballs at cars.' I did. 'He threw apples at tractor-trailer trucks.' I never hit the cab, but I hit the boxcars. We jumped trains. I went to the high school many a day and walked by the principal and walked out the back door and went fishing. That's all Cub and Boy Scout Honor. I did that. These guys are taking me back to pay for that."

In public, he had everything the people wanted in their head coach. He was kind and decent and wasn't a threat to bolt on them. In private, he was just as popular. He had everyone believing WVU would win. Not *could* win. Would. There was a difference, and he wanted his players to note it. Practices were quick and crisp, and everything had a purpose. He was loading up his holster, too. Oklahoma lost a first-team all-conference cornerback to injury when it beat Missouri in the Big 12 championship game. The Sooners were going to move a safety/nickel back to play corner, but that plan was ruined when the safety/nickel back was ruled academically ineligible for the bowl. He would be replaced by a redshirt freshman, the very player the defense wanted to avoid featuring and the very reason the safety/nickel back was to be moved to corner.

Stewart saw a weakness and decided he'd try to exploit it with aggressive pass plays. The players liked the attacking approach, one they had wanted for a while, and they bubbled over at times and spilled some details. Receivers were running reverses and throwing passes in practice. The I-formation was suddenly back and wildly effective. This was a team that was a lot more confident than it probably should have been given everything else that was going on around the program, all the things they'd gone out of their way to avoid. The Mountaineers were going to win the Fiesta Bowl, and they wouldn't listen to any argument.

There were many who would argue. Brian Jones, an analyst for what was then College Sports Television, now CBS College Sports, gave the Mountaineers no chance, not even with all the emotion they figured to take into the game. "They can take whatever the hell they want to take," Jones said in a preview show. "They're going to get blasted by Oklahoma." He explained that an Oklahoma defense that handled top-ranked Missouri's offense would have no problem against a WVU offense Jones said was one-dimensional and had but one receiver, Darius Reynaud. "Too many weapons for Oklahoma's offense," Jones said. "And plus, last but not least, West Virginia lost to Pitt." Fans of the Mountaineers could quibble with the premise of what Jones was predicting. They had no counter to how he concluded his argument.

And that was nothing. The worst came from ESPN's Lee Corso, whom just about every WVU fan thinks has a deeply rooted and biased disdain for their school. He, too, was analyzing the Fiesta Bowl for a preview and he, too, gave the Mountaineers no chance, not necessarily because of who they were, but because of who they were facing. Like Stewart and Jones, Corso was very high on the Sooners, but he had no respect for the Mountaineers. How, he wondered, could the team that lost to Pitt and then lost its coach beat the Sooners? "If WVU thinks the Big East, Marshall, and Western Michigan are good, wait till they see Oklahoma live and in living color. Oklahoma will destroy them by at least three touchdowns. Destroy them. Mark it down: by at least three touchdowns. I'm telling you, Oklahoma is a wonderful football team. They will stick it to them by three touchdowns at least."

Never mind WVU beat Western Michigan by 38 points and Marshall by 25, or that the Mountaineers outscored Big East opponents by 117 points, even with two losses. Corso and Jones clearly illustrated that the Mountaineers were short on believers.

Rodriguez once remarked that if a WVU fan had a tank of gas and a case of beer, then that fan would make it to the game. Yet WVU was allotted 17,500 Fiesta Bowl tickets and sold only about 10,000. Returning 7,500 was a big blow, one that would have cost the school about a million dollars had a booster not made a donation to essentially cover the bill.

An ESPN.com poll again revealed the doubt of the nation, just as it had on the eve of the Sugar Bowl two years earlier. This time, 84 percent of the nation picked the Sooners. For visual proof, the network showed a map of the United States. Forty-nine of the states were red, meaning each had picked Oklahoma. Only one state was in blue: West Virginia. The Mountaineers saw that. They used that.

"The greatest state in the nation," Owen Schmitt said afterward as the band played and the celebration percolated behind him. "That's why we won this game."

When the game was over, Charles Pugh and Antonio Lewis sneaked up behind Stewart and emptied the Gatorade cooler on their coach. And once Vaughn Rivers and Stewart were through with an extended, emotional embrace, when Dingle was done waving a huge WVU flag to the delight of the fans, after linebacker Andy Emery and fullback Sam Morrone had lifted Stewart onto their shoulders, when various other players had run over to the front row behind their bench and slapped hands with fans who brandished a sign that read "WE WILL NEVER LEAVE YOU," it was receiver Dorrell Jalloh who found a dry-erase board and a marker. He scribbled a message and then raised it high above his head.

"84% WRONG"

As incomprehensible as the Pitt game was, the result of the Fiesta Bowl was equally befuddling. The eight-point underdog won the game 48–28 and left no doubt about which was the better team, though there was one substantial explanation. The Mountaineers didn't screw up as often as Oklahoma, which committed 13 penalties, threw an interception in the end zone, stalled on a fourth-and-short, misfired on a two-point conversion, and failed to recover a surprise onside kick that actually invigorated the Mountaineers, who sensed the opponent's desperation. WVU didn't have it easy, though. Right tackle Selvish Capers was secretly hurt all week and couldn't play. He was replaced by Stephen Maw, a theretofore anonymous player who figured he had played about 40 snaps all season. The running game took another hit, it seemed, when Steve Slaton left the game in the first quarter. He carried one time and lost two yards and later felt his hamstring pop when he tried to catch a pass. He limped from his last game with the Mountaineers and handed the torch to Noel Devine, who scored twice and racked up 108 yards on 13 carries.

It was an extension of the overall theme. All the Mountaineers did was find ways to make big plays, averaging 8.9 yards per rush and 9.1 yards per snap. This was a clinic. Schmitt ran from the I-formation and to the empty right side of the field for a 57-yard touchdown. Reynaud scampered 30 yards on a reverse and punctuated it with a dive into the end zone. White took a shot deep and connected with Tito Gonzales for a 79-yard score. Devine handled a toss outside in that I-formation and zoomed 65 yards for the final score. As a sidebar to all of that, the defense attacked from odd angles and hit people hard. WVU sacked Sam Bradford three times and hit him a bunch more, so that the nation's leader in passing efficiency never quite got comfortable.

The Mountaineers were as jubilant after the game as their coach was before it. White grabbed the trophy handed to him for being the game's most valuable offensive player and said of Stewart, "I speak for all the players who say he needs to be our coach at West Virginia." Schmitt, who was stricken with tears of joy and sadness after his last game, thought it would be stupid not to hire Stewart. The kicker and punter, Pat McAfee, vowed to make a T-shirt that read, "Stew for the Head Job." It meant that much for McAfee to help Stewart, who had coached the special teams and who had mentored McAfee. It mattered that much for McAfee to feel good after a game; the one before the Fiesta Bowl hadn't treated him quite as well. His home and his Jeep were vandalized after he missed two field goals in the Pitt game. Angry fans were harassing his girlfriend. This is what that Pitt game did to people. Some were crazily certain Rodriguez threw the game to get out of a debt. Others made death threats against the kicker.

The day after the loss, McAfee hopped in his Jeep and drove for four or five hours, just to clear his mind. Time passed and the emotion faded, but he was still embarrassed by his performance, and still eager to fight the people who had pestered his girlfriend. It was the people within the program who helped him then. Before long, he was joking around and having fun again. "I think old Coach Rod took that target right off of my back and decided to put it on his," McAfee said upon arriving in Arizona. "I really appreciate him for that. Everything's calmed down."

McAfee missed two more kicks in the Fiesta Bowl, pushing one to the right on his first attempt, a 50-yard try in the first quarter, and then having a 44-yard attempt blocked to end the first half. He made two field goals in between, though, and punted the ball almost perfectly throughout the game, averaging 58.5 yards. He wouldn't let himself off the hook, and no one else could ever push all the other haunting memories of 13–9 from their minds. The participants grew to accept that beating Oklahoma and proving the majority of a nation wrong wasn't a bad consolation prize. The Mountaineers finally beat a notable team after falling in so many battles before. WVU and Rich Rodriguez were no more. Those who remained were left to move forward and create their own legacies.

"The Pitt game will haunt me probably for the rest of my life," McAfee said. "That was a game we should have won, and I'm the one who stepped up in the first quarter and missed two kicks that were very easily makeable. I know winning that game would have defined our team. We had Pat White, Owen Schmitt, Steve Slaton. All those guys were so good. We ran everything for three years and that would have been what defined our careers—and in a way it still is. It was a bummer, but once you get out of the state and get out of college and look back, you think to yourself, 'You know what? We still went to two BCS games. We beat the living hell out of Oklahoma. A bunch of us won four bowl games. We still did some really cool stuff.'"

11

DOUBT

"Hey," Bill Stewart said, pacing very brief laps back and forth in front of his football team, rubbing his hands together as he relished the opportunity that awaited him as the interim coach for West Virginia University in the Fiesta Bowl. "We've got a great opportunity. We've got a dandy out there waiting on us."

Us.

For both Stewart and the Mountaineers, the opportunity was to prove people wrong, to convince the cynics who underrated them. As far as Stewart was concerned, there could be nothing worse than standing on the outside and believing you could see inside another man. His players could play. They could win, too. But this man could coach, despite what those who seemed to have forgotten that may have said, and he was going to prove it on that night in the desert. He was going to lead WVU to the win, he was going to take up a permanent residence in the hearts of fans, and he was going to strut to the front of the line of successors and sit before them in the throne Rich Rodriguez had abdicated two weeks earlier.

But this was not about Stewart. It was about the team, the program, the fans—or as they all called it, *Us*. All the time between the Pitt game and the Fiesta Bowl had passed. The distractions were off in the distance. Their moment, the memory they could make and no one would ever forget, was right in front of them.

Stewart had been waiting to give this speech for far longer than the time between his appointment as the interim coach and when he started to speak to the Mountaineers inside the locker room at University of Phoenix Stadium. He hadn't been the head coach for a football game since November 23, 1996, the last time he led the Keydets of the Virginia Military Institute onto the field. The final score was a 26–14 loss to the Appalachian State Mountaineers, and the final record was 3-8. It was an obvious disappointment. A year before that, Stewart's team was 4-7, which was hardly much better, but that was a major jump from the 1-10 record in the coach's first season.

At the end of three seasons, the record stood at 8-25, but his fate had already been decided. Words that came out of his mouth, not the things he did to win or lose games, cost him his job. But that didn't matter before the Fiesta Bowl, behind the doors that were pulled closed when all the players and assistants and support staffers had made their way inside and found a place to pause for a moment. The players sat in front of their lockers and tried to calm themselves, to contain the thunderstorms raging in their heads, to prepare for the brutality they were about to endure. Some stared straight ahead and at absolutely nothing. Others draped towels around their heads to block out their surroundings and focus only on the game. Many closed their eyes and stretched their necks or slowly nodded their heads or took slow, deep breaths. A red digital clock ticked down toward the moment WVU was to leave that room and head back onto the field. Time was running down, but Stewart was just getting started.

"Offense, play fast. Assignment free, man," he said. "Defense, swarm. Swarm and tackle. Punch that ball out every chance you get and keep busting them. Special teams, lay it on the line. Attack your responsibility. Attack it."

The words were coming out faster now. He was leaning over slightly. He shook his head slowly from side to side, as if to suggest there were no other way to play than the way he was suggesting, that there was no question this was how things were to be done that night. He was in the middle of that speech he had thought about for so long. Everything felt right, even if he didn't know what to do with his hands as he spoke. In one moment, he was tugging at the waistline on the back of his pleated khaki slacks and quickly pulling his pants up, even though he was wearing a belt. He clenched his fists and then unfolded them quickly. His arms hung low, like a fighter dragging his fists to the ring.

Then the right hand rose up and the index finger fired out.

"We've got to out-block them. We've got to out-tackle them. We've got to out-hit them and hustle them," he said, flicking out another finger at each point. "It's real simple. You out-block them and you out-tackle them and you out-hit them and you out-hustle them."

The hand was pumping up and down now, and the index finger was there to add a point of emphasis to everything he was saying. It was beginning to get through to the audience. The players had been thinking about this speech, too. They liked Stewart and admired and respected him, but he also amused them. They knew he'd have something to say, but they figured he was just as likely to entertain them as he was to inspire them. But this was very different. Was that a chill? Were those goose bumps? How hard was the heart thumping? They picked up their heads. Some made eye contact with others. They nodded. "Yes sir," one bellowed.

"And you stay within the legal limits of the game," Stewart said. "It's Mountaineer pride. Nothing cheap. From the heart. Straining."

Stewart was rolling. He was pacing quicker. He was staring at players as he spoke. His eyes were wide and filled with a wild emotion. Passion. Desire. Life. The fists were clenched again as he pinched his bottom lip between both rows of teeth.

"Damn I'm proud to be with you. I'm proud to be with you," he said, again shaking his head and shedding any notion that what he said was not the God's honest truth. "Picked you a good one, didn't I, huh? We got a good one."

More players answered this time: "Yes sir." They were smiling and pulsating in place now. "Yes sir!" they yelled again.

Stewart smiled briefly and quickly licked his lips. He shot the index fingers out on both hands, as if what he was about to say was doubly important.

"We are gonna out-strain and out-hit these guys," he said. "Let them know. Leave no doubt tonight. Leave no. Doubt. Tonight. No doubt!"

Stewart was yelling now. His face was reddening. His right hand hammered through the air and punctuated his words. Those wild eyes were narrow now. His stare was sharp. His focus was contagious.

"They shouldn't have played the Old Gold and Blue. Not. This. Night," he roared, pointing at the ground. "Not. This. Night!"

There was a pause and a brief silence until a few players started to thump their thigh pads or tap their feet on the floor. They were bubbling over and couldn't wait to erupt from that locker room and overwhelm Oklahoma. The confidence and the intensity had overtaken them, and they smiled and nodded their heads and looked around the room to make damn sure everyone felt the same. These were the guys once left for dead. Stewart just brought them back to life.

"Don't leave your wingman. Never, ever, ever bail out on your brother. You help, you strain, and you just fight," Stewart said, now abandoning the clenched fist and instead clapping his hands together. "Start fast. Stay on top of them. It's a game, lads. Let's have fun and go get us a big victory."

He clapped his hands one more time and then balled up his right fist and threw it at the locker room door. The Mountaineers jumped to their feet. They screamed and cheered and yelled and subsequently destroyed the Sooners. Forget what would happen on the field. Stewart got that coaching job with that speech, that unforgettable assembly of words that made the hairs on the back of your neck stand tall and salute, that 95-second infusion of everything the previous month had tried to take away from the players. WVU was not going to lose that game, and Stewart had made sure of it with the finest moment of his career.

The game was a reminder of how good the Mountaineers could be and how fun it was to root for that team and those players, of what it was like to see passes fly though the air and players take the ball and run away from defenders. It was a validation of all the things Stewart had said before the game. WVU was aggressive and diverse and just plain scary. The players showed up and they were not bullied. They played fast and hard and with pride, and they left nothing in reserve.

Above all else, the game was a 60-minute audition for Stewart, who hadn't interviewed for the job at all before the game and hadn't made much of a deal out of that, even if he was miffed by the omission and by some of the names of those who were getting interviews or being mentioned as possible replacements.

Many believe Stewart was hired early in the morning after the game by a blend of drunken politicians and administrators. It's not true. The decision was heading that way well before the Gatorade flowed down Stewart's back. The plan was already in motion when Patrick White stood on the stage in the middle of the field and endorsed his interim coach.

Before the game was officially over, but as the celebration began in the stands and the suites, the very important people in and around WVU were beginning to talk about giving the job to Stewart. Had bottles been popped and ice cubes been dropped into snifters? Absolutely, but the fact remains that the decision was not some drunk idea, but one conceived, and executed, before all the booze was gone and done by and large without consent of the top guy in the university.

For Mike Garrison, the university president, the moment that reality arrived had to be terribly upsetting. He'd taken a beating for not doing enough to keep Rodriguez, and then for conducting a coaching search that many thought was pedestrian in both pace and appeal. He wouldn't defend himself in public, but in private he was deeply bothered by how he was doubted so easily.

"The people who say we didn't talk to anybody would be shocked at the people we talked to," he'd say years later.

Through it all, Garrison stayed quiet, trying to keep the details concealed and hoping he'd have the last word and the last laugh when he shook hands with the new coach as his critics nodded their heads in approval. He'd talked to an old Mountaineer linebacker and assistant coach, Doc Holliday, who was part of the 2006 national championship staff at the University of Florida. He'd talked to another former player, former Auburn coach Terry Bowden. Shortly before Christmas, WVU had connected with Jimbo Fisher, a Clarksburg, West Virginia, native who had just signed a contract at Florida State to be first in line to succeed Bobby Bowden. His people in Harrison County let WVU's people know Fisher would be interested if the Mountaineers were interested in Fisher, but it never worked out, mostly because WVU was going to be asked to handle the $2.5 million buyout included in Fisher's deal with the Seminoles.

Butch Jones, an assistant for two years with Rich Rodriguez and then the head coach at Central Michigan, had an interview just days before the game, which was right around the time WVU enlisted the services of professional headhunter Chuck Neinas. Garrison was supposed to meet with East Carolina coach Skip Holtz and Illinois assistant Mike Locksley when he returned from the bowl. He even assured people who asked that he had talked to a dozen or so people and even heard from coaches at BCS programs, men he wouldn't name because he'd assured them anonymity or because they had not yet interviewed for the job. By winning the game, he hoped a few of those people might agree to talk and figured a few others who hadn't been considered might make themselves available to discuss what had become a much more attractive opportunity. It would be easier now to arrive at that triumphant photo op and the handshake with the new coach.

And Garrison was right, just as sure as what everyone around him did that night was wrong. Garrison wanted to be slow and measured. The others wanted something immediately.

The people who had some sort of authority that night were indeed drunk. They were intoxicated by the thrill of the win and were not capable of walking a straight line toward the proper conclusion, not able to make a rational decision right in the middle of the celebration. Yet that's exactly what happened. In the immediate hours after the game, Garrison said a gang of people teamed up to sway him, and together they handed the football program to Stewart.

Just a day before the game, Garrison would only call Stewart a "very viable candidate."

"We'd like to have it wrapped up here quickly, but again, more than anything else, we want to make sure it's done the right way and that we've surveyed all the national interest," Garrison said. "In addition to some names mentioned already, we've had plenty of names out there that may or may not be candidates. We also have plenty of folks who may have interest that are not mentioned."

A day after the game, the photo op happened and he shook hands with his coach as the watching heads shook, though for a very different reason than Garrison projected. It was a stunning and sudden end to a prolonged and much-criticized coaching search, but it was what everyone either figured or feared might happen.

Well, maybe not everyone.

Garrison discovered right after the game that Stewart had some significant supporters. The lobby at the team hotel was packed with fans waiting for the team to return, but it was also occupied by WVU people: administrators, members of the Board of Governors, politicians, boosters, and anyone else who was ready to let go of more than a month of pain and frustration. Garrison thought about it all and how he'd deal with it as he sat in the back seat of a courtesy car that took him from the stadium to the hotel after the game. Shortly before he arrived, his cell phone rang. Robert Wells, then a member of the university's Board of Governors, was on the other end with some advice.

"Go straight to your room," Wells said. "Straight to your room. Don't come to the lobby."

"Why?" Garrison asked.

"They're cooking it up right now," Wells said. "They're going to hire Stewart."

Seeing that Garrison was in charge of the university and the hiring of the football coach, this was news to him. Startling and unnerving news. It wasn't going to happen that way. Not this night.

"There was no reason to do it then," Garrison said.

Actually, there was one reason, one unstoppable reason. Important people wanted it to happen. Unfortunately for the president of the university, Garrison couldn't conceivably heed Wells's advice, sneak in through a back entrance, slip into an elevator, and disappear underneath the covers for the night. He had to make an appearance. Within minutes, Garrison was swept into the hospitality suite and seated on a couch as the other four men in the room brought him up to speed on where things had gone in his absence. Those four people were Athletic Director Ed Pastilong, Board of Governors chairman Steve Goodwin, super booster Mike Puskar, and the governor of the state, Joe Manchin, who'd previously endorsed Holiday and then Bowden and then Fisher. They wanted to hire Stewart.

"I was by no means the only voice in the process, but when you've got the chair of the Board of Governors and the athletic director and the governor meeting unto themselves and with who knows who else, it's challenging to try and unravel that thing," Garrison said.

Garrison sat and listened, but he wasn't able to shake the truth that Stewart would not have been a candidate if WVU had lost. He said he wasn't against the idea, that he knew Stewart wanted the job and he thought the world of Stewart after what he'd done before and then during the game, but Garrison wanted everyone to wait.

"Let's just enjoy this," Garrison said.

His appeal for patience was denied. He pleaded for the Mountaineers to take their time. Garrison believed that he and the team of people assembled to conduct the search—Goodwin, Pastilong, chief of staff Craig Walker, general counsel Alex Macia, and deputy athletic director Mike Parsons—had done a fine job thus far, and were capable of doing even better work with the bowl win in their pocket and Patrick White and Noel Devine coming back. He was met with arguments that time was a commodity WVU should not be wasting—even though Garrison hated the notion that WVU had to be working on a needless deadline.

Before WVU was in need of a coach, Garrison watched one school make a mess of its coaching search and do all the things Garrison and Walker hoped to never do, should they ever be in that situation. That school, oddly enough, was the University of Michigan, which was publicly rejected by LSU coach Les Miles, and then Rutgers coach Greg Schiano.

"I thought it was foolish," Garrison said. "I had commented to Craig well before Rich ever went to Michigan that their search looked terrible. They were trying to race against what they perceived to be the standard out there. I never believed we should have to comply with that standard. The whole thing is driven by the coaches and should be driven by the universities. I was very comfortable doing things the way we were doing them."

That didn't matter to the four others in that room, who thought the sooner Stewart was hired, the better it would be for everyone. Garrison reminded the men that the university had interviews left with other prospective coaches, and that it would be unprofessional and unbecoming of the school to bail on them on such short notice. Why, Neinas had just been contracted and hadn't even started to do what he does, which is assist schools by identifying candidates. None of it worked. Garrison was the only one affiliated with WVU that night who felt defeated.

"It was clear to me that the train was on the tracks," Garrison said. "That was the decision. It was a decision I didn't think was a bad decision, but I thought the timing was bad."

Stewart was called to a room to meet with Pastilong, and the two old friends needed about two hours to go through the process of offering and accepting a job and negotiating a contract. Employees of WVU's sports information department began calling beat writers and national columnists who covered the game and telling them to be at a press conference the next morning. There, they were told, WVU would make an announcement about the coaching vacancy.

Around 100 of Stewart's fans, friends, and family members were at that press conference. They applauded him and cheered his name as he was introduced as the 32nd coach in school history. In one regard, Stewart was the right man for the job. He'd taken over during an impossible time and turned the attention away from Rich Rodriguez and the buyout and the lawsuit, and he pointed it toward the team. He respected the opponent, but would not undersell his team. He was a West Virginian, humbled by the honor and appreciative of the opportunity to coach the team. He made everyone feel good again. That made Garrison feel good.

"I can't disavow myself, I can't say there weren't too many people involved, but there was a big part of me—and I believe this to be correct now just as I believed it to be correct then—that thought we needed someone at the helm who was the polar opposite of what we had," Garrison said. "We needed humility. We needed love for the state. We needed love for the institution. We needed someone who was not afraid."

That was Bill Stewart. He was a lot of things, but he wasn't Rich Rodriguez and perhaps nothing mattered as much as that.

Rodriguez was waging a war against his school, his state, and his people, one that began when he refused to pay his buyout. A few days after the Fiesta Bowl, the *Charleston Gazette*'s Dave Hickman reported that the remaining staff had returned to work and discovered that files containing critical information related to the program and its players, files that were supposed to be in Rodriguez's office, had disappeared. Gone were all the files that tracked boosters, recruiting, summer camps, and the like. Gone were files on players that held their contact information, scholarship particulars, and records for things such as class attendance, discipline, and community service. Gone from the weight room office were files that included everything a player had done in the strength and conditioning program, be it the history of 40-yard dash times, the increases in the weight a player could squat across his career, or anything else that had to do with how the Mountaineers became physically prepared to play. Athletic department sources told Hickman they saw Rodriguez and his sidekick, video coordinator Dusty Rutledge, in Rodriguez's WVU office shredding papers on December 18—two days after he resigned at WVU and the day after he was introduced at Michigan.

Rodriguez was furious. On a hastily arranged conference call the day after the report, he fired back, "You get tired of getting beat up over stuff. It's crazy."

He believed WVU's sources not only lied to the *Gazette*, but that they embellished things to make Rodriguez look bad. "I've obviously kept notes that are part of my current game plan or current coaching philosophy that I've developed and changed," he said. "The things I threw away were completely useless to anybody. I wanted to clean up my office and didn't want to have personal notes and things I thought were easily accessible—whether it's notes on players and things like that—just out there. Honestly, it was part of my cleaning up."

He countered accusations that he was destroying documents to knowingly hurt WVU by saying WVU's assistant coaches and secretaries had copies of everything he discarded and shredded. By now, Rodriguez was fed up with what he deemed to be a "smear campaign" against him. He understood the anger, but he didn't understand the actions of those siding against him.

"There is disappointment and I can understand that," he said. "I know there are hard feelings. It's a small state and the program was sort of surprised, but from my point, the program is in great shape and will continue to be. One of the things I've said is this campaign is not helping West Virginia's program. It's trying to hurt Rich Rodriguez, but it also hurts West Virginia."

Yet one month later, Rodriguez was on ESPN, confessing with a teary-eyed conviction that family members in West Virginia had been harassed and bullied and had even received death threats. "I wish some of the people that are ignorant and that don't know or don't care what they're saying, what they're doing, would see what it does to young people that had no impact in this thing, in this decision," Rodriguez said. "My kids are 11 and nine. They shouldn't have to endure things like that. My nephews and my nieces, to put a death threat on them because their uncle changed jobs? Give me a break."

That was heavy talk on a major platform, the sort of place millions would listen to Rodriguez and shake their heads in sympathy. Those things he said were things the media and especially law enforcement took seriously, but could never corroborate. To West Virginians, it just seemed like he didn't care, that he wasn't listening to his own words when he was saying things about being fair and honest and remembering a history so that there might still be a future.

Neither Rodriguez nor anyone he chose to surround himself with ever looked back to see the wreckage they left in their path. Mountaineer fans got a clear message about Rodriguez's true feelings, from Calvin Magee's claims of racism to explain why he was never considered to replace Rodriguez at WVU, or Rodriguez talking about Michigan as "the biggest and the best."

Why would anyone act that way toward his alma mater and home-state university? The answer, perhaps, came in the deposition Garrison gave as part of the legal battle to collect the buyout. He was asked by Rodriguez's bumbling lawyer, Marv Robon, about that fateful final meeting with Rodriguez the night before Rodriguez resigned and left WVU for Michigan. Garrison had wanted his coach to stay and encouraged him to remember how special a place it had been, still was, and could always be. "He was angry enough to say it wasn't that special—and he used an expletive before 'special'—to be in West Virginia," Garrison said.

That wasn't the sort of thing Stewart would ever say. He was the pipe fitter's son, a ragamuffin from New Martinsville, West Virginia, who skipped classes in high school, who stole turnips from neighborhood gardens, and who threw snowballs at cars and apples at tractor-trailer trucks. He'd always wanted to play for the Mountaineers, to say nothing of being the actual head coach. He was on the freshman team in 1970, in awe of the WVU coach, Bobby Bowden, and in love with just being one of the Mountaineers. He was on the sideline for the 1970 game against Pitt, when Bowden had coached a hell of a first half and taken a 35–8 lead into the locker room, only to lose 36–35. Forty years later, on the verge of coaching his third and final game against the Panthers, Stewart refused to revisit the painful game except to say he remembered it "very vividly" and felt bad for the seniors.

By 1971, Stewart was no longer at WVU. He transferred to Fairmont State, lettered for three years, and was a captain on the 1974 team that won the West Virginia Conference championship. He funneled into coaching and was a student assistant with the Falcons for a year and then an assistant at Sistersville High in 1976. A year later, Stewart had his first full-time college gig as an assistant at Salem

College. He'd spend the next 19 years doing the same, peppering his résumé with stops at North Carolina, Marshall, William & Mary, Navy, Arizona State, and Air Force. Finally, in 1994, Stewart had a head coaching job. He took over a deflated Virginia Military Institute program and seemed like the perfect match there, too. He marched right along with the Keydets, aligning himself with the military way by drawing upon his experience at Navy and Air Force.

There was an ugly ending there, though. Stewart was accused in October of his final season of making a racial slur as he tried to coach a black player out of what Stewart perceived to be bad habits. Stewart had no time for showboating and he didn't like watching his linebacker, Kelly Cook, high-step the final few yards into the end zone after he'd made an interception in practice. Years later, Stewart told ESPN.com he remembered pulling Cook aside after practice and saying to him, "Don't let your actions give people reason to call you a n-----."

Cook, who was from the small town of Ettrick in southern Virginia, not far from Petersburg, remembered the situation differently. He told the *Roanoke Times* in 2008 that Stewart sprinted 50 yards or so and yelled to him in the end zone, "You're acting like a n----- from Petersburg. You don't go to Virginia Union. You don't go to Virginia State."

Whatever the words, Cook went to the VMI administration, which then called Stewart in for a meeting. Stewart confirmed there had been an incident when that one particular word had been used. Cook told the *Times* the situation became difficult to manage when "the majority" of the Keydets got together and decided they didn't want to play for Stewart. VMI told Stewart that December he needed to resign or he'd be fired. He resigned soon thereafter. Stewart didn't coach football in 1997. He sued VMI in 1998 and saw the suit dismissed in 1999, but by then he was coaching in the CFL. By 2000, he was back in college football when WVU coach Don Nehlen had a need for a quarterbacks coach and a respect for what Stewart had accomplished for various peers Nehlen knew quite well.

When the time came for WVU to make a decision about Stewart and to promote him from interim coach to full-time coach, there were no reservations. The school knew about what happened at VMI and actually knew it when he was hired by Nehlen so many years earlier. His season with Nehlen and seven seasons with Rodriguez left no doubts about his character. You wanted your son to play for him. Enter a kid, leave a man, and learn a few things about football along the way. The fans abandoned by Rodriguez and haunted by all the close calls before his exit were comforted by Stewart. He was one of them and would never leave them. It wasn't his style, but even if it were, he wouldn't know what to do.

"I don't have a lot of experience in these negotiations and things. That's my agent right down there," Stewart said, extending his right hand and assuring everyone he was a man of his word and his handshake was all the security he and his bosses would need in the future.

And then he said the thing that would follow him for three seasons, 27 wins, and 12 losses, the thing he meant to be harmless and endearing, but the thing he never, ever should have said.

"This is my last job," he said. "I won't leave here. And they won't have to tell me when I'm not doing the job. I'll tell them."

That was something people would never forget, especially the critics and the cynics and those who felt like Ken Kendrick did. A WVU graduate and a generous donor who works as the managing general partner of Major League Baseball's Arizona Diamondbacks, Kendrick donated the money to cover WVU's unsold Fiesta Bowl tickets. After Stewart was hired, Kendrick said Stewart was "so overmatched it's not even funny." He complimented Stewart for being so kind and so fatherly, but also made the analogy that WVU hired a painter (Stewart) to build its house, rather than an architect (Rodriguez).

Strong prophecy, but it was Stewart's words that were forever locked within suspicious minds as ammunition to use in the future. To them, the Mountaineers had given the job to a career assistant, a failed head coach, a man who was never interviewed for the job and never championed by the donors and supporters. Yet he'd just been put in charge of the football program, the marquee football program in the Big East—one that was expected to do well every year, one that was expected to be talented again in 2008, one that bore a lot of the financial responsibilities in a self-supported athletic department with an annual budget in excess of $50 million. This better be good, they thought. If not, they'd tell Stewart it was time to go.

"The process was unfair to Bill Stewart and it did haunt him for a long time," Garrison said. "I think it followed him through his [WVU] career. He wasn't hired the right way and I was afraid that would become a part of his body of work."

12
CONFUSION

Given the occasion and the outcome, Bill Stewart should have been a happier man. West Virginia was ranked eighth in the 2008 preseason poll and had just beaten Villanova on the first Saturday of the season. The final score was 48–21, and all the reasons to retain Stewart seemed to be justified. That was a fun game.

Pat White threw 33 passes, much to the enjoyment of the fans who had been begging to see the ball in the air just a little more frequently. Those same fans hadn't seen as many attempts since 2004. In his 86 games in seven seasons as WVU's coach, Rich Rodriguez had a quarterback throw more passes just four times—and not once since Rasheed Marshall let it rip 35 times in Rodriguez's fourth season. White passed for five touchdowns and launched numerous, picturesque throws fitted into small openings. Only Marc Bulger had thrown more touchdowns in a game, but by the way things looked and felt that day, White might soon match Bulger's six scores against Pitt in 1999. These were the things Stewart had prophesized. He'd tuned out the detractors, the people who were upset by his appointment and worried about the future of the program. He knew more than they did. He was going to dictate how the game would be played. He wouldn't be handcuffed by stubbornness. If you tried to take away his left, he'd bloody your nose with his right. His was an adaptable offense with an unstoppable vision.

Yet there he was in the postgame press conference, fairly disappointed in himself, even as the words he used to explain the way he was feeling were muffled by the sounds of victory spilling out of the locker room doors across from where he stood. Oh, Stewart was tickled with the win. He was delighted White, who was Stewart's favorite player and his prized pupil when he was the quarterbacks coach, had his career day. He couldn't say enough about some of the touchdown passes White had thrown. One was placed perfectly as Alric Arnett executed a double move, one went to a spot where only Will Johnson could catch it and run with it as he slipped out of the backfield on a play-action pass, and one arched over the shoulders of Jock Sanders and fell into a bucket. Stewart was happy to point out that White's numbers would have been better if not for some legitimate drops by receivers and a bobble that turned into an interception. He even took the blame for that, saying it was Bill Stewart's interception and not Pat White's interception because while there was no need to be passing with a lead, there was also no need to run into eight- and nine-player fronts.

"He could have been 31-of-33 with no picks," Stewart said.

That wasn't what bothered him, though. Stewart was upset with himself because of what had happened in the fourth quarter. White played the first possession and threw four passes. He completed three, including that excellent 17-yard pass to Sanders into a snug spot in the back-left corner of the end zone. Hardly anyone put much stock into Stewart's lament. It was still somewhat early, certainly early enough in the first game for White to be playing, and that touchdown created some distance and made the score 41–21. On the very next play from scrimmage, linebacker Mortty Ivy returned an interception for a score to clinch the outcome. Stewart pulled White in favor of Jarrett Brown and he, too, threw a pass, but it seemed insignificant to everyone but Stewart.

"I tried to say way back and nobody listened, particularly most of the experts in this room, but if you put nine people in the box, we're going to throw the football," he said. "That's the only thing I know how to do. I don't know how to run the ball with nine people in the box. I'm not that smart."

He was driving home a point he'd been trying to make throughout the offseason. No longer would the Mountaineers run into walls. They'd throw over top of them. If those walls started to show some holes, then the Mountaineers would run through them with White and Noel Devine and whoever else could get the ball. That was the plan and, unfortunately, Villanova was the victim. That's the part that pained Stewart. The Wildcats were a nice, competitive Division I-AA school and it wasn't necessary to put one on them like Stewart felt he had. This went against who he was and what he stood for as a man and as a coach.

"My mom and dad would not be pleased for throwing the ball at the end of the game," he said. "But we had to do what we had to do. If you're going to put nine down [defenders near the line of scrimmage], we're going to throw the football. That's what I said we'd do and I told the lads I'll never lie to them."

Trust mattered so much at that time, and it was trust that connected Stewart to the players before the Fiesta Bowl and to the decision makers immediately after it. They'd all been abandoned and wanted to believe in a leader again. Stewart was that man, an honest man, a good man who was determined to do what he vowed to do, but a man who also valued sportsmanship and would never dare show up an opponent. He was a little ashamed and felt so badly about doing what he'd done to someone he liked so much, Villanova coach Andy Talley, who had been at the school for 23 years. This game was Stewart's first impression, and while it had been fun and emphatic, while he knew opponents would lean forward and notice how he'd coached the game with a purpose, he also wasn't entirely true to himself and all of his values.

"I hated to throw the ball because Coach Talley is a dear friend," Stewart said.

This all sounded so kind, so becoming of the coach and the man WVU had hired in part because he had no shame in possessing and displaying these emotions. There was just one problem with it: Talley said he and Stewart had never met before that game.

First impressions? Now that was a pretty good one. Puffing up his supposed relationship with Talley didn't really reflect the way Stewart managed games or prepared a team, but it did show how much Stewart had to learn about his role and his responsibilities in that position. But, hey, it was one time, his first time, and he could be forgiven for getting a little carried away and embellishing something for a noble cause. Was it shameless? Sure, but that was Billy. Sometimes the mouth moved faster than the mind could cope with, but what one called embarrassing another might call endearing. Plus, he won. He threw the ball. He capitalized on the defense's vulnerabilities. He had White posing two threats. He had Devine crafting highlights. He had Arnett streaking down the sideline and Sanders sweeping across the field. If one game was an indication, this was going to work.

That was unbelievably important. The months of the winter, spring, and summer were spent revisiting WVU's decision and fretting about whether or not it would work. The school had been hit incredibly hard by reactions to the hire from all directions and very few of them were positive or supportive or even understanding. Stewart Mandel, of SI.com, wrote the words that throbbed the most and, in the end, read the truest. Days after Stewart was hired, Mandel commented on WVU's decision in a blog post that previewed LSU versus Ohio State in the national championship game. He called WVU's hire a "fitting and, most likely, disastrous end to what had already been one of the most dim-witted coaching searches I've ever witnessed." Then came a paragraph that spooked fans for three seasons.

Maybe Stewart will turn out to be the next Bill Belichick, but I'd guess he has a much better chance of becoming the next Bill Doba. Promoting an interim coach based on short-term success (Bobby Williams at Michigan State), or promoting an assistant just because he's popular with the current players (Larry Coker at Miami), doesn't usually work out in the long run. With Pat White and Noel Devine, it would be hard for any coach to screw up next year's team, but two to three years down the road, the school will likely rue its hasty decision.

That didn't comfort anyone in West Virginia or anyone who cheered for the Mountaineers, people who seek acceptance and approval, and who are susceptible to criticism and prone to panic. Yet these people also thought Stewart deserved the benefit of the doubt and just needed a chance. He couldn't win any games in February. Wait until the fall. Until then, everything was opinion without the presence of fact. No one could reach any conclusion until the Mountaineers started playing games. In between, what stood as Stewart's strongest defense was that the best way to continue the program's ascent was to manufacture continuity. The future mattered, but the present could not be ignored. Keeping Stewart made a lot of sense.

I believed it.

Truly, there was no one else for the job. As hard as it may be, forget Stewart's kindness and his appreciation, that he is as much a teddy bear as his predecessor was a grizzly bear, that he gave an entire fan base, state and university a hug to begin January after a nightmarish December.

Everyone has questions about this hire, but only one matters: What is the goal in college football? There is only one answer and only one team can explain it. That team resides in Baton Rouge, La.

You play to win the national title. Not to build a program or to sustain success. Are those goals? Sure. But that ugly cut crystal trophy is the top goal.

There's no way you could witness the way WVU rolled with Stewart and say that team isn't a contender for the national title next year. It's not even worth arguing. You don't gamble on those odds, either, just because you think somebody else might be able to keep it going and set up a similar situation a few years from now.

This was less about positioning the program for future success and much, much more about maintaining the current position as one of the country's best programs.

Today, that's not one of my proudest moments. At the time, I thought it was a very viable justification. In many ways, I still do. White had unique skills and Stewart knew them very well. Devine was a complex kid, forever affected by a tough childhood and by losing both of his parents to AIDS by the age of 11, and he really liked Stewart. Stewart knew the roster and what it could do. He had specific ideas on offense, things he wanted to change, things he wanted to continue, and things he wanted to feature. He wouldn't run the offense, but he would hire who he thought were the right coaches to get that done. Yet that's where the problems started.

Stewart was fortunate on defense. Defensive coordinator Jeff Casteel chose to stay with Stewart and the Mountaineers rather than follow Rodriguez to Michigan. He was from Paden City, and won a state championship with the Paden City Wildcats when he was a high school senior in 1979. He'd leave the state for coaching jobs in college in Pennsylvania and high school in Miami before returning and working 12 seasons and winning six West Virginia Conference titles as an assistant at Shepherd University. He left again in 2000 for the University of Texas-El Paso, but it reaffirmed his affinity for being home. His family was comfortable in West Virginia and his family's family was never far away.

He'd come to WVU in 2001 and beaten Louisville and Georgia and Oklahoma, topped Chris Johnson, Ben Mauk, and Calvin Johnson, but telling Rodriguez he wasn't taking the 3-3-5 to Ann Arbor was not easy. How could Casteel not reward the man who'd rewarded him with the biggest break in his career? How could he gamble on the unknown at WVU when he knew quite well the men who were joining Rodriguez at Michigan?

"I spent more time with those guys than anyone else and you get really tight when you spend that much time together," Casteel said. "It was really tough not going there, but it's a situation where I'll always be grateful to Coach Rod for the opportunity he gave me here. It was difficult to tell him, 'No, thank you. I'm staying here at West Virginia.'"

That was a huge victory for Stewart, though one he predicted the day he was named coach. Bill Kirelawich stayed as the defensive line coach, and Stewart had little trouble getting David Lockwood and Steve Dunlap to leave their jobs to work as the cornerbacks and safeties coaches at WVU, where they'd been coaches and players before.

Stewart had a harder time assembling his offensive staff. He shocked many when he hired Doc Holliday, the front-runner for a time for the head coaching position, to coach fullbacks and tight ends. He had to give Holliday a lot of money and a lot of responsibility, but about $400,000 annually and the title of associate head coach and director of recruiting were enough to lure Holliday back home and away from the Florida Gators. Suffice to say, Holliday had an eye on the head coaching job, too, and a hunch Stewart might fumble. If so, he'd be right there so the administration could recover and promote him, the guy many of the same people wanted to hire in the first place.

Chris Beatty was named the running backs coach. Beatty was a star high school coach in southern Virginia who prepped Percy Harvin for the University of Florida, but had spent only two years coaching in college, and just one at the Football Bowl Subdivision level, before Stewart called on him. Lonnie Galloway was named the wide receivers coach and, like Beatty, was a respected recruiter, but he, too, was relatively unknown. He'd spent 17 years coaching, but just seven at the FBS level, all at East Carolina.

Stewart pointed to another former WVU player when he hired Dave Johnson, a former center who had snapped the ball to Oliver Luck, as the offensive line coach. Johnson was the tight ends coach at Georgia and had done a pretty good job there mentoring Ben Watson and Leonard Pope to NFL careers, but he had never coached the entire offensive line by himself at the FBS level. He spent 10 years doing it in Division II, but was no more than the tackles coach during his four years at Marshall. The Mountaineers lost a lot when Rick Trickett left the offensive line position for Florida State in 2007; they needed to find someone the players feared and respected. Johnson, who was a terribly nice man, was never that guy, much like Greg Frey was not before him.

Inexplicably, Stewart made his most important hire last. He took advice from a friend in the business, Wake Forest coach Jim Grobe, and hired Grobe's longtime assistant, Jeff Mullen. Another kind and gracious person, Mullen was Grobe's quarterbacks coach after following Grobe from Ohio University to Wake Forest. He'd just never been an offensive coordinator and had never called plays. He liked the option and White could do so much with that, but Mullen was also into motion and shifts and numerical advantages and developing a passing game and vertical routes and screen passes and using tight ends and—well, you get the picture.

Mullen wasn't Stewart's first choice, either. Stewart first targeted Charlie Taaffe, who Stewart had known for years. They had gone up against each other when Stewart was at VMI and Taaffe was at The Citadel. He hoped Taaffe would leave his job as the head coach of the CFL's Hamilton Tiger-Cats. It was going to happen, and the procedural background checks were underway when the Tiger-Cats pretty much forced Taaffe to stay north of the border. Taaffe stayed but was later fired; he moved on to be a very successful coordinator at the University of Central Florida. As Mullen's offenses did little to distinguish themselves through the years, you had to wonder what might have been had Taaffe been the guy from the start.

That season-opening win eased the early worries, though, and the Stewart hire was starting to make sense. Keep the guy who rode shotgun through the years. Keep the program aimed at the top. Don't mess with the defense. Change a few things on offense and keep the critics quiet.

Then everything changed. The Mountaineers ran into a buzz saw in week two and were soundly beaten on the road against East Carolina. The Pirates, coached by Skip Holtz, who was supposed to interview with WVU after the Fiesta Bowl, were hot after they opened their season with a win at Virginia Tech. ECU never trailed and never really had a problem with WVU in a 24–3 win. The Pirates started with an 80-yard touchdown drive that rocked WVU's young defense, but the offense, which had beaten ECU 48–7 with breathtaking bravado a year earlier, would surely respond. The Mountaineers had White. ECU did not.

Sure enough, White and the Mountaineers took the ball and within five snaps were at ECU's 39-yard line. White raced right on a third-and-5 and reached for the first down. He shifted the ball to his left hand and the ball hit the ground as his right hand landed out of bounds. The ball bounced loose and rolled to a stop in bounds. While the offense hurried back to the huddle, an ECU player picked up the ball. The officials awarded ECU possession.

"That was a big, big turning point, daggone it," Stewart said afterward.

He was right to say that, but he had no right to imply he couldn't have done anything about it. It was, at the minimum, a curious call. White's knees could have hit before the ball came free, in which case he would have been ruled down before he fumbled. The right hand might have touched out of bounds before the ball was jarred lose, and again he would have been ruled down before the fumble. No fewer than two possible outcomes were in WVU's favor and a challenge could have also examined whether the ground had caused White's fumble, in which case the Mountaineers would have had the ball and a first down. Stewart had a hunch momentum was there for someone to snatch. He chose not to grab it. He let someone else control the game.

White wanted to call a timeout and seemed close to doing so, but he stopped. The WVU offense hesitated before giving way to the defense. ECU hurried its offense onto the field and snapped the ball to eliminate any chance for a review. Stewart defended himself afterward and said the officials told him they'd checked the play, even though only a few seconds had transpired. He was allowed to challenge the play and if he was right, he would have retained that challenge to use once later. At the very least, he could have called a timeout and given the replay officials, who do review every play, a chance to get more looks at it.

"I didn't have the best view in the house, but if seven officials and TV can't figure it out, they don't need my input," he said.

Stewart quickly earned the distinction of coaching WVU to its first game without a touchdown since 2001. The Mountaineers plummeted in the national rankings to No. 25. It was then that fans remembered this team led Villanova only 34–21 early in the fourth quarter, and only built the larger final margin with Stewart showing up his dear friend with a throw into the end zone and then a defensive touchdown.

Things got no better a week later. In a nationally televised Thursday night game in Boulder, Colorado, WVU was again slow out of the locker room and trailed Colorado 14–0 in the first quarter. The Mountaineers evened the score late, but Stewart suffered another inglorious sideline moment, this time at the end of the game, which ESPN's sideline reporter Erin Andrews characterized as "mass confusion."

After Colorado's two scores, the defense flipped a switch and began growing into its potential during the game, getting 10 straight stops. The last one handed the ball to the offense at its own 20 with two minutes, nine seconds to go and the score tied. WVU was positioned to use the clock and its two timeouts to get the 50 or 60 yards needed to kick a field goal through the thin air. Pat McAfee had been hitting with ease from 50-plus yards during warm-ups.

And then, the team that was down 14–0 so quickly, and worked so hard to get the game even and to keep it that way, managed just 32 yards on eight plays. The eighth was a Hail Mary into the end zone that went unanswered and sent the players to the sideline and into overtime with one unused timeout left on the scoreboard. It was a stunning display of disorganization, and players were again entirely unsure what to do, or if their coaches knew what to tell them to do. The Mountaineers lost in overtime after McAfee's short kick from the hash bounced off the upright and then Colorado's kicker won the game with a field goal on the Buffaloes' possession. The story seemed so clear. WVU had botched the end of the game, and the head coach, in his third game, simply mismanaged the situation.

The question afterward was obvious: Bill, would you change anything about that last drive in regulation?

"No," he said. "No. I don't second guess. No. I don't want anybody second guessing me. No. We're going to do what we do. Run. Try to kick the ball and win the ball game with a field goal. I absolutely wouldn't change a thing."

WVU ran the ball very well against Colorado. White had 143 yards and two touchdowns. Devine added 133 yards. The Mountaineers ran 52 times and passed just 15 times because the run was working, and because the run kept the WVU defense on the sideline and gave those players a chance to recover and eventually take over the game. It worked well enough that the suspense at the end shouldn't have been necessary. WVU could have won the game a possession earlier. The offense moved inside the Colorado 40 when receiver Bradley Starks caught a quick pass behind the line of scrimmage on the right side of the field and drew the defense, then stopped and threw across the field toward a wide-open Jock Sanders. The pass was weak and fluttered to the ground yards short; rather than walk in for a touchdown, Sanders had to scurry back and make a fruitless dive toward the ball. Then came penalties for a block in the back and a hold, and McAfee ended up punting from his 48.

Short-yardage situations were a mess throughout the game, too. White gained nothing on a fourth-and-1 at the Colorado 18 in the third quarter. In overtime, on a third-and-1 from the Colorado 4, the Mountaineers tried to run tiny Sanders for the conversion, but he lost two yards.

None of that would have mattered, though, if Stewart and Mullen had handled that final possession in regulation better. The run continued to work. The first two went for 11 yards. White passed to Devine for four yards before Devine ran for nine and another first down. White again completed a pass to Devine for four yards and then hit Arnett for five more. Arnett stayed in bounds to set up third-and-1. White picked up his hands with 40 seconds left to suggest calling one of the two remaining timeouts. He was told not to call it, so a dozen or more valuable seconds ticked away. Devine then ran the familiar outside zone play from the shotgun and lost a yard. WVU then called its first timeout of the drive with only enough time to throw one into the end zone from 48 yards away. Rodriguez's once-explosive offense had been reduced to banking on a 50-yard field goal from McAfee. At least, that was the explanation from Mullen.

"We felt like if we could get to the 35 and in, Pat was going to win it," Mullen said. "We felt like we were running that outside zone play pretty good all night and we'd get the first down. We'd be across the

50 and then we could burn our timeouts and take our shots with some 15-yard passes and send Pat out to win it."

The length of a coach's honeymoon isn't measured with a calendar, but by actions. Stewart's honeymoon ended as he walked off of Folsom Field. WVU hadn't lost back-to-back games since the 2004 season crumbled. WVU had been ranked for 48 straight weeks, but Stewart would end that after three games. A fan screamed from the stands, "What are you gonna do with those timeouts now?" The players strolled off that same field, and one mouthed to someone in the stands "What the f---?" Another player, this one on defense, said clearly and with enough volume for anyone around him to hear, "Not our fault." Stewart was angry these details were made public. It didn't change the fact they were true. That hurt most.

Stewart and the Mountaineers beat Marshall the next week in a game that was as important as it was unfulfilling. Stewart had to win that one, or else, yet a win would not acquit him, because WVU is *supposed* to beat Marshall.

In the next game, WVU beat a bad Rutgers team only 24–17, and Stewart was giving people panic attacks. Up 17–3 after scoring a touchdown with 47 seconds to go in the first half, he decided to squib the ensuing kickoff. Rutgers took over at its 44. The Scarlet Knights had 112 yards of offense to that point. Rejuvenated by the field position, they drove 56 yards and scored a touchdown.

Stewart defended that error after the game in a totally unprompted monologue. "I will always squib the ball or sky the ball. I will never kick the ball deep and let them take it back with under a minute to go. That's why I did what I did."

White was hurt in that game when he was hit in the head. Jarrett Brown, who had been asked to help the team fix its biggest problem a week earlier by becoming the team's short-yardage back, played the rest of the way. Late in the fourth quarter, it was fourth-and-1 at the Rutgers 46. Stewart called a timeout with two minutes left and found what he thought was the best play in that situation. Brown ran and lost nine yards, and Rutgers took over with a great chance to tie or win the game. Stewart was passionate in his own defense after the game, even if it contradicted what he'd done at Colorado.

"I will always play to win the football game," he said. "I'm never, ever playing not to lose."

In the days that followed, Stewart said White did not suffer a concussion against Rutgers and would play against Syracuse. White missed the Syracuse game with a concussion. Stewart would lose a second quarterback after the 17–6 win against the Orange—Tajh Boyd, a can't-miss recruit from Hampton, Virginia.

Boyd, of powerhouse Phoebus High, was to be the cornerstone of the 2009 recruiting class, the sort of superstar prep player Stewart could sign with Beatty and Galloway on staff. Beatty scouted Hampton Roads and forged a rapport with Boyd, and Boyd himself was determined to lay a pipeline from the talent-rich region that had fed so many great players to so many great Virginia Tech teams. The Mountaineers were going to get in there, and Boyd was going to help. He had some Division I-bound teammates in running back Shawne Alston and defensive lineman Dominik Davenport, who would follow Boyd to WVU, but Boyd was a big enough name that he had made some high-profile friends. One was receiver Logan Heastie, from Chesapeake, Virginia, who was a top-100 prospect like Boyd. So sure were they about their future success at WVU that Boyd's mother designed gold T-shirts that read "BOYD TO HEASTIE."

The way the 2008 season began was concerning on many levels and recruiting was one of them, especially with White playing his senior season and Brown ready to take over during his senior season in 2009. The offense needed a quarterback, which meant the offense needed to keep Boyd committed. After the stumbling win against the Orange, Boyd decided he was no longer interested in playing for the Mountaineers. Boyd worded his decision to decommit politely and spoke highly of WVU and his relationship with the coaches on the staff.

Stewart decided he was going to roll up his sleeves and address the state of his program.

"I will tell you I will call the plays, Jeff Mullen will call the plays, Jeff Casteel will call the plays on special teams, offense, and defense.

No player will call plays. They will play," Stewart said at his weekly press conference. "I'm glad I found that thing out sooner rather than later. No player's daddy is going to call plays."

More than three years later, with his Clemson team preparing to play the Mountaineers in the 2012 Orange Bowl, Boyd said he had decommitted to convince the rest of college football he would be willing to listen to their offers. Privately, he said he was still interested in the Mountaineers and, in particular, how the offense might still evolve and eventually develop him into a NFL quarterback. Stewart's shocking salvo changed all of that.

"In all honesty, my dad never directed anything toward anybody," Boyd said. "We wanted the gist of how the offense was going to work and everyone there took it the wrong way. That was one part of the situation I never understood. At that point, I was like, 'Man, this is how it's going to be before I ever get there? How's it going to be when I do get there?' I had a lot of respect for Coach Stewart, but at that point I felt like I had to look somewhere else."

Boyd was off the board for good. Davenport and Heastie both enrolled, but they left after one year and neither played for the Mountaineers. Alston stuck, though, and became a contributor. Stewart signed no more players from Hampton Roads before his resignation in 2011.

"I'll never know how much my decision not to come to West Virginia deterred Logan or my high school teammates or other guys from down there, but it's something I really wonder about all the time," Boyd said. "I think about how things would have worked out and how the scenario would have went. I know we would have been great."

That was the first recruiting snafu for Stewart, who nevertheless talked up his recruiting success. He said the 2009 and 2010 classes were the highest rated in school history, that both were top-25 classes, presumably in the nation, though no one could ever find the organization that awarded WVU any such distinction for back-to-back years. No fewer than 25 players he signed between 2008 and 2011 either never showed up at WVU or left before contributing for a variety of reasons, be they academics or ability. That's the equivalent of an entire recruiting class. He even signed a few players, most notably receiver Deon Long and defensive lineman Tevita Finau, more than once and was burned more than once.

Stewart would constantly be questioned about the small size of his recruiting classes, too. He had 23, 24, 19, and 18 players in his four recruiting classes, which left no margin for error—and obviously losing more than two dozen of those players created a large deficit. He signed four, five, two, and four offensive linemen, but by the end of the 2011 season, three of those 15 weren't with the team and a fourth wasn't in uniform for games.

Boyd's flip-flop and the style of the Syracuse game intensified fans' examination of the product on the field. But the Mountaineers perhaps could be forgiven for struggling in that game. White was out, and Brown was beat up after playing running back for parts of the previous two games. While no one outside the locker room knew it, Brown could barely run because of a deep thigh bruise, and couldn't lift his right arm very high. That made life demonstrably difficult for the right-handed backup, who nevertheless battled through the game. He completed 14 of his 20 pass attempts, but for only 52 yards, and none of his passes had the heat someone with Brown's size and skill usually provided.

Brown was struggling, the offense was sputtering, and Syracuse's defense was actually playing well for a group that had been allowing more than 36 points and 460 yards per game. Syracuse's coach, the extremely embattled Greg Robinson, then took control. With 90 seconds left in the third quarter and WVU ahead just 7–6, the Orange had a fourth-and-3 at WVU's 43. Rather than ride the defense and use a punt to place Brown and WVU's anemic offense deep, Robinson gambled on his unreliable offense. He opted for a pass that fell incomplete. The field position swung and WVU managed a short drive and a field goal. Syracuse drove again, this time all the way down to the WVU 5, where the Orange faced another fourth down. Robinson went for it again and the pass was incomplete again.

The Mountaineers took over at the 5, ahead 10–6 with 4:42 left in the game. They ran twice for three yards with Syracuse calling a timeout after each down. On third-and-7, WVU ran an ordinary zone play left. Alric Arnett motioned right to left and dragged a defender with him, and left tackle Ryan Stanchek cleared out a linebacker on the second level. With the safeties hovering around the line of scrimmage and giving no thought to the possibility Brown might pass, Devine worked around that one block and was gone. The game was over and Stewart escaped. Afterward, he hailed Mullen's play call as though he'd witnessed Phil Brady's Sugar Bowl–sealing fake punt again. A voice arose from one of the perplexed reporters in the room. "Bill, what else was he supposed to call?" Mullen came out a while later to talk to the media. He was asked if he was worried about his job. It was getting that bad that soon.

To be fair, there was a timing element behind the question posed to Mullen. Auburn was headed to Mountaineer Field for the next game, and the Tigers were dealing with an offensive makeover that wasn't working out, either. Their newly hired coordinator, Tony Franklin, had been pried from Troy University to give coach Tommy Tuberville one more shot at restoring his job security. It didn't work; three days before WVU's close call against Syracuse, Franklin was fired with Auburn at 4-2 and ranked No. 104 in total offense. Mullen was visibly and understandably bothered by the question, and he answered it as calmly and concisely as he could inside the huddle that had surrounded him. Eleven days later, he put an exclamation mark on the response.

Paul Rhoads, the engineer of Pitt's 13–9 victory 10 months earlier, was now Auburn's defensive coordinator. The Mountaineers just weren't going to relive that nightmare. They were going to do what they should have done that awful night the previous December. They'd tried to forget that occasion, and Stewart had done so much, both good and bad, to otherwise occupy their minds. He had no choice but to revisit that game, if not in spirit, then in strategy. He and Mullen knew what Rhoads was going to ask Auburn to do and they found ways around it.

The result was extraordinary. The Mountaineers scored 34 points and had 445 yards of offense.

"They studied the heck out of what we had done at Pitt and they were ready," Rhoads said. "What we'd done the year before, the stuff we did in the 2007 game, we hadn't showed it at Auburn but just a little bit. We ran it exclusively that night."

WVU trailed 17–3, but changed nothing and stuck with a plan that was, in truth, a deviation from what they had established to be the norm. They spread the field and squared off with the defensive backs and snapped it to White in the shotgun and trusted the blocking could hold on long enough to let the receivers run drag routes and crossing routes.

White was only 2-for-3 for 62 yards in the first half, but that included a 44-yard touchdown pass. White shuffled to the right, set himself in the face of an oncoming defender, and then threw a dart to Alric Arnett, who was slanting deep across the field and behind the secondary. That made it 17–10 at the half, but White would go 11-for-18 in the second half for 112 yards and two more touchdowns to Dorrell Jalloh, one from two yards away on a corner route in the end zone and one on a short throw on a drag route that went for 32 yards. White would set the NCAA record for career rushing yards by a quarterback three games later, but he added just eight yards to his total that day. His passing forced the defense to step away from the line of scrimmage, regard the pass, and, as a result, forget about Noel Devine. Devine then had 207 yards on just 17 carries. His 30-yard touchdown up the middle in the fourth quarter came without a hint of the Auburn defense that had once crowded the line.

"We had to loosen them up a little bit," Stewart said. "They played a lot of people down in the box and they played a lot of man-to-man. They've got a good defensive coordinator and a good scheme, but that passing game I'm thrilled to death about. Absolutely thrilled to death."

WVU never sustained it, though. The team rallied and rolled Connecticut a week later, 35–13, but lost a showdown for first place in the Big East at home against Cincinnati when the Bearcats played that familiar defense with great success. Cincinnati also returned a kickoff for a touchdown to start the game—after the return man, Mardy Gilyard, watched WVU's very bad coverage team on film and openly predicted he would do it. The Mountaineers beat Louisville, but lost again to Pitt. Devine rushed for only 17 yards on 12 carries, while White threw a brutal interception late near his own end zone to set up the game-winning score for the Panthers. The game ended with the offense scurrying again at the end, and White throwing a desperation pass into the end zone as time expired.

Stewart then became a very different, very determined man during the final week of the regular season. His conference calls and his press conference featured crisp and sharp replies. He benched Devine and safety Robert Sands and said he was sending a message. He was altogether different within the game, too. He hollered at officials. He went nose-to-helmet with players. He pointed at this guy and knocked on that guy's shoulder pads. He stepped into huddles and allowed hardly anything to happen without his involvement, which was a major change. And then things got really weird. The Mountaineers beat the University of South Florida Bulls, the team that had tormented WVU the previous two seasons.

The game was given special attention by the fans as well. It was to be the last home game for senior Patrick White, by this point considered by many to be the best player, or at least the best quarterback, ever to lead the Mountaineers. The game was declared a "White Out," and fans were asked to show up in white clothing (Stewart insisted, understandably, that the white out was meant to honor all the seniors). USF graciously agreed to wear its green home uniforms on the road, which allowed WVU to wear its white road jerseys. Even Mother Nature obliged, sending a coating of snow down upon Morgantown to enhance the scene.

That win, in that setting, meant to world to Stewart, and it explained his irregular behavior. He took the occasion seriously from the start of the week to its finish, when he was bizarre in a postgame press conference. He said transition seasons are not fun. He patronized reporters by asking them to take his first season and compare it to what other first-year coaches have done. Then he said something that was completely unprompted and puzzling before he left the room.

"We've got enough coal in this state to heat the world. We've got enough oil in this state to lubricate the world. We've got enough brains in this state to run the world. Good evening," he said.

Days later it came to light that Stewart had referenced a nineteenth-century speech by another Wetzel County native, William Olliver Gallahue, who had been asked to come up on stage at the Fairmont Opera after a production of *Uncle Tom's Cabin*. In a monologue of his own, Gallahue said, "Glorious old Wetzel! Whose sons are brave and daughters fair, and which today produces gas enough to light the world, oil enough to lubricate it, and brains enough to rule it."

In the most unusual way possible, Stewart had punched back.

WVU was invited to the Meineke Car Care Bowl, the very outcome Mandel predicted in his January takedown, but it gave Stewart a chance to throw the knockout blow. As the Mountaineers studied their opponent, they noticed North Carolina's secondary gave up a lot of big pass plays. Arnett was most vocal and he pleaded for the offense to throw the ball. A lot.

"I know it's just a matter of going up and making a play against these guys," Arnett said.

Mullen made it so with an aggressive attack that empowered White to throw it 34 times. He completed 26 for 332 yards, both career highs, and four touchdowns as WVU rallied for the win.

"This," White said afterward, "doesn't seem real."

The Mountaineers really seemed to have fun from the beginning of the game to the end, and it was then when Stewart stood on the stage in the trophy ceremony, grabbed a microphone, and started shouting out to West Virginia cities and asking for them to make noise. Meineke pitchman George Foreman looked on from a few feet away with the same surprised expression he had on his face after he knocked out Michael Moorer.

Stewart was relieved. He was proud. He knew the offense looked powerful again and he said those were his orders. He had demanded it and Mullen had executed it. Then Stewart offered up one more quizzical defense of his approach, the one that would change from one game to the next in his first season, by saying there was a method to his madness that would become very clear in the next year or two. He knew things were rocky at times and people and players were frustrated. A 9-4 record wasn't what anyone was used to, but he didn't think anyone would be getting used to it, either. The win sent the Mountaineers into the offseason with momentum, and those frustrated fans were filled with excitement and optimism about a future that suddenly looked a lot more fun. Maybe they could learn to live with one another. After all, they'd accepted certain flaws in Stewart's predecessor. Who knows, maybe this would work.

"About half of them would like to hang me and the other half would like to make me governor when Joe Manchin leaves at this point because we won, but I'm not mad at any of them," Stewart said. "You know why? Because I'm one of them. They have such a passion for football at West Virginia, and all they want is for us to be the best. I want to be the best with them."

13
KICKOFFS

More often than not, a Bill Stewart press conference was an experience. None of Stewart's three seasons offered more or better examples than 2009. On any occasion, you had as much of a chance to learn about Appalachian history, military strategy, traveling to Provo, old-school brawls at Sistersville High, dog soldiers, mine mules, jutting one's jaw, how to rule the roost, and other things only loosely affiliated with football as you did to learn about things inextricably attached to the game and the way it had to be played. It was like the Wild West. There was the loquacious cowboy with his holster he vowed to empty, and there were no rules except one he would never, ever disobey. In those weekly press conferences before a game, Wild Bill would never look back at the game that had been played a few days earlier. There was a reminder of this before he started, and then another whenever someone would ask Stewart a question that encouraged him to engage in retrospect. Those conversations were reserved for the postgame press conference, and later, a conference call after the game.

And that was a shame when the media filed into the team meeting room inside the Puskar Center on Monday, November 16, 2009. The Mountaineers had lost three days earlier at Cincinnati, which was undefeated, leading the Big East Conference, and ranked No. 5 nationally entering the game, but hadn't had a scare quite like the one the Mountaineers gave them. The visitors, led by quarterback Jarrett Brown and his bad foot and running back Noel Devine and his bad ankle, were ahead 14–7 in the second quarter, and the defenders were giving the Bearcats fits their powerful offense was not used to.

On a goal-line play, running back Isaiah Pead tried to jump over the pile and into the end zone, but WVU safety Robert Sands saw it coming. He, too, jumped and swung down on the ball to knock it loose. His teammate, nose guard Chris Neild, came out of the chaos with the football and Cincinnati was in trouble. Driving against WVU's defense, with star quarterback Tony Pike injured on the sideline and only able to come in for spot snaps in the red zone, was hard for the Bearcats, and they'd just squandered a promising opportunity. The Mountaineers were surging and had just added a wrinkle when fullback Ryan Clarke rumbled through the middle for a 37-yard touchdown. WVU went into the game feeling like it could play power football against the Bearcats. That score only reinforced the confidence. Now the offense would take the possession near the goal line, run the ball, drain the clock, quarantine Cincinnati's offense, and give life to this silly idea WVU could beat the unbeaten.

Then came a whistle. The officials would review the play. Was it a fumble or was it a touchdown? The Cincinnati fans took a deep breath on a cold night. WVU fans, the ones who remembered so many things going bad in the past, feared the worst and prepared to accept it. There was nothing on the replay that made it clear Pead had crossed the goal line and entered the end zone. If anything, it looked like Sands had leaped forward to meet Pead before the goal line and didn't retreat until the ball was out and finding its way into Neild's grasp. There was no way to conclusively reverse the call and award Cincinnati a touchdown. The opinion in the press box among the WVU writers who were witnessing a stunner develop before them, the Cincinnati writers who had an interest in covering a team that might play for the national title, the national media there for the occasion, and the employees from both teams who had their obvious allegiances was that

WVU had forced the turnover and Cincinnati had lost possession.

None of that mattered when the officials reversed the call and gave Pead a touchdown. John Marinatto, the Big East Conference commissioner, was in the press box that night. A few reporters made their way toward his suite to ask about the obvious implication of the conference protecting its national title contender. Cincinnati had tied the game and would take the lead in the third quarter on Pike's second cameo touchdown pass. WVU was too angry to go away quietly, but the Mountaineers were once again undone by decisions that boggled the mind. Down 21–14 late in the fourth quarter, the Mountaineers drove from their 20 to the Cincinnati 26 after Brown bravely scrambled on his bad foot for 23 yards on third-and-12. Devine was out, though, after aggravating his injury early in the drive, and Jock Sanders, the receiver, was again called upon to play running back in reserve, which robbed the offense of its best route runner and pass catcher. He gained a yard on first down, and Brown was hurried into an incomplete pass on the next play. On third-and-9, Sanders again got the ball and ran into the middle of the line to gain nothing. More inexplicable than the play call was the explanation. Offensive coordinator Jeff Mullen said later that he was trying to set up a "manageable fourth down," and used a play he said had worked all night, but also one Cincinnati sure seemed to be expecting. The fourth down pass then went into the end zone and fell incomplete as WVU turned the ball over on downs.

The good thing, if one could exist in the scenario, was WVU knew Cincinnati would run the ball with just 5:23 to go. On first down, Pead gained 43 yards. The Bearcats kicked a field goal for a 24–14 lead with 2:09 remaining, and then played a soft defense that allowed WVU to piece together a touchdown drive. With 39 seconds left, Stewart ordered up an onside kick and sent out no one taller than 6-foot-3 defensive end Zac Cooper. The Bearcats had a hands team filled with skill players and, not surprisingly, 6-foot-4 receiver Armon Binns recovered.

There was plenty to talk about in Stewart's press conference before the rivalry game against Pitt, which would be a second straight top-10 opponent for WVU. The press conference was again preceded by a request to limit questions to the upcoming game, but that had to be ignored. Stewart, who often discussed bad and missed calls of his own volition, was asked early on about the still-unfathomable replay reversal. He threw up a stiff arm that belonged on the Heisman Trophy.

"I have no comment on someone who made a judgment that maybe differs from my judgment," said the man whose record was then 16-7 and who had quite possibly been screwed out of a chance to change everything everyone thought about him with a win at Cincinnati. His reply wasn't good enough. Reporters would circle back and he would decline to opine except to say he thought it was a great call "on the field." He laughed with the others after he said that, and then leaned over to his right and said something to the team's play-by-play announcer, Tony Caridi.

Stewart fielded another question from a reporter, and then Caridi asked a question about something many had probably forgotten, about something that was meaningless toward the outcome, about something that was nevertheless embarrassing. After Brown tied the score 7–7 with an eight-yard run in the first quarter, the Mountaineers were penalized on the kickoff for using an illegal formation. WVU started with four players on the left of kicker Tyler Bitancurt, and six on his right. A player on the left then started in motion to the right before the kick, and he was on Bitancurt's right side when he kicked it to the right side of the field. It broke the rule that says at least four players must be on either side of the kicker before the kickoff.

WVU backed up five yards and kicked again. WVU did the same thing again and was penalized again. This time the Bearcats declined the penalty because the Mountaineers, for some strange reason, insisted on kicking to Mardy Gilyard, who had taught everyone in America, most notably WVU, not to do that. Gilyard returned the short kick to midfield, even against the plan designed to overwhelm him. The Bearcats ended up punting, which made the penalties meaningless footnotes, but Stewart wanted everyone to know how smart he was. He and Caridi worked out a plan before the press conference so that Caridi would ask Stewart about the goofy sequence. Stewart remembered and leaned over to Caridi and said, "Ask me about kickoffs. Kickoffs."

Caridi did, and Stewart would then say it was his idea to send a man in motion and then kick to the side with more players in an attempt to outnumber the blockers on that side and quickly tackle Gilyard.

And he said he made that call twice.

"We kind of got caught with our hand in the cookie jar, and I said, 'Do it again. They won't call it a second time,'" Stewart said.

Never mind it made no sense to kick to Gilyard, who a year earlier told his teammates and coaches he'd return a kickoff for a touchdown against the Mountaineers—and then did. Stewart had a plan to outsmart the obvious. The players would confess afterward they rarely worked on it in practice before that week, and had never done it in front of officials. A few said they didn't even understand the penalty because it was never pointed out to them. But Stewart said he called it twice in a row, basically because he thought he could get away with it and that it would work. He also pointed out, in alarming detail, exactly what the penalties meant toward the outcome. Stewart, who had that rule about not talking about the previous game, was a lot like a lot of other coaches who can't remember plays or sequences or statistics from the old games, but he knew all the particulars for that one episode.

"After that, it was they had three plays, minus seven yards. They had the ball for one minute, 38 seconds, and they did what to us after that double penalty kickoff? What did they do? Anybody remember? They punted," he said. "We got the ball, went five plays. What did we do? We punted it back and changed field position. They got the ball and missed a field goal. We got the ball and scored and went up 14–7. That kick with the two penalties had no part, in any way, shape, or form, any bearing on the game. I was just trying to use a little sandlot to spice up the coverage and got caught."

It wasn't an important part of the game, but Caridi later confessed Stewart staged the explanation. Caridi found his way to The Smoking Musket, a WVU sports blog that had written a post about the incident. In a comment on that post, Caridi wrote, "Before the press conference I asked Stew what had happened on those two kickoffs that resulted in penalties. He said I wasn't alone, and he wanted to talk about it during his press conference. I forgot to ask and he remembered that he wanted to talk about it. That's when you see him asking me to ask him about it."

And when Stewart was done defending himself, he closed the discussion on the irrelevant topic that had nothing to do with the final score from the previous game everyone else was asked not to mention by saying to Caridi, "Thanks for asking that question. That clears up some things."

That was Bill Stewart. Some coaches are sensitive to criticism. Stewart seemed scared of it. And he was the guy in charge of several bad moments and bad losses. Maybe it wasn't really surprising the Mountaineers were already stuck with three losses with two games left in the regular season, and had no chance of getting their hands on the conference title.

After all, WVU had to play its starters the entire season-opener against Division I-AA Liberty. The Mountaineers struggled in the first half of the rematch with East Carolina and led 21–20 despite a very poor first half by the Pirates, but won 35–20. They went to Auburn and followed Devine to a 14–0 lead in the first quarter on short and long touchdown runs, but fell apart when Brown kept throwing the ball to the wrong team. Two of his four interceptions were on middle screens, which is hard to do, and the second was returned for a touchdown when the Mountaineers had the ball and were aiming to drive for a go-ahead score. Six turnovers helped produce 24 Auburn points in the 41–30 loss.

WVU recovered and avenged its loss from the year before by beating Colorado. The Mountaineers had to survive four more turnovers, including a fumble by a linebacker after he forced a turnover. They then thumped Syracuse inside the Carrier Dome. Brown's freshman backup, Geno Smith, played virtually all of the next game against Marshall after Brown was brained by two defenders in the first quarter, but the Mountaineers won 24–7.

Brown was never the same the rest of the season, but the team stuck with him in his diminished state. Next was an emotional game against Connecticut, days after their star cornerback, Jasper Howard, was stabbed to death. It swung early on freshman Tavon Austin's touchdown return on the opening kickoff, and then later when Devine again saved the day with a 56-yard touchdown with 2:10 to go. It was a thrilling reversal after WVU had intercepted a pass that seemed to clinch the game, but lost a fumble when cornerback Kent Richardson decided to work for extra yards on his return. The Huskies pounced and scored on an 88-yard touchdown, but couldn't keep Devine from bailing out the Mountaineers yet again.

After seven games, Devine had 535 yards and seven touchdowns in the second halves of games. Twenty-three of his thirty-five 10-yard runs, and thirteen of his twenty-one 20-yard runs, came after halftime. In his fourth quarters, he had 39 carries, 253 yards, and five touchdowns. Suddenly, Devine was a Heisman contender, and the Mountaineers were ready to be mentioned with Pitt and Cincinnati when the discussion turned to the conference championship. The next opponent was South Florida, but the only history that mattered was recent history. Stewart had beaten the Bulls in 2009, and the Bulls had lost their previous two games, 34–17 to Cincinnati and 41–14 to Pitt. The Bearcats won when their backup quarterback was forced into emergency action. The Panthers, a team not known for offense, had almost 500 yards. Surely, the Mountaineer offense would be successful.

WVU lost 30–19 and their pass defense was again suspect, just as it had been in 2006. The Bulls, with an erratic but athletic quarterback in freshman B. J. Daniels, completed three passes of at least 45 yards and had 232 yards and three touchdowns on just 17 completions. WVU's previous three opponents managed 292, 300, and 378 yards; the Bulls noticed the trend and took aim.

"It's something we looked at," said USF's offensive coordinator at the time, Mike Canales. "It is a trend."

Stewart was stoic and steadfast after the game. He tried to protect his cornerback, Keith Tandy, who had a hard time covering Carlton Mitchell, and said Mitchell was better than Tandy in one of those moments when Stewart said he wasn't singling a player out, but singled him out nevertheless. He then left his audience with a warning: "Remember November."

That was an odd month, though. The Mountaineers beat Louisville 17–9, and could thank defensive end Julian Miller for a fantastic finish against a team starting its third-string, walk-on, 5-foot-9 quarterback. On Louisville's final series, Miller sacked Will Stein on first and second down to move the ball from WVU's 42-yard line to the Louisville 46. Two incomplete passes later, the first with Miller closing in on another sack, and the game was over. That preceded the heartbreaker at Cincinnati, which served only to motivate the Mountaineers as they entered the Backyard Brawl against No. 8 Pittsburgh. On a brutally cold night at Mountaineer Field, Devine again offered a major assist with an 88-yard touchdown run. The defense survived an equally significant letdown when it let Jonathan Baldwin get deep for a 50-yard touchdown reception to tie the score 16–16, with just under three minutes to go.

But in a sign of growth, Stewart directed his offense on a game-winning drive. The Mountaineers converted a fourth-and-1 by giving the ball to Clarke for the first down and then ran the clock and used two timeouts to allow Bitancurt to kick a 43-yard field goal as time expired. Stewart had his signature win, and his adversaries had one less thing to point out when they made a case against him. Now early in December, he was asked what he, the coach who had sparked the curiosity weeks earlier, remembered about November. He introduced Ferdinand Foch, an obscure French military hero revered for his calm amid chaos, to college football.

"Hard-pressed to the right, out-flanked to the left, my center is yielding. Impossible to maneuver. Situation excellent. I am attacking," Stewart said. "That's what I remember about November. You think about that."

It would have been brilliant if it weren't so bizarre, so beautifully and bewitchingly bizarre. With those words continuing to serve as their marching orders, the Mountaineers closed the season with a 24–21 victory against Rutgers. That secured a spot in the Gator Bowl against Florida State and outgoing head coach and former WVU coach Bobby Bowden, for whom Stewart had such deep and sincere admiration ever since Stewart was on WVU's freshman team in 1970.

The Gator Bowl arrangement may as well have been guaranteed to the Mountaineers before the Rutgers game, though. Cincinnati completed a ridiculous comeback to beat Pitt, clinch the BCS bowl, and relegate the Panthers to second place in the conference. But the Gator Bowl, which had the first selection of Big East teams after Cincinnati earned the BCS game, wanted WVU, the third-place team, to set up the so-called Bowden Bowl.

It wasn't as though the Gator Bowl reps liked what they saw against Rutgers, though. The Mountaineers scored touchdowns on their first two drives and led 21–3 after safety Sidney Glover returned an interception for a touchdown. Then the special teams again collapsed and Rutgers returned the ensuing kickoff for a touchdown. Brown started 6-for-6, but finished 10-for-20 and lost two fumbles, and the offense ended up 2-for-14 on third down.

The game, with the strong, misleading start, the lull in the middle, and the escape at the end, was symbolic of the entire season. So I asked about it. I wondered if Stewart could appreciate how the season ended with a game that was a complete representation of everything before it. Wasn't it fitting his Mountaineers had come out on top during a game that could have knocked them down? Didn't it seem appropriate that the game and the regular season ended with WVU on a high after so many lows?

Stewart didn't want to hear that, didn't want to admit bad preceded good, didn't concede struggles, wouldn't even remember November. He saw red and instead ended a second straight regular season with a monologue.

"I'll tell you what I've seen the entire season," he began. "I've seen four quarters of not great football for West Virginia. Let me slow this down for you real good, everybody. Listen to me: we're 9-3. We're 9-3. You understand how many teams in America would like to be 9-3 now? I'm not scolding you. I'm telling you. I've been keeping this in too long. Bill Stewart is going to punch back a little bit today."

There were nervous looks in some parts of the room and smirks in others. No one would dare interrupt. No one would dare miss recording what he might say next. Stewart basically claimed that, if not for 60 ultimately decisive minutes, the Mountaineers might be playing in a much bigger, much better bowl game.

"We're 9-3. We're going to the Gator Bowl. OK?" he said. "We had a bad fourth quarter at Auburn. OK. I didn't throw that kid under the bus. We didn't do very well. We had a bad fourth quarter at Auburn. We had three bad quarters at South Florida. That's what Mike's alluding to. Mike, I'm not scolding you either. You're my buddy. But write that. Write the truth.

"We had four bad quarters of football. We took a Cincinnati team to an onside kick. Fifth in the country. Three points. At their place. We lost to them by three points at our place last year and they were conference champs. There were some ups and downs, you betcha, but a whole lot more ups than downs.

"Don't tag my name to anything other than this is a 9-3 football team. And that's from my heart and as businesslike as I can be and it's fair. I'm not going to let people keep telling me my players and my boys are not good. They're 9-3. I told you about the four quarters. I told you about Cincinnati. Now, did we win pretty all the time? No, but, by God, that was pretty to me today. Next."

Fantastic.

Next was the Gator Bowl, where the Mountaineers were merely invited guests, the sentimental choice to hold Bowden's hand as he crossed the finish line and entered retirement. Not that there was anything WVU needed to apologize for. The Seminoles were a 6-6 team and had one of the nation's very worst defenses. They were No. 94 in scoring defense, No. 108 in rushing defense, No. 77 in pass defense, and No. 108 in total defense. Yet WVU's offense wasn't any more threatening, any more accomplished, any more effective than it had been 12 or 25 games earlier. It started out nicely once again as Brown ran 32 yards on his own for a touchdown and Devine dashed 70 yards to set up a short touchdown run and a 14–3 lead. WVU had 149 yards and 14 points in the first quarter and looked every bit as good as Florida State's defense had looked bad all season long.

Then it unraveled just as things had unraveled for the Mountaineers throughout the season. Brown threw an interception to set up a Florida

State touchdown. A drive reached Florida State's 22 and was undone by a holding penalty and an intentional grounding call against Brown. The senior quarterback never made it to halftime, hurting his ankle late in the second quarter.

WVU's special teams then made their contribution. They began by allowing a 69-yard return on the opening kickoff of the second half to set up a field goal and Florida State's first lead. Bitancurt missed a field goal, and Scott Kozlowski had a punt partially blocked before the Seminoles took control with a touchdown for a 23–14 lead. The Mountaineers would score one touchdown in the fourth quarter on an 80-yard drive; that accounted for all of the scoring and more than half of the 155 yards the offense managed in the final three quarters of a 33–21 loss.

No Football Bowl Subdivision opponent had fewer yards against Florida State's bad defense, and only one FBS opponent had fewer points and passing yards. Bowden went out a winner and got away from the things that stacked up against him in his final few seasons with the Seminoles, things like that defense. For Stewart, the end was about to begin.

14
LUCK

Right up until the day before Oliver Luck was hired and named the next director of athletics at West Virginia, he was *not* going to be hired and named the next director of athletics at West Virginia. At least, that was what you were made to believe when Luck said a few days before he was hired, "I couldn't be interested in that position at this time." A couple of days would then pass before Luck even interviewed for the job. A day later, it was his.

There had been a hope among the masses that the Mountaineers would bring Luck back home, back to where he was a really good quarterback who would make it to the NFL, back to where he was a Rhodes Scholar finalist. It always means a lot for WVU to have one of its own in one of its high-profile positions, be it the football or basketball coach or the president at the university, and Luck was an immediate favorite among the people when the school needed a new athletic director. He wasn't their top choice; he was their only choice.

Luck came to WVU in 1978 from Cleveland's St. Ignatius High School. He played for two different coaches with the Mountaineers, Frank Cignetti and then Don Nehlen, and had two very different experiences. He was an option quarterback for Cignetti's veer offense, and as a sophomore he ran the ball 204 times and scored five touchdowns on the ground, as opposed to 103 pass attempts and eight touchdowns through the air. As a senior, his second season under Nehlen, he ran just 40 times but threw it 394 times and had 16 touchdowns. He liked the variety, and it drew him away from Cleveland and the well-worn paths to the Big Ten schools and the traditional offenses of Woody Hayes and Bo Schembechler and others they influenced.

"I thought, 'Why go to the Big Ten and hand the ball off for four years, when I can go somewhere else and do a lot of different things?'" Luck said.

Luck was named the team's most valuable player in 1980, when he passed for what was then a school-record 19 touchdown passes, and again in 1981, when he helped WVU to an 8-3 record and a Peach Bowl win against an especially confident Florida Gators team led by a coach, Charley Pell, who didn't even know Nehlen's name. Luck left 43 touchdowns and more than 5,700 yards passing on the field for the Mountaineers, and twice was a first-team Academic All-American.

He continued to make his people proud after graduating from WVU. He had the NFL career, collected a law degree from the University of Texas, and built his executive experience in professional football and soccer. He also had the proven ability to raise funds and organize major projects as the CEO of a community development group in a major American city.

As WVU's longtime athletic director, Ed Pastilong, grew on in years and entered a gradual retirement plan, the stage was set for a transition. The pressure was on the university's new president, Jim Clements, to make it happen. Clements entered office not quite a year before he hired Luck, but he learned right away what everyone wanted him to do.

"Anywhere I'd go in the town or in the state the people would say, 'Go get Oliver,'" Clements said.

There was an issue, though: Luck wasn't all that interested in the job. Oh, he was intrigued. It was his alma mater, after all, and that kind of work just seemed like a perfect match for his background. Luck is a thinker, a tactician, a problem solver, a builder. He does with his acumen and his approach what others do with their cranes and their bulldozers. If all the fans knew that, Luck did, too. Yet he was also the president and general manager of a Major League Soccer franchise, the Houston Dynamo. Luck liked soccer after all the years he spent in Europe, and he really liked assembling a winner. He'd had the job since 2005 and he was good at it, too. The Dynamo won two league titles, and were starting a $95-million project that would give the club a new facility. Luck was entrenched, but his roots were even deeper in Houston. From 2001 to 2005, Luck was the chief executive officer of the Harris County-Houston Sports Authority. He was in charge of evolving and then managing the $1 billion project that built the professional baseball, football, and basketball facilities there.

Luck and his family had a life in Houston; he'd already bounced around a bunch in his time after college, and taken his wife and kids with him as he pursued various professions. He was a pro quarterback in Houston, and then a lawyer in Germany. He went to Washington, D.C., for a job, and then ran for a congressional seat in West Virginia in 1990, when he got in a little trouble with the state's ethics commission for securing a Mountaineer Athletic Club mailing list so he could send voters a letter and a picture of himself as the WVU quarterback. Then it was back to Germany as a general manager of two teams in the World League of American Football, and later as the president and CEO of NFL Europe.

He returned to Houston in 2001. He and his wife Kathy settled in, and together they raised their two sons and two daughters without having to leave the continent, let alone the city or the state. By 2010, the oldest son, Andrew, was poised as perhaps the nation's best college quarterback and the oldest daughter, Mary Ellen, was about to join Andrew on campus at Stanford and play for the volleyball team. At the very least, Luck wasn't neglecting WVU—he did have a seat on its Board of Governors. Things were in order and everyone was happy.

Clements just really wanted to hire Luck, and wouldn't give up on the idea. Clements knew getting Luck would be a tremendous endorsement of the athletic department, how it was operated, and what it could do for young student-athletes. He also knew WVU would be facing major issues in college sports, none greater than conference affiliation, which was the sort of problem best managed by someone who understood the law and business, and either had a lot of friends in college sports or could make them easily. Clements knew Luck was his best and only option.

"Jim is a silver-tongued recruiter," Luck said.

Pastilong, a quarterback at WVU from 1963 to 1965 and later a recruiting coordinator in 1976, had been the athletic director since 1989 and helped the school get into the Big East Conference in 1991. He was supposed to step out of the full-time position on July 1, 2010, and enter a two-year emeritus position, but there was no movement toward hiring and installing a replacement. The calendar turned to June and patience turned into panic. There were names out there, college athletic directors and executives from pro sports, but there were no interviews. None.

The closer Clements got to July 1, as Luck maintained his seat on the Board of Governors, the more it looked like Luck was indeed not interested in the job, that he was committed to his family and the Dynamo and the building project, and that Clements was in a tight spot. Why would Luck leave Houston and all its security to begin a new line of work at a school with the looming threat of NCAA sanctions in the football program, a football coach who was appointed by the previous athletic director and president, and membership in a conference that just wasn't very stable? No, Luck was safe in Houston and his reasoning was sound.

Clements would not be deterred. He knew better. This was nothing new to the president who had only been named to his position on March 6, 2009, and entered office on June 20, and that familiarity was the source of his curious calm amid imminent calamity. Clements had been extremely popular and accomplished, to say nothing of comfortable, at Towson University. He was a provost and a vice president the students voted faculty member of the year four times. He made moves and made splashes, too, and a lot of people pointed to him as a reason why the public school outside Baltimore, a part of the University System of Maryland, was able to renovate Johnny Unitas

---

Football Stadium and build a $45 million basketball and concert arena.

"Only Oliver can speak for what went through his mind, but when I was nominated for this job, it was, 'I'm in the middle of a major project now. I'm really happy now. I love my family. I love my house. I love my job. Why would I want to leave?'" Clements remembered. "Then it became, 'Oh, my gosh. What a great university. What a great opportunity.' Then you start to think about things. How do you transition your family? How do you transition projects? There are so many things you have to think through until you get to the point where you say, 'You know what? I'm interested.'"

Clements relived the process, this time projecting his experience on Luck's emotions, relying on his patience and trusting Luck would have a similar moment of clarity when he would admit to himself that he was indeed interested. The president always fell back on one thing to keep his hopes up. "I don't think Oliver ever said no to us," he said. He was right, and Luck never moved past the possibility. He thought a lot about it and he began to see some similarities he shared with Clements. The president had four children. The president had a wife, Beth, who understood the unknowns associated with the life they had chosen. Luck and Clements were both professional men, but they were both family guys, and whether by the president's persuasion or Luck's awareness, he saw the possibilities in Morgantown.

"The most important thing in my life certainly is my family, and there was a lot of thinking by my wife and I in terms of making a decision: 'Can we do this? Is this possible?'" Luck said. "Because of the affirmation of Jim and Beth, we thought it was possible."

Luck quietly resigned his post on the Board of Governors, a major prerequisite to becoming the athletic director, a few days before things took an even bigger step toward the conclusion. On Wednesday, June 9, Luck formally interviewed for the job. It was his first and only interview. It was the first and only interview Clements would conduct. This was sudden, and Luck was by no means a certainty, so much so that WVU had scheduled interviews in Pittsburgh that weekend with a handful of candidates. Those were canceled shortly after Luck's interview. Luck and Clements worked out an arrangement so both could get what they wanted. Luck was allowed to stay with the Dynamo through the end of the year to oversee the construction that was to begin in October, while WVU was left to navigate a completely uncertain time without an athletic director on campus at all times. That concession mattered little to Clements. He had his athletic director and WVU had the biggest thing to hit campus since the PRT.

15
LA-LA-LA-LA-LA

For many years, West Virginia fans could count on a few things to deflect or disarm much of whatever criticism was lobbed their way. The Mountaineers could dominate Marshall in their state and beat Rutgers, Syracuse, and Connecticut in the Big East Conference; all of that went a long way toward establishing an elite position in Eastern football. The Mountaineers ran a clean program, played by the rules, and had a coach people admired, either as an accomplished veteran bound for the Hall of Fame in Don Nehlen, or a dynamic up-and-comer in Rich Rodriguez. All of that was compromised during the 2010 season, the last season with Bill Stewart.

The end approached before the beginning. The mess Rodriguez had made with what were then only alleged NCAA violations at the University of Michigan finally breached the borders back home. Nine months after beginning a broad and detailed investigation of WVU, and three days before Stewart would open his third preseason camp, the NCAA sent the university a notice of allegations. A day later, the school had a press conference, and Oliver Luck revealed the program he had been in charge of for barely a month was looking at five major violations and a secondary violation.

The secondary violation belonged to Rodriguez for practicing too much during the open week before the loss at Louisville in 2006. He also owned two of the major violations for letting too many of his underlings do too many things they were not allowed to do. Rodriguez was accused of allowing some of the noncoaching graduate assistants, staffers, and student managers to perform football-specific coaching duties and also conduct and supervise offseason workouts, all of which were against NCAA rules. That left two major violations for Stewart, basically for continuing to do the same things Rodriguez had done before. Stewart didn't change his practices or even bother to look and see if they were flawed, not even after Rodriguez was implicated in a *Detroit Free Press* investigation on August 29, 2009.

Before the dark clouds and foreboding music could fade away after that press conference, Stewart presided over another embarrassing mistake. During the first two days of fall practice, a bunch of players wore protective pads NCAA rules specifically prohibit. WVU had to self-report this as a secondary violation.

While many would roll their eyes because it was such a minor error, and WVU was only guilty of wearing pads on the first two days that were legal beginning on the third day, the rulebook is very clear about that topic and very helpful in avoiding trouble. I found out about the problem with the pads not because I had recognized it during practice, but because another school did when it saw pictures online. That school knew WVU already looked bad and could be made to look worse, so it offered a tip. I needed about two minutes to locate the rule in the NCAA manual.

Rule 17.9.2.3 covers the "five-day acclimatization period," meaning the first five days of practice for all players, no matter if they start on the first day of camp or some time afterward. It sets regulations for those first five days to keep schools from going too hard and subjecting players to too much, too soon. If WVU, or any school, was doing something that necessitated pads on the first two days, that was a violation of the rules and a violation of the goal to protect players.

Within the rule is subsection (d), which states, "During the first two days of the acclimatization period, helmets shall be the only piece of protective equipment student-athletes may wear."

That's not vague. That's transparent. The NCAA manual is thick and oftentimes unnecessary, but it exists for a reason and it explains the particulars. If for some reason a school is unclear about a rule, it can use the phone or email to ask the NCAA a question.

Supporters and defenders of WVU wanted to parse and argue the term "protective equipment." Is a mouthpiece protective? What about a knee brace? Surely "protective equipment" was open to interpretation and pointing that out was a fair tactic, except that those two words are preceded by two other words: "only piece." The rule specifically refers to the helmet. Sure, it seemed severe to shame and punish the Mountaineers for letting players wear these spider pads, as they were known, but the act of commission didn't matter as much as the act of omission. WVU broke the rule because WVU never researched the rule.

Subsection (d) then goes on to generally eliminate confusion. "During the third and fourth days of the acclimatization period, helmets and shoulder pads shall be the only pieces of protective equipment student-athletes may wear."

Shoulder pads! Are spider pads shoulder pads? Probably. Some call them vests, which is a different word, but they serve the same purpose and protect the upper body. If WVU wasn't absolutely positive—and clearly WVU was not because it broke the rule—then it was the program's duty to its players and to the rules to seek a clarification. That was the issue.

Wearing pads two days early was wrong, but it was completely inexcusable to commit a violation right after receiving the notice of allegations. It was a major failure that WVU's compliance department, football coach, and equipment manager didn't sit down between the athletic director's press conference and the first day of practice to go over every detail. That a compliance person wasn't at the first practice, which WVU admitted, was just about as inappropriate. As the spider pad story was breaking, a Big East official told me it was surprising WVU didn't have its entire compliance department out at practice and circling the field, just to make a point.

WVU had a problem and Stewart knew it. He knew I was aware of the violation and that I needed to pull him aside to ask him about it. Rather than get out in front of the issue and handle it as the head coach should, Stewart tried to evade it. He had a public relations messenger request that I not make a big deal of it because things were already bad enough.

That was Stewart's reaction. WVU's reaction was no less outlandish. A few days later, some employees were actually going to reporters with pictures they said showed players at other schools wearing protective pads during the prohibited days and violating the same rule. The reporters were then asked to write stories that told on those other schools—and worse than that, at least one did. Two weeks later, the school hired an associate athletic director for governance and compliance and simultaneously reassigned the assistant athletic director for compliance to work the NCAA case until his contract expired.

That was the start of the season, one that began with a new indignity. During 2010, even accomplishments came with asterisks, and the case against keeping Stewart was assembled by the masses. There was defeat in victory, exasperation in losses, and often embarrassment no matter the outcome.

The Mountaineers started their season with a 31–0 victory against Coastal Carolina of the Football Championship Subdivision, but nearly bottomed out a week later. WVU trailed Marshall—Marshall!—21–6 in the fourth quarter and looked beaten, when WVU quarterback Geno Smith was sacked by unstoppable Marshall lineman Vinny Curry, and Smith lost a fumble at his 16-yard line.

Marshall was a few plays away from putting the game out of reach. For some reason, it handed the opportunity to freshman running back Tron Martinez, who hadn't carried the ball all game. He ran for a yard on first down, and then two on third-and-2, to put the ball at the 6. On the next play, Martinez was stripped of the ball and lost the fumble. The Mountaineers had their miracle with eight minutes, 28 seconds remaining. Nine plays and 96 yards later, they were in the end zone and ready to play defense to get the ball back one last time. Marshall gained 28 yards on its first play to move to its 48, and ended up with a fourth-and-1 at the WVU 43 before deciding to punt rather than take the gamble. The punt was downed at the 2. The Mountaineers had just 3:09 to again march the length of the field, score a touchdown, and then force overtime with a two-point conversion. They did it in 15 plays and with 12 seconds to spare.

WVU kicked a field goal on its first overtime possession; Marshall missed its kick to somehow give away a game it had no business losing and WVU had almost no business winning. Almost. Smith was phenomenal in the final two possessions. The first 10 drives of the game gained all of 245 yards. The final two covered 194, and Smith did nearly everything, completing 14 of 17 passes for 151 yards and getting another 37 yards rushing. Most significantly, he picked up an offense that was supposed to belong to Jock Sanders and Noel Devine and twice carried it into the end zone.

Five years earlier, it was Pat White who arrived with a magnificent, late comeback against Louisville, but there was one difference here: No one was happy about what had happened that Friday night in Huntington. It was, as far as the fans of the Mountaineers were concerned, an unnecessary diversion and a sour celebration. Still, that didn't stop the team's star cornerback, Brandon Hogan, from getting arrested the night after the game for driving under the influence when he was spotted driving the wrong way on a one-way street.

Something therapeutic seemed in the works a week later, when WVU ambushed Maryland and led 21–0 at the half. But it should have been better. One fumble was lost at Maryland's 15, another drive ended on downs at the 34, and a second fumble was lost at the 22. A long punt return preceded a short touchdown pass to make it 28–0, but the Terrapins singled out Hogan's replacement, Pat Miller, who was up against their all-conference receiver, Torrey Smith. Touchdown passes of 68 and 80 yards, the second when a safety got lost and left Miller no help, had Maryland back in the game. WVU responded with a gadget play, but the double pass blew up when Sanders had his throw intercepted and returned to set up a field goal. Stewart had seen enough and was so concerned with his team's three-seasons-long inability to finish an opponent that he ordered a drive that used 12 runs on a 16-play march that took no chances. The drive ticked 8:55 off the clock before a field goal left Maryland with less than three minutes to attempt a two-touchdown comeback.

One of WVU's biggest supporters on the sideline that day was Hogan, whom Stewart allowed to be with his teammates. Stewart never justified his decision except by stating it was just that. He let Hogan watch the game, and then practice on the first opportunity after the Maryland game. Stewart didn't promise Hogan anything, but said he'd let Hogan participate and he'd keep an eye on the former state player of the year from Manassas, Virginia. Stewart had personally recruited and maintained a special preference toward Hogan through the years. It was completely inconsistent treatment: Sanders had been arrested and charged with a DUI in what surely looked like a similar situation in the 2009 offseason; he was suspended from February to August that year. Asked to explain what made one different from the other, all Stewart could muster was, "There is a difference because the situations are different. Different case, different scenario, different offenses." Hogan traveled to LSU for the next game, dressed, and was allowed to start, though no notice or explanation was given. He was a nonfactor in the game, but he was nevertheless there for the Mountaineers.

The game inside Tiger Stadium involved all the things that defined Stewart's tenure. On the seventh play of the game, Devine was tackled by the facemask. On the next play, Devine was tackled out of bounds and hurt the big toe on his right foot while Stewart raged. Devine was never healthy again, never the same the rest of the season. Stewart and the offense no longer had the home run hitter who could bail them out of tough spots like he had so many times before.

Later in that first quarter, Ryan Clarke lost a fumble near his goal line to set up LSU's first touchdown. Another turnover, this time an interception, preceded an LSU field goal. Then came the special teams meltdown, which by this point was all but expected. A punt intended for the numbers went instead to the hash. One player ran out of his lane to let All-American Patrick Peterson sprint unencumbered for a 60-yard score and a 17–0 lead. Peterson struck a Heisman Trophy pose in the end zone, guaranteeing the Mountaineers would be on the wrong end of another highlight reel.

WVU didn't roll over, though. The Mountaineers closed to 17–14, but punted, missed a second field goal, and then had a critical short-yardage failure on a third-and-2. With the crowd roaring and the Mountaineers backed up near the LSU end zone, Smith lined up behind the right guard before Devine stepped forward to tell him to move over. Smith had to hurry, and then ran a very rare option play for no gain. That led to another punt as the 15th-ranked Tigers held on 20–14.

"It sucks to have that feeling that you were the better team and you couldn't come away with the W," linebacker J. T. Thomas said.

Stewart changed again after that game. He kept repeating his team had the ball at the LSU 30 with 12 minutes to go, and that so many other teams who have played the Tigers in that stadium would have liked to have had that chance and would welcome that scenario in the future. He knew his team had played hard enough and long enough to win, and he knew what a win in that environment would have meant. But he knew the same old story was again true. The Mountaineers weren't good enough and gave back just as much as they were given. Had they done this one thing or not done another, had they exploited a small variable even a little bit, they would have won that game.

Stewart was short and sharp with replies to questions that he didn't agree with, or that weren't meant to agree with him. He answered yes and no questions with a yes or a no, though sometimes he would liven it up a little and offer up a stern "absolutely not." He flatly denied Smith lined up behind the right guard on that one key third-and-2 play, and seemed genuinely bothered that he had to explain a loss he thought explained itself. And even though the nearly unanimous feeling after the LSU loss was that the Mountaineers were a pretty good, though not great, team and they were capable of much more, Stewart insisted outsiders were finger pointing and trying to tear the team apart. He had virtually no ground to stand on to make that accusation—except in the little corner he'd backed himself into as he felt the walls compressing around him.

The following week, the Mountaineers smoked a very bad UNLV team, 49–10, and scored more points than in any other game with Stewart in charge. A week later they beat USF, 20–6. WVU ran for just 79 yards, but won thanks to a hook-and-ladder play that worked for a decisive score.

WVU was 5-1 overall and 1-0 in the Big East with the conference's best defense, best quarterback, and most explosive assembly of players on offense. Games would follow against Syracuse, which had lost eight straight in the series, and Connecticut, which was 0-6 all-time against WVU. Surely the Orange, who had just lost 45–14 at home against Pitt, would capitulate, and the Huskies, who had never really even been competitive against the Mountaineers, would bow down once again. Suddenly, WVU looked as though it was ready to put itself in a very good position—ideal for the team still perceived to be the elite outfit in the Big East, but that hadn't had first place all to itself since the end of the 2007 season. The Mountaineers were ranked No. 19 in the coaches' poll and No. 20 in the Associated Press poll and the BCS, and no one else in the Big East was even close.

Then Sanders put a stamp on the season without ever knowing it. "Twenty points, we win. It's in the book. Book it," he said after the USF game. It was a ringing endorsement for the defense, but anything but a vote of confidence for the offense, which just couldn't click without Devine. He was hurting and he wasn't explosive or threatening. Devine had just four runs of 20 yards or more to that point in the season. He had 34 in his first three seasons. Devine averaged a 20-yard run once every 16.5 attempts his first three years. He was getting one every 25.9 carries after six games in 2010. Devine's injury robbed WVU of the only way it could score on any snap.

The Mountaineers promptly lost to Syracuse and Connecticut in succession. The losses certainly couldn't be blamed on the defense: the Orange completed only five passes. They made it inside WVU's 16 four times, and kicked four field goals. They did hardly anything to win on the road against a team like WVU, but they won nonetheless. Smith threw three interceptions, one in the end zone, and WVU scored just twice in four red zone possessions. It was a 19–14 loss.

Mickey Furfari, the longtime, resourceful writer who's been around the program for a generation and doesn't really hide the fact he's a fan, called it "one of the most pitiful performances … a guy in his 65th year of covering the Mountaineers can recall." After seven games— and really, this was 33 games into Stewart's tenure now—this was an offense with nothing to lean on, with no identity, with no way to rescue itself from itself, not even with two chances late to either kick two field goals or score one touchdown to win the game. "I disagree with that," Stewart said. "It's been short passing, deep passes. We were 5-1. We were passing the ball, and putting a lot on our skill guys because our running back is hurt. That's your opinion and that's my opinion. I'm not going to debate you on that."

Short passes. Deep passes. Running game; despite the fact the star back was hurt, Devine carried 24 times that day for 122 yards. Unfortunately, 66 of those yards came on three carries. The other 21 gained 56 yards, and six carries either lost yards or gained no yards. It was clear Devine didn't trust his body like he once did.

Clarke, the rugged fullback who could have helped on a day WVU was admittedly outmuscled, carried four times for eight yards. Stewart said he kept using Devine because he thought Devine would make someone miss and break a long run, that a kid who hadn't been right for weeks would turn a handoff into a horse race. This was an offense that was trying to do so many things, but wasn't really good at any one thing. "I see a lot of good we're doing; I just don't see consistency," Stewart said. "That's as calm and as honest as I can answer that question. Are we masters of any one thing? No."

Stewart again turned the attention elsewhere and put weight on the shoulders of outsiders, specifically the media, again, for building up Smith into something that, apparently, Stewart did not believe his sophomore quarterback was yet. "He had a real tough outing. When that happens, he needs help. You cannot have an offsides here, you can't have a hold there, you can't have a dropped ball here. When this young man, whom people were writing ballads about, is not clicking, never throw a slant over the middle. He'll learn that. In seven college starts, that's the first time it happened."

I frequently thought Stewart, who read the newspapers, was singling me out when he'd reference things like that, and I had written something of a ballad about Smith after the Marshall game. What he did that game, in his second college start and with the terrifying reality of being the first quarterback to lose to Marshall staring right at him, was impressive. I wrote it. I believed it. I even quoted Stewart, who said, "I thought he was methodically in tune with what we were thinking and how we were being defended. Geno took what they gave us. He hit under routes, he hit the outside routes, he hit the hole routes, and he spread the defense. He made Marshall defend the 52-plus yards wide on the field. I thought that was excellent."

Nevertheless, as people tired of Stewart spinning stuff after losses, *Pittsburgh Post-Gazette* writer Colin Dunlap produced an original version of "The Ballad of Geno Smith" to the tune of "The Ballad of John and Yoko."

> *Standing in the Pocket in MoTown*
> *Trying to push the lads down the field.*
> *The man in the vest said, "You got to bow your back."*
> *You know they didn't even give us a chance*
> *Hickman, you know it ain't easy.*
> *You know how hard it is to QB.*
> *If I don't get this offense together,*
> *They're gonna keep blaming me.*

On it went for three full verses, but when the laughs were done, it remained true that WVU had only one conference loss. Whoever would become the Big East champion was not likely to go unbeaten—not when the teams were as average as they were in 2010. WVU's pride could be restored so long as the coach and the players treated the final five games as they had the first seven. In the coach's weekly press conference, a reporter reminded Stewart that the Mountaineers were still contenders. Even if they believed it, they didn't want others to know they believed it.

"I don't want to hear that," Stewart said. He put his fingers in his ears and continued, "If I go, la-la-la-la-la, would that upset you?"

That was before the Mountaineers lost to UConn for the first time ever. This was WVU at its very worst, finding a way to lose with 414 yards of offense and a clear speed advantage the UConn defense could not handle. The Mountaineers lost to a team playing its third quarterback, and playing for a coach who was answering questions that week about whether he should be fired. The Huskies had just lost 26–0 to Louisville, but beat the Mountaineers because, again, the Mountaineers beat themselves. WVU fumbled seven times and lost four, and the final one was decisive. Clarke was stripped on UConn's 1-yard line in overtime and lost the ball. The Huskies promptly kicked a field goal to win 16–13.

It wasn't the fact WVU was losing that mattered most. It was how WVU was losing. It followed a script of penalties, turnovers, missed chances, and a critical inability to put away the opponent. This was the beginning of the end for Stewart, and he was asked afterward if he was worried about the future. He gave a soldierly answer, but afterward he went up to the inquiring reporter, Dave Hickman from the *Charleston Gazette*, and said, "I'm surprised by you, Dave."

The surprises were just beginning. Stewart's boss, Oliver Luck, who had been watching and wondering and shaping an opinion from the moment he was hired, began to make up his mind.

16
CONVICTION

One day somewhere in his first two months as the athletic director at his alma mater, when Oliver Luck was in town—and not back in Houston being a husband and father, or helping the soccer team with its stadium plan—he decided to go to work at around seven o'clock in the morning. On a Sunday. He parked his car outside in the empty lot and walked toward the Coliseum, where a few steps in the main concourse area would take him to a set of stairs that led to his office on the second floor.

As Luck hopped up onto the sidewalk and neared the entrance to the 10.5-billion-cubic-foot facility, he had to pause for a moment to understand exactly what he was seeing.

"The lights in here were burning like a Christmas tree," Luck said. "So I was curious. Do we have systems in place where the lights kick off? Do they kick on automatically at a certain time of day?"

For all Luck knew, there was a computer somewhere that flicked on the lights at 6:30 every morning. As populated and as popular as the Coliseum was, that seemed conceivable. It wasn't unusual to go inside early in the morning and see an older couple walking circles for exercise. It wasn't unusual to see athletes sneaking in a workout while they had the time or the opportunity. It wasn't unusual to see a crew setting up for an event. It wasn't unusual to see teams forced to practice at unusual times.

Surely if the lights were on, if they were programmed to come on, there was a need and thus an explanation. The Coliseum was at times overbooked and overcrowded, and its lack of availability was the overriding reason money was scraped together to build a basketball practice facility in the same complex. Build that thing, and then the men's and women's basketball teams could take their activities out of the Coliseum and free up all sorts of time in a place that is otherwise packed.

Luck knew about all that. He'd sat on the Board of Governors and watched the practice facility come together, and he understood the benefits, not just for the basketball teams to have a place to call their own, but for everyone else who could, for example, work on bump-set-spike practice at the Coliseum at an ordinary hour of the day and not when Luck was slipping in on a Sunday.

"Have we told our student-athletes if they want to play basketball Sunday morning at 7 they can come in because the Coliseum's lit up?" he thought. "Do they have to reserve it?"

Luck got inside, dropped his stuff off at his office, and engaged his curiosity. He looked out onto the floor and saw something startling: Nothing. No one. Nowhere. He was alone with his thoughts, which were now developing quickly. If the lights were supposed to come on automatically, there was no need that morning. If someone operated the lights, then he was witnessing human error. Luck smirked, sighed, and added that to his list of things to look into.

"Because stuff like lighting up the Coliseum not only costs money, but I'm old school," he said. "If you're not in the room, turn the lights off."

Luck would dig in and learn more about things at WVU. Not big things, but still significant things. He was kind of surprised about how the baseball team didn't have a place to change before or after the game. The Mountaineers and their opponents usually arrived at Hawley Field in uniform and later left that way. If a changing area was needed, they used the Shell Building, which is beyond the outfield fence and serves as the indoor home of the track and field teams. There were plans in place for a clubhouse in the home team's dugout, but that made the Mountaineers only more comfortable and no more hospitable. It was a minor blemish when people looked at WVU's résumé, but appearances mattered so much to Luck, who knew very well that his tenure might be defined by the imminent threat of conference realignment.

It was along those lines that he took a look at attendance at home matches for volleyball, gymnastics, and wrestling at the Coliseum, and men's and women's soccer matches at Dick Dlesk Soccer Stadium. The numbers were inconsistent and never impressive, and Luck knew and accepted that. There wasn't much he could do to dramatically change that and make the sports universally popular, but he did discover a problem. Those smaller sports, the ones that will never have the following of football or basketball at WVU, were played on the Evansdale Campus. A lot of students lived on the Downtown Campus on another side of town. Walking from the dorms on Evansdale wasn't easy, either, especially in the winter months. Some students had cars, but many did not. There was a bus system on campus, but Luck discovered the schedule wasn't synched up with the start times for the smaller sports.

So he had his people talk to the bus people, and they worked out a way to get the buses to run a little later so they might take students to and from games. One night that September, WVU played Marshall in volleyball. The Mountaineers beat the Thundering Herd for the first time since 2001, and with 625 people in the Coliseum, which is a gigantic crowd for volleyball.

If Luck was so attuned to power management at the Coliseum, accommodations at Hawley Field, and bus schedules for students, it stood to reason he wasn't going to allow the football program to underachieve without his involvement.

He watched a lot of football in person in 2010. His oldest son, Andrew, was quarterbacking Stanford to dizzying heights, and dad tried to make the games that his schedule would allow. He saw a Cardinal team without elite talent, but with an unconquerable drive and discipline. He saw a completely competent coach in Jim Harbaugh and an identifiable system that never wavered and, as such, rarely failed. He saw a team win the games it was supposed to win, and then win some games many thought it might not.

Luck also saw the Mountaineers give away four fumbles and lose for the first time to the University of Connecticut. There was no way for Luck to attend that game, whether he sat among WVU's people at Rentschler Field or in the visiting AD's seats, without being deeply bothered by what he'd seen, by what those around him voiced, and by what the future held for football at WVU.

The fact that WVU lost that night wasn't as significant as the way WVU lost. This loss was an illustration of all that was wrong at that time. The Mountaineers fumbled seven times, and by then—deep into the third season with an offense that lacked a strength, an offense that couldn't get out of its own way, an offense that conspired against its own success with turnovers and penalties—you had to openly wonder if another team valued possession less than this one. Despite the final score, despite the fact the Huskies went on to represent the Big East Conference as its champion in the Fiesta Bowl, there was really no arguing the Mountaineers had better talent. For proof, you only had to watch Bradley Starks zip through the UConn defense on a reverse for a 53-yard touchdown in the first quarter. Starks was a second-level player for the offense. He was never featured because he was never relied upon, and he was never relied upon because he was never healthy long enough to make an impact and then sustain it. But he was undeniably talented, and that second-level player had the ability to just rip through and then run away from the defense. Rarely will you find a receiver run for a long touchdown with as little trouble as Starks had on that play.

WVU had just too much talent for the Huskies. WVU knew it. The Huskies sure looked like they knew it. I was writing a live blog post that night and after three possessions I wrote, "WVU is far too fast for UConn to defend, unless WVU helps. And WVU helped twice on that drive with an unnecessary chop block behind the play that erased a touchdown, and then another formation penalty—third in the past two games. Still, the Mountaineers have 10 points and

UConn has seven yards and no visible spirit." On that third drive, Noel Devine had a nine-yard touchdown run wiped out by right guard Eric Jobe's chop block on the opposite side of the field. On the next play, a perfectly appropriate second-and-21 at the UConn 24-yard line, a 13-yard gain was nixed by an illegal procedure penalty. The Mountaineers ended up settling for a field goal for a 10–0 lead.

My live blog post that night was titled "Greetings from a Breezy Rentschler Field," and featured a picture of the stadium flags being straightened out by the wind, which was so strong that Stewart wanted to force the Huskies to kick into it one last time in the first quarter. He even used two timeouts to make sure it happened. It was bizarre and pretty much unsuccessful, as the punt traveled 43 yards and pushed WVU back to its 34.

Then on third-and-10, the offense was scrambling and Geno Smith couldn't call a timeout because WVU wanted to keep its remaining one for the rest of the half. That drew a flag for a delay of game and on third-and-15, Smith's pass to Starks was good for only 14 yards.

For years and years with Rich Rodriguez, the Mountaineers had an offense that turned first downs into touchdowns. This team was turning touchdowns into field goals and first downs into punts.

There was no doubt Stewart's job was in the balance. After the game, Colin Dunlap of the *Pittsburgh Post-Gazette*, a national newspaper with a circulation greater than 243,000—roughly as large as the circulation of all the papers that cover WVU combined—wrote this as his lead about the loss:

> *Now, coach Bill Stewart could be in deep trouble.*
>
> *The kind of trouble, no matter what happens the rest of this football season, he might never be able to sway the fan base— and more importantly the decision-makers at West Virginia University—back onto his side with their full faith.*

It was bold and it was presumptuous, and it was wholly accurate. The loss to the Huskies ended a stretch of 13 games that included just about everything WVU would find in a typical season. There were seven conference games, seven home games, five road games, 10 games against teams from Bowl Championship Series conferences, and a New Year's Day bowl. Stewart was 8-5 in those 13 games, 4-3 in Big East games, 2-3 on the road, 5-5 against opponents from BCS conferences, and 0-1 in a bowl. And worst of all, WVU was tied for last place in the conference it was supposed to at least threaten to win every season. This was bad, and everyone in the room that night for the postgame press conference knew it, seemingly except Stewart.

"Am I worried about the program?" he repeated. "No, I'm not. I'm worried about just righting the ship and making sure we don't fumble the ball, and getting things better so we can finish strong."

Privately, Stewart was worried. He sensed the trouble, and spent an open week coordinating and conducting a "total self-evaluation of the program." He cited problems and vowed to fix them, but he never really said what he'd do. It was a good moment for him because, at the very least, he showed an awareness detractors were certain he did not possess, but without stating his findings, the same moment was otherwise empty.

The Mountaineers won a week later, 37–10, against Cincinnati. The same day a plane flew around the stadium towing a banner that read, "Mr. Luck. Leave no doubt. Fire Luther." Stewart would be Luther, of course, because he resembled Jerry Van Dyke's bumbling character on the sitcom *Coach*. It was amazingly clairvoyant.

Luck called Stewart in for a meeting the next day. He told his football coach he wasn't satisfied and would be making a change. On November 23, nine days later, Luck met the replacement for the first time. On a trip to Kansas City to see Jerry West enter the National Collegiate Basketball Hall of Fame, he took a side trip to meet Dana Holgorsen, the offensive coordinator at Oklahoma State. Holgorsen was someone Luck thought was as good as anyone at what he does, which was score points, win games, and sell tickets. Luck knew who was running his football program, and he knew he needed someone different.

"As I looked at a guy like Dana Holgorsen, I thought to myself that he will be a head coach somewhere soon, and I wouldn't want to prepare to play against his offense," Luck said. "I want him to be at this university and to lead us in the long term."

The same was not to be said of Stewart. Luck couldn't shake the gripping feeling that if Stewart were allowed to continue, then Luck's football program would not have an opportunity win a national championship. For a program that had played for a title in 1988, had been undefeated in 1993, and was one win away from playing for the championship in 2007, Luck thought that was unacceptable—especially in 2010, when the Big East was as weak and nonthreatening as it had been since it was reformed in 2005. Miami, Virginia Tech, and Boston College were gone; Cincinnati, Louisville, and South Florida were not the Hurricanes, Hokies, and Eagles of old. WVU was 2-2 in the Big East, and Luck figured even three more wins wouldn't change anything, least of all his mind.

With three games to go, the decision was made. Stewart was out, though with conditions. Luck created some wiggle room and some more time to reach a conclusion about exactly when Stewart would leave. He reserved the right to fire Stewart at the end of the season and install Holgorsen right away, but he also gave Stewart a chance to hang on for one more year. If that were the case, and if Stewart wished, he would be allowed to come back for the 2011 season to work one year with Holgorsen, who would take over in 2012 for the first time as a head coach at any level. If that wasn't cool with Stewart, then he would be let go after the 2011 season and Holgorsen would take control. Whatever the decision, Luck would announce it after the Mountaineers completed their schedule. Until then, WVU's coaching situation would not be publicly discussed.

The now-official beginning of the end for Stewart was also the beginning of a strange and sad time for WVU. Stewart kept his situation and decision to himself, but there were signs something was happening. He entered the final phase of his career with whimsy surely empowered by his emotions. After beating Louisville, Stewart revealed he'd given his team a message the night before the game.

"Match the mountains," he said. "The pageantry, the majesty of West Virginia. Match the mountains. I said, 'Just think about three things with me: where you are, who you are, and where you're going by being a Mountaineer. That's all I want you to do. Where you are in life, who you are in life, where you're going in life.' And by doing that, if you match the mountains, the pageantry we have—I didn't invent that. I saw that when I was flying out and I said, 'Look at these beautiful mountains.'"

Stewart paused. He took a deep breath. He scanned the room. He stood up. He spoke.

"That may not mean much to some," he said. "It means a lot to this kid right here. Take care and God bless."

WVU thumped Pitt 35–10 a week later while wearing special Nike Pro Combat uniforms that were tributes to the coal industry and to the state. The combination of the win and the theme meant everything to Stewart. He left that postgame press conference with another oddity, and another clue that something wasn't right.

"It's about four very simple things," he said. "I told the guys last night. No. 1: an appearance. An appearance that is impressive. No. 2: a foundation. A foundation that's rock solid. No. 3: a people that are resilient. And No. 4: a reach that's high. Thank you very much. Today the Mountaineers matched the mountains."

Then the Mountaineers beat Rutgers. With the win, they now had scored 70 points in two games. Stewart had done a wonderful job improving the Mountaineers after learning he was losing his job and telling no one. He followed the program's first two-game losing streak since 2008 with four straight wins. At times, WVU looked a whole lot like the team everyone wanted to see.

Stewart bragged a little after the fourth win when he paraded around the postgame with a T-shirt rightly labeling WVU the Big East champions. True, it was to be a shared title, but it was something Stewart had not yet done, and it meant a whole lot with him knowing what he and no one else but Luck and Holgorsen knew.

"It's been a fabulous four weeks, the ride of my life, and I'm so grateful we've come out the way we have," Stewart said after the 35–14 win against the Scarlet Knights. "Not many people thought that shirt right there would have been handed out."

And who was he speaking of there? Perhaps the guy who was going to get rid of a coach who was 9-3, ranked in both polls, and in possession of a 5-2 Big East record and a share of the title? Stewart would go home that night to watch UConn and USF play in Tampa, Florida, knowing full well if the Bulls beat the Huskies then he would take the Mountaineers to a BCS game—and just imagine that, for a moment. Luck was nevertheless spared the notoriety when UConn's Dave Teggart made a 52-yard field goal to win the game and clinch the Huskies' BCS bid. A bad snap or hold, a little gust of wind, or a really athletic play by a USF player and Luck could have had a problem on his hands. Stewart would let his boss off the hook. The coach who masterfully handled the time immediately after he was told he was on the way out, who truly did well enough to convince Luck to keep him around one more year, went on to badly botch the events that happened after word got out that Holgorsen was on his way.

Secrets can be hard to keep in Morgantown, and when someone is spotted touring around campus with the athletic director and the football-savvy town doesn't recognize the guest to be a part of the staff, people start to talk. Meetings between Luck, Stewart, and Holgorsen were planned, cancelled, and planned again, and enough insiders were so excited or bothered by the decision that the secret couldn't be kept.

By December 13, the staff at the *Charleston Daily Mail* knew enough to act. I work in Morgantown, two hours north of the paper's office in Charleston, which was where Luck was scheduled to speak to the local Rotary Club that morning. I huddled with my boss, sports editor Jack Bogaczyk, over the phone, and we decided it was time to corner Luck. All we knew for certain was that there was an interest in Holgorsen, but we suspected it to be much more than that. Only the insiders knew the particulars of the arrangement, but Bogaczyk pulled Luck aside, brought up Holgorsen's name, and explained what we believed to be true. Bogaczyk relayed to me afterward that Luck's face flushed before he chuckled and said, "I'm just not going to say anything."

The next day, the word was spreading, and newspapers in Charleston, Morgantown, and Pittsburgh alike were reporting the story. Luck was hiring someone to change the offense, and change the football environment. One day later, WVU announced Holgorsen's hiring as the offensive coordinator for one year and then as the head coach beginning in 2012.

Luck explained everything he did and thought along the way. He detailed his lack of faith in Stewart and the reasons why he believed so much in Holgorsen. He justified why it was necessary to keep the decision quiet for a month, and said he would have preferred to wait until after the Mountaineers played their bowl game. He even made a good case for keeping Stewart in place for one additional year and having Holgorsen on the staff as the coach-in-waiting.

That was by far the riskiest part of this decision. Luck was trusting that not only could Stewart and Holgorsen coexist, but that the offensive coaches Holgorsen was going to hire would fit in with the defensive staff Holgorsen agreed to keep in place.

Luck showed everyone his homework, and pointed to the coach-in-waiting models he studied at Oregon and Wisconsin. A bunch of schools had tried this approach before, but a bunch of them had seen it go wrong, too. The Ducks and the Badgers did it right, and Luck said he believed the same could happen for the Mountaineers. There was a major difference, though. At Oregon, Mike Bellotti willingly stepped off the sideline to become the athletic director after he was able to hire and groom his successor, Chip Kelly. Barry Alvarez did the same thing at Wisconsin and picked and prepared Bret Bielema. Kelly was at Oregon for two years after being at New Hampshire at the FCS level. Bielema spent two seasons learning about Wisconsin after working previously at Kansas State in the Big 12 and Iowa in the Big Ten.

What Luck was saying made sense. Holgorsen had moved around a little more, working at Texas Tech from 2000 to 2007, Houston in 2008 and 2009, and then Oklahoma State in 2010, but he, like Bielema and Kelly, had never been a head coach. Holgorsen could use the time constructively. He could learn about West Virginia and its people, its characteristics and its history, and its tradition.

It wasn't a fatally flawed plan, but no one knew it was to be doomed by one important participant. Then again, maybe everyone should have anticipated trouble. As much as Luck said in his remarkably revealing press conference the day he announced the Holgorsen hiring, when he plainly pointed to dwindling attendance, a depressing offense, and no likelihood of winning a national title with Stewart, he was noticeably brief when addressing one thing.

Neither Jeff Mullen, the offensive coordinator, nor Dave Johnson, the offensive line coach, had been informed they were going to lose their jobs, even though they were already supposed to know. When Luck and Stewart had flown to Houston to meet with Holgorsen on December 9, when Luck maintained the ability to get rid of Stewart after that meeting if he felt things might not work, Holgorsen said he would replace Mullen as the coordinator and quarterbacks coach, and find a replacement for Johnson. Luck directly instructed Stewart to tell Mullen and Johnson. That would have given both time to find a job, but it never happened. When Luck was asked about Stewart's failure to inform Mullen and Johnson, all he could say on a day when he was so honest, open, and thorough was, "I don't have any reaction to that."

Mullen, who had interviewed for the head coaching position at Kent State, found out his fate at WVU from the media. Johnson, who was a candidate for a head coaching job at a Division II school, was on a recruiting trip for the Mountaineers when Colin Dunlap called Johnson and told him Holgorsen would be bringing in a new offensive line coach. Johnson was spinning and tried to confirm the news, first through Stewart. Johnson couldn't reach Stewart, though, and grew tired of waiting on the head coach to return his calls, so much so that he called Dunlap back and asked for Luck's cell phone number.

Johnson had gone to the top of the football program, to no avail, and was now going to the top of the athletic department. Luck was surprised and disappointed that he was the one who had to tell Johnson he was being let go. Johnson had played center at WVU in the early 1980s, and had snapped the ball to Luck and tried to keep his quarterback safe. They were close, and Johnson thought he deserved to learn his fate in any way other than how he had. He grew to understand why Luck had withheld the information, but it was harder to understand Stewart's actions. From the very beginning, though, the arrangement between Stewart, Holgorsen, and Luck was compromised—and seemingly only because Stewart couldn't play along and follow orders.

During the previous days, when it looked like Holgorsen would be hired, I spoke to Stewart a few times and asked him if certain things were happening. I left every one of our conversations thinking he didn't know what was going on, and I was equally curious and amazed by that possibility. All along, I was positive something was up and almost as sure Stewart was about to be blindsided. Later, we'd find out that Stewart knew all along.

I don't blame Stewart for keeping the truth from me. He had a duty to keep his fate a secret. After all, the plan was to masquerade until after the bowl game, and you can forgive the coach and the athletic director for trying to preserve what remained of the season. But while Stewart had no obligation to tell me the truth, he had an order to tell Mullen and Johnson they were about to be fired. The two acts of deception are totally different. The first was acceptable, but the latter was the most uncooperative way to start his final year, and probably should have worried Luck. The potential for a power struggle, for a personality clash, for a stubborn Stewart to torpedo things, was definitely there.

If it wasn't clear then, the bowl game experience took care of that.

The time between the end of a regular season and the bowl game is precious for football programs. There's no limit to how many times a team can practice, as long as it doesn't work more than four hours a day, or 20 hours a week. There's usually no school in the weeks before a game, and that means there are no distractions—coaches and players are dedicated to just football.

Most teams give young players a chance to learn and shine and even audition for next season. Many coaches tinker with, refine, or even add to the offense, defense, and special teams. If a team has the time, if the game is far enough away after the end of the regular season, there are usually around 15 practices, the same as there are in spring football and about as many as there are in fall camp. WVU's 2010 regular season ended December 4, and the invitation to the Champs Sports Bowl came a day later. That game would be played on December 28 in Orlando, Florida.

A break for exams and for Christmas cut into that, but the Mountaineers started practices on December 11 with a wealth of distractions already in place—before anyone knew anything of Holgorsen. Kent State was interested in Mullen. Junior safety Robert Sands was mulling the NFL draft. Backup quarterback Barry Brunetti announced he was going to transfer, and Stewart refused to acknowledge it. Cornerback Brandon Hogan tore the ACL in his left knee against Rutgers, and Stewart refused to acknowledge that, too.

Still, WVU worked out on the 11th, and then planned to break until returning the 19th. Then they would work out that day and every day up until the walkthrough at the Citrus Bowl on the 27th.

The team returned December 19 and practiced that day and then the next two, but only inside the indoor practice facility because of winter weather. That building presents challenges because the field is 70 yards long with two 10-yard end zones, and its low ceiling really hinders kicking and punting. Stewart decided to give the Mountaineers a break on December 22 and had them lift weights and watch film before letting them go for the rest of the day. That afternoon, Holgorsen was ceremoniously introduced at a press conference. WVU flew to Orlando the next day, did not practice, and then spent Christmas Eve at the Universal Orlando Resort. On their third day in Orlando, the Mountaineers finally practiced and then did so again a day later. The walkthrough was cancelled on December 27 with the explanation that the stadium wasn't prepared. That didn't stop the opponent, North Carolina State, from doing its walkthrough, that after a fun day and three practice days.

Privately, the players, who'd seen tense and awkward interactions in and out of practice between grown men who didn't like one another, were a little spooked. They're partial to routine; every road game in every normal week they had three practices and a walkthrough. Even if a walkthrough on the road is overrated, the Mountaineers could still find some value in treating the sixth road game like the five before it, in finding the play clock locations, or in testing the new turf at the stadium. In 16 days, Stewart managed to practice only seven times, and only outside and in Orlando twice. On the second day, the wind was so bad that kicking and punting practice was just about useless. Asked if he might add kicking to the walkthrough, Stewart said he would not make any changes because, ironically, he believed in "routine, routine, routine."

"It did get to us," said linebacker Najee Goode, who was a junior on that team. "Football is as much mental as it is physical, and that messed us up mentally. We had guys [that] year who could just go out and play, but you started to see at the end of the game, at key points in the game, something you're normally focused on get messed up and it's not because of the day of the game, but the practices before when we didn't get a chance to go over it."

The game was one more mess for the Mountaineers. All the things people were saying and wondering about WVU once again came to define the defeat. Everything that was bad or suspect about that team that year was on display one last time. The 23–7 loss was the first time WVU allowed more than 21 points in a game all season. Ironically, the player who professed WVU could not lose if the offense scored 20 points was responsible for North Carolina State's final score. Jock Sanders muffed a punt and turned the ball over at his own 7-yard line in the fourth quarter, in a mistake you almost expected when you consider the team hadn't really worked on special teams since before the Rutgers game. Tyler Bitancurt missed two field goals, too, and WVU added five more turnovers in just the second half to go out in a familiar style. Geno Smith was sacked twice and hurried eight other times as the Mountaineers, playing without academically ineligible center Joe Madsen, struggled with the pressure they said they anticipated.

Stewart had no better handle on the team off the field, either. Tailback Shawne Alston, who played so well when called upon in the final four games, but who carried just twice against the Wolfpack, found the opportunity to update his status on Facebook during halftime of the game. Mullen packed his bag in the locker room after the game and headed directly to the bus without speaking to the media. Stewart was as unorthodox as ever in the press conference, combating reporters and dismissing questions designed to address important parts of the game. Asked about North Carolina State's pressure, he said, "Did you see the zone blitzes I saw every play? Thank you." Asked why Smith threw the ball 39 times when Stewart said WVU would run, he said, "If we don't turn the ball over, I think we would have had great results." Asked what came next for him, he said, "I'm going to have more games."

That was something Luck was going to have to think about over the next several months—right up until Stewart left Luck with no choice but to make the change he should have made in the first place.

17
HOLGORSEN

The true irony of Bill Stewart's exit as the head football coach at West Virginia University is that while he seemed to create the conditions that preceded his departure, he actually set the whole thing in motion years before without ever knowing it. Until WVU or Stewart decides to specify why Stewart submitted his resignation on June 10, 2011, people can go back and forth about what caused that decision and whether Stewart was guilty of the things he was accused of, or if WVU simply decided the distraction was too easy to extinguish before it turned into something very ugly. What no one can ever debate is Stewart unknowingly heightened the profile of his successor the night his Mountaineers defeated Oklahoma in the Fiesta Bowl in 2008.

The co-offensive coordinator for the Sooners that night was Kevin Sumlin, who had previously agreed to become head coach of the University of Houston Cougars beginning in 2008. Sumlin fulfilled his obligation to the Sooners for the bowl game while working on his transition to Houston and Conference USA on the side. Sumlin also had a premium seat that night in the desert to see what WVU did to a pretty good Oklahoma defense, how the Mountaineers' no-huddle offense established a blistering pace, how the brief amount of time that passed between the end of one play and the beginning of the next gave the Mountaineers a dangerous rhythm, and how easy it all looked from start to finish.

Sumlin embarked on his new life the next day, and flew to meet with some of the coaches he'd hired. Sumlin was also eager to meet with someone he really admired and really wanted to hire as his offensive coordinator. His name was Dana Holgorsen.

Sumlin knew Holgorsen pretty well by then. They frequently bumped into one another on the road while recruiting, and they battled for many of the same players who played high school football in Houston. Then there were those matchups between Oklahoma and Texas Tech in the Big 12. Holgorsen was becoming a commodity in the industry, and he was open to moving on from Texas Tech and the control head coach Mike Leach had over the Red Raiders offense. Holgorsen, after eight seasons in Lubbock, Texas, wanted to start being his own person. He'd grown tired of asking Leach to punt on fourth down rather than going for the first down.

So Holgorsen accepted Sumlin's offer, knowing many would wonder what he was thinking moving from the Big 12 to Conference USA, but knowing he'd be allowed and empowered to do his own thing. Sumlin's requests were simple, yet profound.

"The two things I was interested in were where he was in terms of an ability to run the ball a little bit more than they had done at Tech, and then I wanted to do it as fast as humanly possible," Sumlin said. "I saw West Virginia do it to us the week before. Dana thought it was an interesting concept."

Sumlin's Houston players weren't very big, certainly not as big as the ones at Oklahoma and throughout the Big 12, and he needed a way to create an advantage. The frenetic offense seemed like a possibility and, at the very least, it made sense to consider it.

The Mountaineers had been working with the same physical shortcomings through the years. They didn't recruit the biggest and baddest receivers. They didn't land the nationally coveted, prototypical spread or option quarterbacks. They didn't even feature running backs schools from other conferences thought very highly of when they took a look. Theirs, as characterized by the participants in their heyday, was the Island of Misfit Toys. Yet Rich Rodriguez and his offensive coordinator, Calvin Magee, who stuck around to coordinate the Fiesta Bowl offense, made the players play fast, fast like their hair was on fire. Sumlin liked it and Holgorsen accepted it. It would become the signature of Holgorsen's offense.

"We didn't play that fast at Tech," Holgorsen said. "We'd huddle sometimes, we'd go slow sometimes, we wouldn't huddle, but we'd still go slow. Every now and then, we'd have a two-minute mode and hurry along, but we never practiced like that. Kevin told me, 'Do exactly what you do, but do it as fast as you can.'"

Holgorsen and Sumlin and their quarterbacks and receivers went on to do some amazing things, and produce astounding statistics that would lead and tantalize college football. Soon Oklahoma State head coach Mike Gundy decided he needed to hire Holgorsen because, as Holgorsen remembered, "he wasn't a very happy guy," trying to be the head coach and improve the offense to preserve his job.

Holgorsen was polishing a reputation that had thus far lacked that marquee lacquer. He wasn't a high school or college star like so many others, like Gundy or Sumlin, for example. Sumlin began as a walk-on linebacker at Purdue, but he's still in the top 10 in Boilermaker history for career tackles. Twice he was honorable mention all-Big Ten. Gundy was a star quarterback when he was in high school in Oklahoma, and was the state's player of the year as a senior. He eschewed Oklahoma, Barry Switzer, and the wishbone for Oklahoma State. While Gundy was the guy who famously handed off to Barry Sanders and Thurman Thomas, he left Oklahoma State and the Big Eight Conference as the career leader in passing. Even Rodriguez had his rise as a player and a leader at WVU, and he had his milestone interception against Penn State in 1984, all of that after a decorated high school career in Marion County.

Holgorsen was just a guy in high school in Mount Pleasant, Iowa, one who wasn't mediocre, but was, by his own admission, "very mediocre." He blended into the tiny town of 7,000 in the southeast corner of the state. He played football at the college in his hometown and it was there, at Iowa Wesleyan, that he met Hal Mumme, a Texas high school coach who said he took the job at Iowa Wesleyan because none of the state's high school coaches would.

When he was hired, Mumme visited Mount Pleasant High and wanted to talk to some of the players on what he remembered was a pretty good football team. Holgorsen wouldn't even leave class to consider the conversation, let alone the pitch. Holgorsen headed instead to St. Ambrose University, in Davenport, Iowa, but didn't care for being moved to defensive back. He traveled back to Mount Pleasant, and told Mumme he wanted to play for the Tigers. Holgorsen became a much better player at Iowa Wesleyan and occupies the school's top 10 with 145 receptions and 1,711 yards.

"Dana was then like he is now: He loved those quick screens," Mumme told *Charleston Daily Mail* sports editor Jack Bogaczyk in 2011. "He had good speed, but he wasn't a game-breaker. He'd come off the field and come up to me and say, 'The quick screen was there.'

"So, I'd put another guy in and call it and we'd get big yardage, and Dana would get really mad at me. So one day we're playing a team, I think from Illinois maybe, and I called the quick screen and finally left him in. He took it 65 yards for a score. He came back and said to me, 'And that's how to carry the cabbage.'"

Mumme and his staff left for Georgia's Valdosta State in 1992, when Holgorsen was a senior at Iowa Wesleyan. Holgorsen joined Mumme's staff a year later, first as a graduate assistant and then a full-time assistant. He became much more familiar with Mumme's offense, which would soon become known as the Air Raid after a player's dad started sounding an air raid siren at games.

Mumme had Leach as his offensive coordinator. They took great care building their offense, taking some of Bill Walsh's practice principles and game plan philosophies and combining them with the passing techniques of Lavell Edwards and BYU. Over time they put their own touches on it, sometimes abandoning the huddle, other times running plays out of the shotgun. After three years with Mumme and Leach, Holgorsen left in 1996 to become the offensive coordinator at Mississippi College. He was 25 years old and on the path that would lead him to Morgantown, changing the offense to suit his preferences along the way, but also to adapt to the more modern style that demands versatility from every system. If you ever want to enrage Holgorsen, suggest he can't run the ball. He's been combating that stereotype for years.

"I don't think there's a lot of difference in the general philosophy—in fact, there's none," Mumme told Bogaczyk. "But where Dana did a great job at Houston and Oklahoma State is in integrating his backs in the run game, taking the skill level of his backs and coming up with innovative ways to get them the ball in space. He's made the run game a little more a part of it than what I did or Mike did."

Holgorsen was at Texas Tech from 2000 to 2007, and worked with offenses that went from averaging 324.8 yards per game the first season to 529.6 in his last season. He was the inside receivers coach his first five years, the co-offensive coordinator in 2005, and then the coordinator by himself the last two years. His 2005 offense led the country in passing yards, and finished No. 4 in scoring and No. 6 in total yards. A year later, the Red Raiders were No. 3 in passing and No. 6 in total offense. In 2007, Texas Tech again led the nation in passing, and was No. 2 in total offense and No. 7 in scoring.

The move to Houston didn't change the results. In two years, the Cougars averaged more than 42 points and 560 yards per game, with more than 430 of those coming through the air. Houston was No. 3 in total offense, No. 2 in passing, and No. 10 in scoring in 2008, and then led the nation in all three categories in 2009. In 2010, Oklahoma State was No. 3 in total offense, No. 2 in passing, and No. 3 in scoring. The year before Holgorsen arrived, the Cowboys were No. 70 in total offense, No. 99 in passing, and No. 56 in scoring.

Holgorsen worked a special sort of magic with the Cowboys. Quarterback Brandon Weeden played minor league baseball from 2002 to 2006. He redshirted at Oklahoma State in 2007, and played just four games the following two seasons. In his season with Holgorsen, Weeden passed for 4,277 yards and 34 touchdowns and broke school records for passing yards, total offense, completions, and completion percentage in a season, and for yards and completions in a game—and he'd better every mark in 2011. Receiver Justin Blackmon caught 20 passes for 260 yards and two touchdowns in 2009. In his season with Holgorsen, he won the Biletnikoff Award as the country's best receiver with 111 receptions for 1,782 yards and 20 touchdowns.

So Holgorsen is a thrower, a chucker, a flinger. Football is cyclical, and the game has witnessed, still experiences, and will always go through phases. The wishbone could have a remarkable return to glory, and a triple option team might win a national title. What Oregon does on offense will always thrill because it can get players who want to be in a system that gives them regular opportunities to make plays. The traditional style, I-formation offenses have worked just fine in recent years, too—they have won national championships at LSU and Alabama, and no one at Stanford complained when that old-school offense won at a very high level and produced an NFL quarterback trained in the classics.

One thing will remain, though: offense excites, and nothing excites like seeing the ball in the air. Woody Hayes coached with a mantra: "There are three things that happen when you throw the ball and two of them are bad." Holgorsen might counter, "Yeah, and one of them is awesome."

Holgorsen's predilection for the pass isn't merely characteristic of a devil-may-care attitude. It's the devil he knows. Hayes might shake his head and frown, but Holgorsen isn't intimidated by the possibility of the incomplete or intercepted pass. He's obsessed with the potential for a first down or a touchdown. One school of thought says there is a 66-percent chance a play ends badly. The other says you complete zero percent of the passes you don't throw. Holgorsen's brand of football is one part high octane, one part high wire. It might invite disaster, but everyone is there for the party. There's an easier way to do things, but there's a duller way to do things, too. He involves risk and there is a reward, but through the years he's learned that you manage and minimize one to enhance and expand the other.

Holgorsen is an artist and the football field is his easel, but life will sometimes imitate art.

This is a man who hasn't exactly taken the conventional approach to climbing the ladder in his industry. He is a self-made success who has taken his risks and been rewarded. It's been a hell of a ride and, quite frankly, he likes to enjoy it. He wasted no time making that very clear at WVU. A day after being elevated from offensive coordinator to head coach, Holgorsen traveled to Beckley with some WVU friends he was just getting to know. On Monday, they fished. On Tuesday, Holgorsen went skydiving with the U.S. Army parachute team.

"We went up about 10,000 feet, and then we just jumped out of an airplane," he said. "It was an amazing view. You could see for miles and miles, just beautiful countryside. Then we came in and we were trying to land on a beach, obviously a small, little beach. It was pretty windy and we came up short and had kind of a crash landing. It resembled something like Bruce Irvin tackling a quarterback."

That's Holgorsen, and really, the only thing that can be surprising about learning he'd celebrated the realization of a career-long goal by jumping out of an airplane is learning Holgorsen actually hadn't been skydiving before. And it probably should have been no surprise, either, that he made a friend in WVU head basketball coach Bob Huggins— and at WVU, there may be no better ally than the basketball coach with some 700 wins, and just as many ways to help a guy find his way.

Holgorsen met Huggins the day Holgorsen was introduced at WVU, and he was genuinely impressed and excited. Huggins would soon invite Holgorsen over to his house, and away they went.

"I like him," Huggins said. "He loves football, he loves coaching, but he's a fun guy to be around. He's a really loyal guy. I think if you look at his staff hires, it's guys he's known for a long time."

It's one thing to get Huggins's seal of approval, but when he signs off on loyalty, the most cherished trait to Huggins and to the people of West Virginia, that says a whole lot more. They have other things in common, of course, such as having a good time and relaxing with a drink or two, things that people see and change the way they talk about you—and frequently behind your back. Huggins had already been through a few of the things Holgorsen would go through in his first six months at WVU, and Huggins could offer some advice on how to handle it in the moment and beyond.

"Probably for a long time I didn't care [what people thought], and that probably wasn't the right move, to be honest with you," Huggins said not long after Holgorsen was named head coach. "He should probably do everything I didn't."

Holgorsen is indeed his own man, defined and driven by his own designs. His hair is perhaps harder to tame than his offense. He's at peace in shorts and sandals behind a podium. He's powered by energy drinks through those endless days, weeks, and months that occupy his calendar. He goes and goes and goes, and only stops to chug a Red Bull so he can go and go and go some more. Sure, he has a title and a profile that require certain roles and responsibilities. Sainthood and divinity are not among them. Holgorsen likes to live, to make the destination worth the journey, to drop back in the pocket and throw it deep from time to time. Maybe it was the constraints of the small town he grew up in, but Holgorsen likes to feel free, likes to live free. When he was on campus at Oklahoma State, Stillwater reminded him of Mount Pleasant. He'd slip away to Tulsa. When he was with Sumlin and the Cougars, Holgorsen could occupy his free time and get away without ever leaving Houston.

"It's no secret I like the city," he said.

And so it was that one night in May of 2011, five months after he was hired but a month before he was promoted, Holgorsen found himself drawn to the bright lights of a dog track and casino in a town called Cross Lanes, north of Charleston, the state capital of West Virginia. Holgorsen and some other representatives and dignitaries from the athletic department had been in Logan earlier in the day for one of the events on the summer's money-making circuit. The event ended but the night had not, and a bunch of people, in an effort to get to know the new football coach, decided to make the trip about an hour up the road to Cross Lanes.

It wasn't Holgorsen's idea, but to him, a new guy in a new place getting to know new people, it sounded like a good idea. Was it? That doesn't matter. The point is that trips like that with people like that at a time like that are kind of necessary. The variables appear with how those people handle those trips. Handled wrongly, those variables create trouble.

That night, everyone was doing whatever it is that people tend to do in a casino that serves beer and liquor as the late night turns into the early morning. Something happened, something many people sought to either cover up or never disclose, and Holgorsen ended up confronted by someone from casino security who insisted Holgorsen needed to leave. Then something else happened, something else many people sought to cover up or never disclose, and the local police were called. At 3:13 in the morning, the casino dialed 911 to report someone who would not cooperate with the wishes of casino management. The police arrived and had a brief conversation with Holgorsen, one in which they said he needed to leave. Holgorsen went outside, sat on a bench, waited on a taxi, and left with the others to go back to their hotel in Charleston.

The implications were obvious, but the actual details of the incident were not. The state's lottery commission declined to release the footage from the facility's surveillance system. The security staff at the casino was forbidden to discuss it with the media. No one who was known to be with Holgorsen would go on the record to discuss it, which then made it hard to fully trust anyone's version of the story. Still, there was no police report because there was no arrest, and there wasn't even verification Holgorsen was belligerent, drunk, or even tipsy. The only mention of a degree of sobriety came from the police officer who responded to the scene. He merely said police are typically called when a patron is drunk, but he never said Holgorsen was drunk. In fact, all the officer did say was that Holgorsen followed all orders, was "very compliant," and allowed the situation to be handled "very easily." The honest, unbiased truth is no one ever came out and said if Holgorsen was hammered and uncooperative or if Holgorsen was just tired, cranky, and out a couple bucks.

It didn't matter. Holgorsen had arrived with a reputation, fair or unfair, deserved or not, and all the trappings of a divorced football coach, not yet 40 years old, who had bounced around to four schools in five years, sneaked away to big cities, and lived in a hotel. Whatever happened at that casino, whether it was as tame as insisted by secondhand experts and by participants who begged for anonymity, or as serious as the involvement of security and the response of police suggests, it was a problem, not only for Holgorsen, but for Athletic Director Oliver Luck, the man who had extended himself and his still-shiny reputation to hire Holgorsen. The story hit the newspaper a week after the incident, and Luck decided "inappropriate behavior did occur." Holgorsen filed an apology, too.

"I learned a valuable lesson from this incident," he said. "As a football coach, I am always in the public eye, and I have to hold myself to a higher standard, which is what I ask our players to do. I'm sorry that this incident has put the university and the football program in a difficult position. I will not put myself in that situation again."

By all accounts, Holgorsen was a different person at the rest of those summer's money-making events. Maybe he'd learned. Maybe he didn't want to give anyone any ammunition. He maintained his role as the newly hired coach, the guy everyone wanted to get to know and to talk to, the main attraction at those cash grabs, but he was reserved and would try to withdraw into the background rather than stand out by word or action. Or maybe it was just simpler that way.

Neither Luck nor the university would punish Holgorsen, and there were no prohibitions placed on his fundraising appearances. Holgorsen didn't opt out either; he's not a guy who shies from the perceptions of others. That he made clear months earlier when he was spotted in town hanging out with Rodriguez and thought nothing of it. Others aggressively disagreed, insisting their new coach couldn't mingle with their old coach, but Holgorsen didn't understand why one coach couldn't socialize with another, why it was wrong to talk about Michigan and Oklahoma State, why people thought it was a big deal.

Most of all, Holgorsen didn't care.

"A couple of his buddies who are supporters of the program, guys that I know obviously as this point, called me and wanted to know where I was. That's something that's not unusual," he said. "They were in town, coming back from a Steelers game, actually, and called and said, 'Where are you at?' I said, 'I'm in town.' So I stopped by and we chatted for a while. Simple as that. Happens all the time."

So, no, Holgorsen wasn't going to disappear for a while after that casino kerfuffle and hope everyone would forgive and forget. It was just easier to go on and be seen and behave, rather than disappear and let everyone make a big deal out of his absences. It was easy to stay out of trouble by staying visible. Rather than worry about the problem, he focused on the solution. It was impossible to fix the problem. It was easy to control the solution. Holgorsen is, if nothing else, a simple guy.

"Life's hard," he said. "If you make it harder, it doesn't make a whole lot of sense."

This is the guy who arrived in Morgantown and made heads explode by stating with a stunning nonchalance that he would need just three days to install his offense, the one that had torn up college defenses for years, the one WVU and Luck desired because it was so unstoppable. On the fourth day, the offense would revisit and refine the first day. The fifth day was there to tidy up the second day. The sixth day addressed the third day. On and on it went, until the Mountaineers went through 15 spring practices by installing the offense in the first three, and rehearsing those three days in order during the final 12 days.

This is the guy who has a playbook that is more like a pamphlet. This is the guy who goes into a game with 20 or 25 plays he wants to run, the only ones the team worked on in practice that week. This is the guy who chooses those plays thusly: "If it works, do it again. If it sucks, you probably shouldn't do it again." This is the guy who lived in a hotel the entire time he coached Oklahoma State and for his entire first year with the Mountaineers.

But again, sometimes life imitates art. Hotel living is simple. The guy who is consumed by positive plays and big numbers is also the guy who spends a lot of time at work. Sometimes it's nice to come home and find the linens have been changed and the bed has been made, towels are fresh and the soap and shampoo has been replaced, the bathroom is clean, and the carpet has been vacuumed. People would make an issue of it and inquire about this nomad, and wonder how he fit in a place that cherishes loyalty and cringes at suggestions it might not exist in the form of a new home and a mortgage. And Holgorsen would once again wonder why it was a big deal that he lived in a hotel.

"It's just easy," he said. "Convenience is a part of what I do. It makes sense. A lot of stuff that doesn't make sense is inconvenient. I try to live like that. That makes sense to me."

Order could only last so long in Luck's head-coach-in-waiting arrangement, and with the emergence of the Cross Lanes casino story, Holgorsen's simple life was about to change.

18
SCUMBAG

West Virginia University *is searching for anonymous contributors to newspaper stories it says contain "blatant inaccuracies" about the football team's head coach-in-waiting and offensive coordinator, Dana Holgorsen.*

Two senior university officials told the Daily Mail *the scope includes members of the entire football program as well as other athletic-affiliated organizations.*

The timing of WVU's internal inquiry, which is a normal procedure in response to such incidents, coincides with a pause in the concluding phase of coach Bill Stewart's separation agreement with the university.

Two sources said the contract has been awaiting signatures for weeks but has been tabled as the athletic department determines who has and has not participated in fabricating stories about Holgorsen and compromising the coaching transition.

After three years as the head coach and 11 years at West Virginia, Bill Stewart saw it all come to a rapid conclusion once the *Charleston Daily Mail* and my byline sent a story topped by those four paragraphs out to the public. What was written June 6, 2011, never says that Stewart was out to get his replacement, Dana Holgorsen, but the implication was as obvious as the outcome was unmistakable. Stewart was being accused of in some way undermining Holgorsen and his transition from coach-in-waiting to head coach. If it wasn't Stewart, then it was someone near him or under him, someone he was expected to control and, in this case, mute. Either there was a burden of responsibility he was being blamed for not bearing, or he was behind a traitorous act and he could not be allowed to survive.

There were no specifics from the beginning of the fiasco to the end. That gray area produced some nonsensical stuff in the black and white of the newspapers, but what began on Monday came to a conclusion on Friday as a press release announced Stewart's carefully arranged resignation. A hastily organized news conference followed later that night, and forced Athletic Director Oliver Luck to discuss it. There were no details there, and Luck was silenced and restrained by a promise made by Stewart and WVU's negotiators to never, ever discuss the matter. We'll never know exactly what happened, what Stewart actually said or did, what proof he may have possessed to acquit himself, or what evidence WVU may have presented to convict Stewart, the man who usually kept his personal feelings about those around him whom he did not like close to his sweater vest.

Stewart didn't care for the way Rich Rodriguez ran a football team or a football program, but he never really publicly said it. He hinted at it from time to time, especially when he mentioned his record against South Florida or the way he preferred to treat his players, but that was about it. Late in their time together, Stewart was not a fan of Doc Holliday, who had emerged as the first candidate to replace Rodriguez, only to accompany Stewart on his first coaching staff. When Holliday had some philosophical differences with others on the staff, when Holliday left for Marshall, and when WVU prepared for its first game against Holliday's Thundering Herd, Stewart said all the nice things for the cameras and the recorders. Off the set, it was different. That was Bill Stewart, the good old boy who only had nice things to say about people in front of other people because it was the only way he knew.

And that's what made his alleged act of treason so surprising. It was completely out of character.

People really believed, or wanted to believe, it could not be true. The *Dominion Post*, the newspaper of record in Morgantown, had nothing in its pages the day after WVU officials told me about their suspicions and gave me permission to write about them. The *Charleston Gazette*, the state's newspaper, followed with a column that addressed the situation but concluded that because the story had been preceded by Internet innuendo, it could not be true. Actually, the official description was 2 percent fact and 98 percent "hooey." This choice of words was later scrubbed away and replaced with something else, but nevertheless it stood as a guarantee: "There is nothing else out there." Three days later, the football coach was gone. This is not a critique of the way the story was covered. It's an illustration of just how sudden and unexpected Stewart's departure was.

Yet in truth, the fast-paced events of that week actually started a full three months earlier. I was in Florida at what was then the St. Pete Times Forum, covering WVU's men's basketball team in the NCAA Tournament, when I got an email from someone I absolutely trust. If this person told me to go to hell and bring ice, I'd be shopping for an ice bucket with flames on it. This person told me that the first person Holgorsen had brought along for the ride, longtime friend Brady Ackerman, had been dismissed from a contracted position evaluating the athletic department's academic support system. A few nights earlier, the basketball team had been in New York for the Big East Tournament, defending its 2010 title at Madison Square Garden. While at a private birthday party for President James Clements and Ben Statler, a former coal company executive and generous donor, Ackerman apparently said some mean things about some important people without realizing he was in the company of friends and family members of those important people. One thing led to another and Ackerman was soon dismissed, well before his contract would expire.

That email was designed to send me down a path that ended with a story about Ackerman being let out of his contract, and it did. But a postscript to that email soon had me following up on a different story: "May want to check on Stewart's contract."

Stewart had signed a modified employment agreement that outlined how he'd spend his final season and then gallop off into the sunset once he'd handed the program to Holgorsen. Most assumed it was final, but I was assured by many others that it was not. That became something to keep track of and later something to fixate upon—there was a reason it wasn't being finalized, even and especially as Holgorsen was getting kicked out of casinos and a columnist in Huntington was writing almost libelous tales about Holgorsen's alleged indiscretions.

What I learned was both sides were working on some minor requests and revisions. What they were, no one would say, but there were a bunch of possibilities. For example, after Holgorsen took over in 2012, the contract stated Stewart was allowed to leave WVU at any point without penalty, and without having to forfeit a $375,000 salary for a 30-month term in a job in the athletic department. He could have, in theory, gone to Pitt to rendezvous with the head coach at the time, Todd Graham, and assistant coaches Calvin Magee, Tony Gibson, Tony Dews, and Paul Randolph, all guys Stewart had worked with at WVU. Stewart could have drawn a paycheck from the Panthers and spilled all sorts of secrets, all while still being paid by the Mountaineers.

Perhaps WVU's leadership would invoke some sort of a clause to prevent something like that. Perhaps Stewart would fight like hell to prevent any provision that would stop him from continuing his coaching career as soon as WVU was done with him as the head coach. Whatever the case, Stewart was working on what the university believed was a terms and conditions sheet, which is the framework of a contract that is completely functional, but not final.

Contracts are pretty mundane, and generally interest no one who wants to read about the Mountaineers. But covering the Mountaineers through the years meant you had to know about, and had to pay attention to, contracts. When Gale Catlett retired after 24 seasons as the men's basketball coach, WVU first hired Dan Dakich from Bowling Green. Dakich was the coach for eight days before he realized

WVU was about to be in trouble with the NCAA for some things highly recruited guard Jonathan Hargett had received from a so-called mentor. So Dakich packed up everything he'd unpacked in the brief time he occupied his office at the Coliseum and went back to Ohio and the Falcons. How? He never signed any kind of a contract with WVU. Why? No one could answer that.

The Mountaineers lucked out and hired a wonderful teacher, tactician, and person in John Beilein. He had a bit of a wandering eye, though, and eventually he locked his gaze upon the University of Michigan. He left for Michigan after five seasons with WVU, and successfully opposed the buyout clause in his contract. He got away paying $1 million less than the $2.5 million the contract stated.

Rodriguez, of course, was G. T. Beauregard to WVU's Fort Sumter in their drawn-out civil war over the buyout in his contract. Even Beilein's successor, Bob Huggins, had a contract story early in his time at WVU. After his first season, he and his people worked out a lifetime contract with WVU, something WVU had never done before.

Stewart's contract was, at the very least, up in the air. Not only that, but it came at a time when the future of football and, specifically, if or how everyone would coexist, was solidly unpredictable. I decided to follow the contract. On occasion, I'd send WVU's legal department a request for Stewart's contract under the Freedom of Information Act, and on every occasion a reply would come back the same: Nothing had changed from January, when Stewart's modified employment agreement was released, which was before both sides sought to make changes. That seemed to suggest the finalized contract was not done.

Then things got weird. Holgorsen was bounced from the casino in Cross Lanes, West Virginia, after 3 a.m. on May 18, and that obviously became the top story on the beat. Stewart's contract never went away, though. It kept popping up in matters you would think were not related. In the first wave of reporting about Holgorsen's incident, I had someone tell me to be careful about what I wrote and how I wrote it because, in this person's opinion, what happened wasn't as bad as it would be made to look. That seemed like a subtle caution, but it

WAITING FOR THE FALL

became a very significant statement later when things were made to look worse than WVU believed was true.

Holgorsen was, on cue and as expected, vilified and mocked for his behavior, behavior we weren't able to accurately define, but behavior we could agree wasn't fit for someone in his position. Then Chuck Landon, a columnist at the *Huntington Herald-Dispatch*, also on cue and as expected, used his space three days later to smear Holgorsen. Without any proof or corroboration, the column said the coach-in-waiting had been involved in "at least three and, perhaps, as many as six alcohol-related incidents" since he was hired. The column further crafted a division in the university's leadership, suggesting Clements had called Luck back to campus early from Big East meetings so he could threaten Luck's job. It was written that Clements was so angered and embarrassed by the casino incident that he vowed to fire Luck if Holgorsen got in any more trouble.

That same column, the one that indicated three to six incidents, actually cited eight. Most were things people had heard about before the column came out—indicating that rumors had been circulating independent of the Huntington paper's column. To me, it seemed the scope of some of those things grew every time they made a trip through the grapevine. Before and after the column was printed, I tried and tried but couldn't confirm any of the incidents. I was actually able to get some people to discredit the stories.

For example, Holgorsen was accused of being asked to leave a bar in Huntington after his Houston team played at Marshall in October of 2008. A football program employee at Houston had heard about this allegation by the time I called. That person knew it wasn't true, and had already looked back at whatever records were available. Those records said Holgorsen flew back with the team after the game. Anyone who covers college football knows coaches don't stick around for the night when the team flies back to campus. The exception is when a team has time off after a game, and the coaches stay on the ground to either recruit the area, or to catch a flight the next day that will take them to an area they do recruit. Houston did have an open week following the Marshall game, but Holgorsen was said to be on the team's charter flight back to Houston. If he were to recruit after the game and during the open week, it was not going to be somewhere near Huntington.

Even the other alleged incidents, at a golf course an hour south of campus, or a bar in the northern part of the state, or even the lounge at the hotel in which Holgorsen lived, couldn't be corroborated. The only event I kind of verified, I also debunked. At a different casino, Holgorsen and a bunch of other figures from the athletic department were indeed at a party that is organized annually by an area booster. There was steak and lobster and cigars and whiskey, and everyone was said to have a good time. Holgorsen was indeed escorted out by law enforcement—off-duty law enforcement that was there to keep things calm and, in Holgorsen's case, merely make sure he got back to his room unencumbered. There wasn't even smoke, let alone fire, there. In other inquiries, I actually angered people I talked to along the way. I was subjecting myself to scoldings and rude replies. I couldn't even put Holgorsen in some of those places when I talked to employees who were WVU fans and worked there five days a week.

Some of them didn't like Holgorsen, or didn't like the way he was forced upon Stewart and the program, but they wouldn't put Holgorsen in their establishment. Not only that, but as a part of a few of those conversations, I was told that people from WVU had also called to check on the validity of these stories, which seemed a little strange. Remember, Holgorsen had not yet been ejected from the casino or assailed by the columnist, but WVU was nevertheless already investigating these stories, which meant WVU was hearing these stories way before they went public in the newspaper. That became really important later.

Before then, though, I couldn't prove any of the incidents happened. WVU also tried and couldn't. I'm sure the columnist couldn't either, assuming he even tried. Whether he had or not wasn't yet the issue. At that time, it seemed WVU had a blemish. The school pushed a good man out of the head coaching position, and replaced him with someone so grateful for the opportunity that he was chucked from a casino while doing fundraising for the athletic department. At the very least, WVU had a problem, if not in reality, then in perception. The question that needed to be answered was simple: What was WVU going to do about this—if anything? So I began to ask around about WVU's reaction to the casino incident, as well as the suggestion Holgorsen had been involved in far more. Would he be benched for the rest of the offseason fundraisers? Would he be suspended for a game? Was his job in jeopardy? How about a fine? Reprimand? Twenty-eight day stay in a treatment facility?

As I asked about responses and punishments, what I learned was WVU, while bothered by the implication the casino incident created, was more upset about the inaccuracy and the foundation of the other allegations. In fact, WVU, a place that was often maligned and turned the other cheek, was reviewing its options for recourse. Was this libel? Could that be proved? The university promised there was no rift between Luck and Clements, but that was one man's word against the other. An itinerary and a prepurchased plane ticket proved Luck was actually due back early from those Big East meetings so he could attend a rifle team fundraiser—that would counter what was written about Luck being pulled out of the meetings so Clements could yell at him.

WVU decided not to respond, decided to let the audience sort fact and fiction on its own. It wouldn't pursue libel. It wouldn't publicly dispute the allegations to support Holgorsen. It would place no restrictions on Holgorsen's appearances and responsibilities—and that was the strongest statement made amid the silence.

Yet to say the university would do nothing was inaccurate. WVU decided it had a liability somewhere within the athletic department, and quite likely inside the football program. Before it all made the newspapers, before Holgorsen was spotlighted at the casino, before he was besmirched in the Huntington newspaper, WVU representatives had already started checking on the stories they had heard about Holgorsen.

When the stories about incidents at various bars and casinos around the state popped up in print after Holgorsen was made to leave the casino in Cross Lanes, WVU's representatives began to wonder how and, more specifically, why that had happened. They couldn't ignore the timing. It was too convenient. They started to work in reverse and find out on their own.

WVU wasn't typically an organization that would combat stuff in that manner. So, WVU's response seemed like a substantial development in the story. I then tried to figure out how and, more specifically, why those stories appeared in print. By the time the athletic department rolled into Charleston on June 2 for an annual fundraiser and a meeting by the Board of Governors, I'd come to learn and believe a number of things that made it seem that the torpedoing of Holgorsen was a case of friendly fire.

That was when the conversation returned to where it started.

Stewart's contract was finished and the terms were defined and agreed upon, but it didn't have the signatures needed to make it a complete document. Why? What was the delay? WVU had been and remained suspicious of what was then believed to be an attempt to damage Holgorsen and his transition to head coach.

Surely, though, it could not be Stewart: the coach who told his players never to bail on their brothers? Never to leave their wingman? Never to betray the Old Gold and Blue? No way.

Then again, think for a moment about the conditions that existed when Stewart was hired: WVU was looking all over the country to find the Band-Aid to heal the wound Rodriguez inflicted with his exit. When the Fiesta Bowl was done, the people who were making the decision stepped back and concluded, "Wait, we had the right guy all along. What's wrong with Billy Stewart?"

Well, why couldn't lightning strike twice? Holgorsen gets bounced from a casino. The voices that supported Stewart when his replacement was introduced would now return with greater volume. The folks who were worried about Holgorsen's reputation coming to life would arrive in force and with firepower. Surely a crowd of people would point fingers at Holgorsen, and many more could wring their hands long enough to pressure Luck or Clements and they might be swayed enough and step back and again conclude, "You know what? We had the right guy all along. What's wrong with Billy Stewart?" Perhaps they just needed a push in that direction.

Of course if you could believe that sort of sedition, you also had to allow for the possibility of something similar coming from the other side. Some people wanted badly to get rid of Stewart. He had delivered low moments on and off the field, and generally steered the program off the path Rodriguez had placed it on before his departure. Perhaps people were working against Stewart by working against Holgorsen. Perhaps they knew a smear campaign would logically be traced back to Stewart.

Then you also had to consider that if Stewart was innocent and someone else was guilty, and that person was within the football program or associated with someone within the football program, then it was someone Stewart should have had control over, someone Stewart couldn't afford to keep around if he or she was going to sully the uncharted waters the program was about to navigate the following season. If Stewart couldn't manage the actions of others, he could not be allowed to stay, either.

Luck and the small circle he incorporated into this informal but critical inspection of the entire operation believed all three options were conceivable. But it was clear one was at the front of their minds, and that meant Stewart was in peril.

So the *Daily Mail* prepared the story, the one that indicated WVU was searching for the source of these exaggerated stories, the one that implied Stewart was involved on some level, the one that suggested his contract was not finalized because he wasn't in the clear. A day before it ran, and then again on the Monday it ran, I gave Stewart an opportunity to comment. He could have denied his involvement; he could have vowed to cooperate with the search; he could have offered a generic comment; he could have offered no comment; he could have told me what to do with myself.

Instead Stewart did and said nothing and went on with business as usual. He went to one of those the summer fundraisers the day the story went out and worked the room with Luck and Holgorsen as if nothing was happening, a surreal scene people in attendance could not believe.

The situation turned in a very bad way for Stewart that night when Colin Dunlap, the WVU beat writer for the *Pittsburgh Post-Gazette* in

2009 and 2010, was a guest on a late-night show on 93.7 FM The Fan in Pittsburgh.

After covering the WVU beat, Dunlap was promoted to cover the Pirates during 2011, but resigned shortly after his wife gave birth to a son and daughter. Dunlap had also been a host for regular and substitute duty at the station during and after the time he worked for the *Post-Gazette*. After resigning from the paper, he had his own weekend show.

Dunlap's full-time occupation was as a stay-at-home dad. The schedule he kept with his twins throughout the day prevented him from doing some ordinary things like going to the office to pick up his paycheck during normal business hours. One night when Dunlap planned to go into the radio station office to get his paycheck happened to be the same day the *Daily Mail's* story about Stewart broke, and the football coach looked like the villain. Because he would be in the office anyway, Dunlap was asked to spend an hour in-studio with host Chris Mueller to discuss the situation at WVU, one Dunlap knew quite well.

Dunlap went on-air at midnight. As part of the conversation, Dunlap reasoned Stewart could be guilty of conspiring against Holgorsen because Dunlap had experienced Stewart's desperation firsthand in December 2010. Dunlap then told the story about when Stewart had asked Dunlap to "flame-throw" Holgorsen.

"He said, 'Can you get the word,'—I think it was 'scumbag' or something—'tattooed on the front of the sports page? You need to dig up this dirt. You need to get it out on this guy.' I said, 'Hey, man, I'm not, like, a part of some witch hunt,'" Dunlap said.

Among the people who covered WVU, Dunlap's account wasn't news. The day Stewart resigned, Bob Hertzel wrote a column in the *Fairmont Times-West Virginian* that said, "Did [Stewart] slip far enough to call Colin Dunlap of the *Pittsburgh Post-Gazette* and another reporter and ask them to 'dig up dirt' on Holgorsen? I don't want to believe that he did, although Dunlap told me at the time that it had happened."

Dunlap also mentioned on the air that a similar thing had happened to a separate reporter, one Dunlap said he'd spoken to, one

Dunlap nobly never identified, one who has never come forward.

To Luck and his search team and the university's legal department, that was a major, major development. They'd just discovered the problem they were dealing with in June, and had suspicions about in March, had actually been happening for perhaps six months.

"In December, I saw him as a man beaten down, downtrodden, who had his dream job stolen away from him, and I passed it off as a desperate act," Dunlap told me the following December. "I was just a reporter. It wasn't personal. He was trying to use me as a platform, not as a man. He wasn't trying to use me. He was trying to use my pen."

A detail Dunlap disclosed with neither malice nor premeditation, something he shared as a guest and not on the show he regularly hosted on his own, sent the pendulum swinging above Stewart.

"I was simply asked a question by an interviewer and answered it honestly," Dunlap said. "Bill Stewart was the one who was acting in a devious form, not me."

When night turned to day, the revelation took off, and in the afternoon Luck released a three-paragraph statement that said he expected his coaches to run a "clean and honest program" and exercise "the utmost integrity and professionalism."

Those were two swipes at Stewart and two strikes against Stewart. If Luck's direction was not yet clear, he then concluded that violations of those expectations were "unacceptable and will not be tolerated."

Stewart and Luck met that afternoon and Stewart denied any wrongdoing. Stewart had breakfast the next morning with my boss, the sports editor at the *Daily Mail*, Jack Bogaczyk. He knew Stewart from his days at VMI when Bogaczyk worked in Roanoke. Stewart again declined to talk about the only thing anyone wanted to talk about, choosing again to let his silence serve as his defense.

In the end, we have no idea if it worked. We don't know if he admitted to anything or if WVU found him undeniably guilty of anything. We don't know if he was able to combat any accusations or suggestions made by WVU. We don't know if what the *Daily Mail* learned and pursued as the premise of the story on June 6 was ever validated. Stewart has never once spoken about his exit.

"If somebody forced me out of my dream job and it was an untruth, if that untruth was said on a FM station in a decent-sized market and it forced me to lose my dream job, I'd sue their ass," Dunlap said.

Whatever happened that preceded Stewart's resignation is a secret both WVU and Stewart agreed to protect with the language of the severance agreement. Even if it was without proof, it was clear Stewart's guilt or innocence wasn't WVU's main concern. Maybe Luck was asking if Stewart did it, but he was surely having second thoughts about whether the coach-in-waiting arrangement with Stewart and Holgorsen could work.

Luck did his homework before hiring Holgorsen and organizing the coach-in-waiting succession plan. He didn't do it because it was the easy thing to do, or because he felt he owed it to Stewart. Luck thought it could work. He really and truly believed that, even though he allowed himself some wiggle room in that modified employment agreement by first reserving the right to get rid of Stewart within 72 hours of meeting Holgorsen, and then by maintaining the option to get rid of Stewart after the regular season. Both times Luck invested in Stewart and, again, not because it was the idea that offered the least resistance or was most popular.

One thing that's clear about Luck is that he isn't afraid of doing something counterintuitive, like proposing selling beer at the Mountaineer Field as a way to improve fan behavior, or to play a home game in Washington, D.C., or sanctioning his son, Andrew, to stay at Stanford for his redshirt junior year when he was all but guaranteed to be the first pick in the NFL draft. Luck did all of that in his first year at WVU, so letting Stewart stick around for one season wasn't shocking. The sad truth is Stewart could have helped Holgorsen, who had never been a head coach, who had bounced around in recent years, who knew nothing of the WVU program and culture, who could have benefited from Stewart's insight on recruiting, the fans, the Big East Conference, and so much more. Stewart could have offered many lessons, but how to wield a knife was not supposed to be one of them.

Luck took a gamble and he bet on the wrong guy. Even without proof to authenticate any allegations made against Stewart, Luck was forced to concede the coach-in-waiting plan would not work. It's a flawed practice, and it had gone wrong for other schools many times before, but, in Luck's defense, it never came undone quite like it did on his watch. He could have projected the worst-case scenario at WVU and, quite likely, never have envisioned what he experienced.

The coaching profession is built on absolute trust and unshakeable relationships; it can collapse when the conditions are even slightly off. Coaches spend an inestimable amount of time together recruiting, watching film, traveling, coaching, raising money, and doing anything else to justify their paychecks. It can be a miserable existence if one coach doesn't like and trust the other. It is impossible to go into a recruit's living room or into the locker room and ask kids to behave like men when you're a man acting like a kid. Given all of that, Luck and probably even Stewart realized it wasn't going to work.

Technically, Stewart resigned. But Stewart also knew Luck hadn't gotten rid of him before, and was going to have a hard time finding the ammunition to use to fire him now. Luck accepted the resignation, but let's not pretend he didn't coerce it either. Luck had a second chance to replace Stewart, like he could have when he hired Holgorsen, either with cause because of the NCAA infractions, or with convenience because he had the offensive wizard he so badly wanted.

It was a terrible experience, an embarrassing lesson in management, a brutal reminder that you can't predict what pride will do to people, but there was something redeeming about the whole thing. That awkward season Stewart and Holgorsen were going to have to spend together was gone, and with it the problems that predicament could pose. Even the players confessed that when it was done it was a major relief. Luck was free of inevitable obstacles.

"The program is more important than any individual, more important than any coach and any player," Luck said. "Clearly, because there were distractions within our football program—and being a former student-athlete, I know one thing you don't want around any program is distractions—I think the totality of the circumstances, the totality of the innuendo and the things being said, were a distraction."

Stewart remained silent to the end, and didn't appear at the press conference announcing his resignation, though he did have Luck deliver a message to his remaining fans and supporters. It offered perfect symmetry from the man who said years earlier he would know when it was time to go, and no one would have to tell him to leave. That thing he never should have said on the day he was hired haunted him for the next three seasons, and then it chased him out the door.

"As I said on the day I was appointed head coach, what is best for WVU is my first priority," Stewart's statement read. "Today, I am doing what I believe to be in the best interest of the Mountaineer Nation."

And then Stewart disappeared, tiptoeing away with $1.65 million thanks to the agreement he'd signed. It was June 10, 2011, the first anniversary of Luck's hiring, and the day before Stewart's 59th birthday. The future had arrived.

19
RESET

Optimism returned in the summer of 2011. Dana Holgorsen was in place as the head coach. Season tickets went on sale to the general public on June 22, following a previous deadline for supporters of the Mountaineer Athletic Club, the athletic department's main fundraising organization. Inside of three weeks, an additional 1,200 season tickets had been sold. WVU was already above the total for the 2009 season, important because Luck cited slipping season ticket sales as a reason to remove Bill Stewart.

The talent was again hard to ignore. Quarterback Geno Smith and receiver Tavon Austin were named to the first ever Pony Express Award watch list for college football's top tandems. Smith was named to the Maxwell Award watch list for the nation's most outstanding player, the O'Brien Award watch list for the country's best quarterback, and the Walter Camp Award watch list for the national player of the year. Many others with a voice and a vote put him on the dark horse list for the Heisman Trophy.

Defensive end Bruce Irvin and cornerback Keith Tandy made the watch lists for the Bednarik Award and the Nagurski Trophy, given to the top defensive player. Left tackle Don Barclay made the

Outland Trophy's watch list for the best lineman. Joe Madsen made the Rimington Trophy watch list for the best center.

By August 1, basically at the end of summer recruiting before high school seniors focus on their season, WVU had 16 players committed to the 2012 recruiting class. They came from Texas, Baltimore, Washington, D.C., Cleveland, South Florida, Eastern Pennsylvania, and New Jersey. They were quarterbacks and receivers and running backs and cornerbacks and defensive ends, the kinds of players that made people take an interest in the future before it ever arrived.

Everything felt right, and it began with Holgorsen. He'd hired assistant coaches to fit his system and his vision. He and those assistants had impressed during spring practice and then in recruiting. His offense was the talk of the town. The Mountaineers, with Holgorsen and Smith and Austin and Stedman Bailey and all the others, had their fans thinking boldly once again.

WVU was the favorite in the Big East even before the preseason coaches' poll at the conference media day made it official. A few analysts and columnists would even give WVU good odds at playing for the national title, provided it won the LSU game at home on September 24.

Most important was the feeling the Mountaineers were again on the right track. Had it been since that week before the Pitt game in 2007 that the fans felt so secure? It's hard to look back and think otherwise, especially when one considers Stewart's first team started No. 8 in the 2008 poll, but was unranked after three games.

In Luck there was an athletic director who had plans to make football big, and the compulsion to see things through. The coach-in-waiting worry was gone. WVU could win the Big East once again.

"I'm a Dana fan," former kicker Pat McAfee said. "I like his style of play. I think it was a great business move by Oliver Luck to make. It's a style of play people want to put on TV. We're going to make money with ESPN. It's an identifiable offense. People know us. We're going to get recruits. Big recruits."

Finally, things made sense again. The only fear among fans was if they'd all be fooled again.

"I really like what's going on with this transition," McAfee continued. "I think it might take a little time. People might expect stuff right away—and I think they will—but hopefully it happens. But history says any time there is change, not a lot of things go right."

* * *

Indeed, nothing was easy for West Virginia in 2011. Holgorsen's stated goal, to keep things simple in life and in football, was challenged and ultimately shelved. In a business where the best game plan is to adapt and advance, Holgorsen was left with no other option. He could continue to do things exactly as he preferred, and risk losses and regression and a waning faith in the future. Or he could realize the shortcomings of his first Mountaineer team and change the way he called plays, ask the offense to play slower, and hope for the best.

Coaching transitions are never a cinch—to say nothing of coaching transitions that occurred like Holgorsen's did—and rarely has anyone traveled the path of least resistance at WVU. That path was especially difficult in 2011, complicated by the opposition and by the Mountaineers themselves.

"The whole thing was hard," he said. "Nothing is ever easy, where you don't face some sort of challenge, or adversity, but look at the season. Before it ever starts—and we don't need to talk about anything that happened, because everything ultimately works out for a reason—but we still have that. Then we start August 1 and start working toward one common goal, because that's the only way you can do it, but you face challenges every week. And we faced them and found a way."

The Mountaineers found a way all the way to the end, where they earned a third of the Big East Conference championship and an appearance in the Bowl Championship Series against Clemson in the Orange Bowl. So if Holgorsen could adjust, and the Mountaineers would change with him and reach a level that for a time seemed out of their reach, then why couldn't the people who live and die with the ups and downs make a few adjustments along the way? That was the hallmark of the 2011 season, a season that delivered the doubts, disasters, and defeats the fans had learned to loathe, but that also showcased the sort of serendipity you could get used to.

The very moment everything changed for the better for Holgorsen and the Mountaineers was also the very moment things looked the worst. It came, oddly enough, in a loss and when the momentum swung and landed a haymaker, as WVU's opponent blocked a field goal and returned it for a touchdown. The fans were again saddled with ·despair, but they shed it when they understood their Mountaineers had finally learned to use the event to get to back into the spotlight. The football team found ways to win by defying the circumstances that conspired against them. The fans then defied their past to anticipate the possibilities of the future.

Getting there was a chore, though. Holgorsen's first game was uniquely difficult. Under threatening skies, the Mountaineers played host to Marshall in the annual Friends of Coal Bowl. The first offensive series with Holgorsen in charge was a three-and-out, and the first punt of the season was returned for a touchdown, which spooked everyone who hoped to exorcise the special teams demons that haunted Stewart's three years in charge. The game was delayed two times by lightning; it started at 3:37 in the afternoon and was cancelled before all four quarters had been played, at 10:24 at night. WVU and Marshall played for two hours, 25 minutes, but they waited through four hours, 22 minutes of delays before the game was called with the Mountaineers leading 34-13.

A week later WVU beat Norfolk State, a pretty good team from the Football Championship Subdivision, 55-12, yet the Mountaineers trailed at the half, 12-10.

"We got booed off the field at halftime, which—well, I would have booed too," Holgorsen said.

The next game was at Maryland. The Terrapins always played tough against the Mountaineers and had just upset Miami the week before, but they finished at an awful 2-10. WVU led 34–10, but only won 37–31 and survived when the defense intercepted a Terrapin pass at the WVU 7-yard line with a little more than a minute left to play.

Next came the game everyone was looking forward to—a rare trip north for the Tigers of LSU. WVU had a 3-0 record and a spot at No. 16 in the Associated Press poll. LSU was also undefeated, having beaten the speedy Oregon Ducks in a much-hyped season opener played in Dallas, and was ranked No. 2. The matchup was good enough to convince ESPN to send its College GameDay set to campus for the first time.

The week leading up to the game should have been nothing but a festival for the school, the program, and the fans, for all the people who constantly gripe about never getting that type of a showcase. Instead it was almost completely overshadowed by the gloomy specter of conference realignment. The uncertainty added an edge of desperation, a feeling like WVU had to prove itself on the national stage, to a weekend that should have been one big, happy party.

Pitt and Syracuse announced the week before that they would leave the Big East Conference for the Atlantic Coast Conference, which threatened the future of the Big East and all its remaining members. The Mountaineers were looking for a way out, but no one, it seemed, wanted them and all of their accomplishments and tradition and appeal. WVU conceded long before that the ACC would not extend an invitation. The Southeastern Conference was more interested in Missouri, an informed opinion that seemed almost irrefutable all the way until it became a fact, but was nevertheless combated by WVU fans who were blinded by either their anger or anguish from again being left behind as major conferences expanded. The only league that wanted WVU was the Big East, but WVU wanted out in a bad way. The school was part of the meetings with the league and its members and its leaders; they all said things about expanding and preserving the league, but the Mountaineers were merely going through the motions as they tried to find a new home.

Maybe, though, WVU would beat LSU and again prove it could compete with and conquer the best of the best, as it had against the SEC's Georgia and the Big 12's Oklahoma. Maybe WVU could use the national stage as an audition. But by halftime, the Tigers had proven to be too talented, too deep, just too much for a WVU team that was still learning the offense, and was still finding the right people to play on defense.

LSU led 27–7, but then things started to change, and it seemed like there might be some more magic in that stadium that tends to cast a spell in night games. The Tigers dropped a sure touchdown pass on their first drive of the third quarter, and then missed a field goal, the first time in 42 trips inside the red zone they hadn't scored points.

WVU's offense then came alive, first driving 80 yards in six plays and scoring when Smith completed a 12-yard touchdown pass to tight end-turned-slot receiver Tyler Urban. The Tigers punted, and the Mountaineers needed just five plays to go 90 yards and score on Dustin Garrison's one-yard touchdown run. In just seven minutes, 40 seconds, the Mountaineers turned a blowout into a showdown.

It was 27–21, and just about all of the 62,056 fans were losing their minds and pumping gold towels in the air as the stadium blared "Seven Nation Army," by The White Stripes. Everything felt so good, so right ... and then LSU's Morris Claiborne returned the kickoff 99 yards for a touchdown. Claiborne did to the WVU faithful exactly what every untimely antagonist had done before him. The final score was 47–21; no one outside of Morgantown would remember it had been a one-possession game, that the Tigers looked vulnerable, if only for a moment.

No matter. WVU recovered and hammered Bowling Green the next week, and then did the same to Connecticut to open Big East play. The Mountaineers were 5-1 overall and 1-0 in the Big East. The only loss was to LSU, which was by then the top-ranked team in the country. The Mountaineers didn't look so bad themselves. They were the only ranked Big East team, and led the conference in the major offensive and defensive categories.

These were the very conditions WVU took into the game against Syracuse in 2010. As they had that year, the Orange beat WVU again, this time by a far more embarrassing final score of 49–23. That 26-point loss went much like the 26-point loss to a far-superior LSU team. Syracuse unplugged the Mountaineers by returning a kickoff for a touchdown to turn a 14–9 game into a 21–9 game. Now there was doubt about WVU and whether anything had really changed other than the leadership. Perhaps the Mountaineers were still the same, still the team that would fall once it stood tall, that would find a heartbeat and then suffer heartbreak. If you weren't sure that that's exactly how things go at WVU, then the following week was an all-inclusive lesson.

WVU was invited to join the Big 12 Conference. This would seem like a triumph, but it quickly became a travesty and seemed on the verge of becoming a tragedy. The Big 12 had lost Nebraska, Colorado, and Texas A&M, and was preparing to lose Missouri to the SEC. In the Mountaineers and Texas Christian University, it would add two programs from the Big East and end up with 10 members.

The Mountaineers were free from the uncertain future of the blundering Big East, which lost Syracuse and Pitt previously, and then TCU after the Horned Frogs agreed the previous November to leave the Mountain West and then abandoned their promise to the Big East in favor of the Big 12. No longer did WVU have to worry whether the Big East would lose its automatic Bowl Championship Series bid. Now the worry would be finding the resources and the personnel to compete with Texas and Oklahoma, finding the funds to travel to Waco, Texas, and Lawrence, Kansas, but those were welcome anxieties compared to the alternatives.

The excitement about a new life in a new league trumped everything else. The future was set. Reported by all the newspapers and websites on Tuesday, October 25, it was to be confirmed, and then celebrated at WVU the next day. The Big 12 and WVU were sending drafts of press releases and fact sheets back and forth. WVU was planning a press conference for Wednesday afternoon, and trying to figure out if a 3 p.m. start was better than a 4 p.m. start. Officials from the Big 12 were planning their travel to Morgantown. Important people at WVU were calling around to reporters to confirm details and share others, and even trade tips for visiting cities such as Austin, Texas, and Norman, Oklahoma. There was no confirmation from the university, but that wasn't relevant. There were no denials, not even from the people who were gushing about the news.

That night, WVU did something WVU never does, and released a statement after 9 p.m. "Contrary to media reports, there is no press conference scheduled for Wednesday concerning WVU's athletic conference affiliation. There are no further comments at this time," it read.

By morning, the partnership with the Big 12 had been derailed in a fashion that defied even WVU's history of dismay. The future was not set, and everything that had been on track to take WVU to this thrilling and lucrative destination had come off the tracks. Worse yet, there was no explanation that made sense, not when the finality had been so clear a day before. This wasn't about whether or not the Big 12 wanted WVU, or whether WVU was having second thoughts. All anyone knew for sure was that the Mountaineers were wanted and ecstatic and optimistic one day, and then stranded and rejected and depressed the next.

Then came the infuriating explanation. *The New York Times* reported Senate Minority Leader Mitch McConnell, a Republican representing Kentucky who happened to be a Louisville graduate and former student body president there, had become involved on behalf of his alma mater. McConnell, it was said, was tapping some of his buddies in the Big 12 on their shoulders and asking them to reconsider WVU's addition, and to give the Cardinals a look. West Virginia's congressional delegation was enraged, and ready to fight back on behalf of WVU. Democratic Senator Joe Manchin held a press conference that night and said he'd ask for an investigation if it was true McConnell immorally impacted the Big 12 after the conference reached an agreement with WVU.

"If someone as U.S. senator interfered after the process took place, then that's wrong and unacceptable," Manchin said.

Wednesday and Thursday were terribly traumatic for the state, the university, and its supporters. They had no idea how the ordeal would end, but they feared what they always feared—the worst. They feared being stuck in the Big East, and not because of anything that happened on a football field or a basketball court, not because of anything related to ticket sales for postseason games or the ratings of televised games. This was about something they couldn't control. This was politics, and it had at least succeeded in getting the Big 12 to pause and think things over at the expense of the Mountaineers and their happiness. There was a road game Saturday against Rutgers, but that was hardly anyone's concern, especially with a home game coming a week later against Louisville. The more the silence lingered, the more it seemed like WVU would be deserted. The melancholy masses remembered that something good couldn't just happen to the Mountaineers. It either had to happen with unforeseen circumstances attached, or it had to seem tantalizingly close to happening, only to be taken away unexpectedly.

Then Friday arrived, and with it, the conclusion. The Big 12 had come back around to the Mountaineers, and again invited and accepted them into the Big 12.

"I wouldn't be completely honest if I didn't say we didn't have a little bit of nervousness," WVU's Athletic Director Oliver Luck said.

There was a conference call in the afternoon and the league's interim commissioner, Chuck Neinas, the same guy WVU hired in 2007 to assist in the search for Rich Rodriguez's replacement, used a whole new language to try and explain the delay, which he said was about logistics. WVU had joined TCU as a future member, and those two were readying to join the nine other schools in the league. Trouble was, one of those nine was Missouri, which, by every indication available at that time, was heading to the SEC. Still, the Tigers had not yet made up their mind and they had options: would they depart and leave the Big 12 with 10 teams, the number of members most of the Big 12 schools preferred? Or would Missouri stay and leave the Big 12 with 11 teams?

Suddenly the Big 12 was puzzled, and a long ordeal that had been dominated by network contracts, the amount of televisions in a state, and the miles between campuses was inexplicably extended by the numbers 10 and 11. Suddenly, the learned scholars and academicians in charge of the Big 12 members realized it would be different putting together sports schedules with 11 teams than it would be with 10. That, Neinas explained, was the nature of the delay. Neither McConnell, Manchin, nor the short runway at Morgantown's airport was offered as part of the explanation. A problem as simple and as identifiable as scheduling logistics was said to have come up at the 11th hour to delay the process for 48 hours.

The Mountaineers, who were told days before that they were

invited regardless of Missouri's decision, had been welcomed to the Big 12 with a fruitcake, but at least it was done. The university would later sue the Big East to get out of the conference early, and the Big East would sue WVU for breaching its contract with the conference, but that was a sidebar all the way through a settlement that paid the Big East $20 million, and freed WVU effective July 1, 2012. The Mountaineers were out and unapologetic.

A day after formally accepting the invitation from the Big 12, the Mountaineers beat Rutgers for the 17th straight season, this time after falling behind 31–21 at halftime on a cold, windy, snowy day in New Jersey. They held the Scarlet Knights scoreless in the second half, scored 20 unanswered points, and won 41–31.

"That was one of the most challenging probably 24 hours of my entire life," Holgorsen said eight months later, still chilled by the circumstances and in awe of the result. "We had to win that one if we wanted to do anything, and we were getting drilled. The weather was miserable. I mean, it was just awful. And we figured out how to win the game."

Next was Senator McConnell's beloved Louisville, which had beaten WVU only once, in 2006, since joining the Big East in 2005. After those first three meetings, the team that won ended up representing the conference in the BCS. But after the Cardinals hired Steve Kragthorpe in 2007 and WVU hired Stewart in 2008, the games no longer meant as much.

The 2011 game was something of a return to the rivalry. It meant something for the present and for the future. There was competition on the field and off of it. Louisville's second-year coach, Charlie Strong, was a known winner who'd burnished his reputation with national championship teams at the University of Florida. Strong was building something with the Cardinals. Holgorsen, similarly renowned, though without the fancy rings, was supposed to be building something with the Mountaineers. And then there was the political football, where Louisville's McConnell was accused of running an end around and WVU's Manchin was throwing penalty flags in the nation's capital.

The Mountaineers trailed at home 24–21 in the third quarter when Tyler Bitancurt lined up to kick a short field goal that would simply tie the score to start the fourth quarter. Louisville cornerback Adrian Bushell slipped around the right side of WVU's line and blocked the kick. The ball bounced into the hands of another cornerback, Arthur Johnson, who returned it 82 yards for a touchdown. The Cardinals won 38–35, and for the sixth straight season the Mountaineers had two losses in the Big East, this time while they were doing everything to get out because they felt the conference was beneath them.

"You can pinpoint that one particular play and it was a 10-point swing and say it's a reason we lost, but that's not true," Holgorsen said.

Actually, that one play was indeed why WVU lost, but it was also why WVU would go on to win the final three games of the regular season, each one decided on the final possession. When the Mountaineers got together to review the film the day after the loss to Louisville, they watched the blocked field goal and saw Bushell make what was just a good football play. While that wasn't an explanation the Mountaineers would accept, it was the reality they had no other choice but to acknowledge.

But nothing Bushell or Johnson did on that play was the focus. When WVU looked the play over, Holgorsen took his eyes away from what happened between the lines and instead placed them on the sidelines. He asked his team to watch how the WVU sideline reacted and how the Louisville sideline reacted. He'd been doing the same thing during the entire review session to get a point across to his players, so that they might see how their investment in a game compared to the opponent's, but it never stung like it did right there.

"Their [sideline] was clearly more energetic," Holgorsen said. "Our biggest goal was to get them to the point they were cheering for everyone."

This wasn't some sort of a motivational tactic. Holgorsen was serious. He'd seen his team confronted by adverse circumstances in each of its three losses, and he'd seen his teams shrink in the moment rather than rise above it. Claiborne's kickoff return started a run of 20 unanswered points by LSU. Syracuse's kickoff return started a 35–14 streak for the Orange. Louisville's score preceded a turnover by WVU, and though the Mountaineers would score a touchdown next, the Cardinals answered with a 13-play touchdown drive thanks to a key fourth-down conversion.

The point Holgorsen was trying to make was the other team was more devoted to the outcome, and thus better able to handle adversity. That had to change, and Holgorsen was going to make sure he did his part to facilitate it. The Mountaineers needed to win their final three games of the regular season and get some help if they wanted to win the Big East and get to the BCS, but they needed to help themselves first.

It began by Holgorsen acknowledging for the first time that he'd tinkered with the way he called plays against Louisville, after WVU had gone only 2-for-13 on third down against Rutgers. Before that, Holgorsen was either stubborn or steadfast in defending his ways, saying the schemes were sound but the execution was not. Yet after the first nine games, he'd grown tired of third-and-long. The Mountaineers had seen 122 third downs, and 55 required seven yards or more. The offense was good, but without that obstacle Holgorsen knew it could have been great. So he changed the way things would go on second down.

"When we got to second down, we tried to get half of it," he said.

His high-speed, high-powered offense was literally not going all-out on second down. That was a shame, because second down had been the best down for his passing offense, where it had its highest completion percentage and passer efficiency rating and its most first downs, big gains, and touchdowns.

"We're not a team that can convert third-and-long," Holgorsen said. "Our pass protection is not very good, which puts us in a bind when we try to throw the ball downfield. Third-and-long has been troublesome, but our third-down percentage was better [8-for-14 against Louisville] for us, based on doing a better job on second down."

That wasn't all, though. WVU's offensive line was everything from a concern to a catastrophe in Holgorsen's first season. It was the unit most impacted by his predecessor and by the transition. Stewart's recruiting practices, his propensity to undersign recruits while the rest of college football was finding ways to sign more athletes than there were spots available, left the Mountaineers without a lot of depth, especially on the offensive line.

Holgorsen's system also asked his line to pass block a lot. Defenses responded by blitzing to attack the line, though sometimes defensive lines could dominate the Mountaineers without extra blitzers, which really discouraged Holgorsen. He finally moved away from drop-back passes and deep routes, and asked for more quick throws.

The initial admission he was going to do things differently would have qualified as a big development on most weeks, but that was also the week Holgorsen got serious about the constitution of his team. That three-game stretch to end the season would begin with a road game against Cincinnati, and Holgorsen wasn't about to make that trip with any excess baggage. He was only going to take players ready to help WVU win; if that meant traveling with 50 or 55 players, so be it. The way he saw things, the Mountaineers had won 60 games in the previous six years, but all that past success did in 2011 was convince some guys they could simply show up and expect to win. A lot of those players either hadn't played or hadn't contributed to those 60 wins. If those players, or if players guilty of a similar nonchalance, didn't prove themselves in practice before the trip to take on the Bearcats, they'd be left home.

"You take who wants to win, you take who wants to pull for their teammates, you take who wants to be all-in on this thing and not guys who pout and mope because they're not playing," Holgorsen said. "We're going to be a united team, and the only way I know how to get that accomplished is to make sure that we take only people focused on heading in the right direction."

Sixty-four players made the trip, maybe 10 fewer than normal. Cincinnati scored early on a short drive, but WVU countered with a touchdown pass from Smith to Bailey, a score that triggered a celebration on the sideline that stopped just short of players pouring Gatorade on Holgorsen. Later in the game, the Mountaineers sacked Cincinnati quarterback Zach Collaros and forced a fumble in the end zone. Defensive tackle Julian Miller recovered for a touchdown—

and that sideline party featured everything that could earn an unsportsmanlike penalty except one of the Mountaineers grabbing the flag from an official and throwing it on himself. On the final play of the game, safety Eain Smith zoomed through a gap in Cincinnati's line and blocked a field goal that would have forced overtime. Instead the game ended with the Mountaineers up 24–21, and the players happily dancing on the field and shamelessly taunting Cincinnati's fans and students.

The Bearcats had lost for the first time in conference play, and Collaros, one of the best players in the Big East, was lost for the rest of the regular season. He'd broken his right ankle when WVU defensive end Bruce Irvin sacked him in the end zone. The same day, Louisville lost to Pitt and now had two conference losses. With Collaros out and the Bearcats ahead of Louisville, WVU, Rutgers, and Pitt by just a game, the conference championship was again within reach. The Mountaineers would need help still, but winning the final two games would help the most. WVU was off the following week, but Cincinnati lost again, this time to Rutgers, while Louisville beat Connecticut. Now WVU, Cincinnati, Rutgers, Louisville, and Pitt had two conference losses.

The Mountaineers returned to the field the following week and returned to their old ways. They fell behind Pitt 14–0 in the first quarter of the 104th Backyard Brawl. In the third quarter, a second turnover fielding a punt led to a second Panther field goal and a 20–7 lead. The WVU defense rallied to dominate the second half and put on a performance that illustrated exactly what Holgorsen had been requesting weeks earlier. The defense had a relentless energy and finished with 10 sacks, nine in the final 25 plays, and four on the final drive when the Panthers had a chance to win the game with a field goal but lost 21–20.

Pitt was no longer eligible for the conference title and Rutgers lost to Connecticut, but Cincinnati beat Syracuse and Louisville beat South Florida to set up the final week. The Cardinals were finished with the regular season at 7-5 overall and 5-2 in the league. WVU was 8-3 and 4-2, and would play the following week at USF, the school that used to always ruin things for the Mountaineers. Cincinnati had the same record, and would finish at home against Connecticut two days later.

To get to the BCS, the Mountaineers had to beat their nemesis, and had to have the Bearcats beat the Huskies. Any other outcome gave the BCS berth to Louisville or Cincinnati. It was typically torturous for the Mountaineers and their fans, who knew they could win and still it might not be enough. WVU's fate was not in its hands, but in the hands of Cincinnati's backup quarterback, who was only playing because the Mountaineers had injured the starter. It was just too ironic that the injury that cost Cincinnati one game, maybe two, and brought WVU back into the Big East race could ultimately conspire to cost WVU the BCS.

The game at USF was no different than any of their previous matchups; the speed the Bulls had on defense foiled what the Mountaineers wanted to do on offense. Yet the Mountaineers found ways to stay in the game thanks to the defense and special teams, both of which had done their damage throughout the season. Cornerback Pat Miller, who had been removed from the starting lineup, returned his first career interception 52 yards for one touchdown, and receiver Tavon Austin returned a kickoff 90 yards for another. That score answered a USF touchdown and gave WVU a 20–10 lead. A sloppy stretch by WVU, with three turnovers on 11 plays, included two interceptions by Smith in four passes. The second was returned 24 yards for a touchdown, and WVU was suddenly down 27–20 with 9:49 to go.

"I'm not going to lie to you," Julian Miller said. "That was ridiculous. We still had 10 minutes left in the game, but that hurt. It really did."

On 12 drives, Holgorsen's 16th-ranked offense had 214 yards and no touchdowns. On the next two drives, that same offense had 140 yards and 10 points and won the game. On the first, Smith and Bailey connected for a 10-yard gain on a fourth-and-1 in WVU territory, and Garrison scored on a five-yard run. That tied the score 27–27, but special teams slipped up at the worst, and yet most predictable time, allowing the Bulls to return the following kickoff 53 yards to give the offense the ball at WVU's 41 with 5:09 left to play.

"Punch in the face," linebacker Najee Goode said.

The Mountaineers were out of timeouts when USF's quarterback, B. J. Daniels, ran for seven yards on a third-and-4. Everything was lining up for a familiar catastrophe until the Mountaineers made something happen, something that never happened *for* them and always seemed to happen *to* them. WVU blitzed but sent the pressure one way while the play went the other way. Goode was held up, but the delay actually helped and gave him a moment to spot Daniels. Goode decided to stray from his assignment and chase Daniels. He put one arm out for the quarterback and the other smacked the ball to the ground. Miller was on the other side of the play and realized he couldn't get to the ball, but he saw his teammate, nose guard Jorge Wright, run toward the ball and dip down to grab it.

Wright ran through the play and past the ball.

"My heart dropped," Miller said. "I saw the offensive linemen get close, but then I saw Doug Rigg curl up on it. I was so happy I jumped in there myself."

Rigg was WVU's weak side linebacker. He'd been a starter early in the season, but he broke his left hand against LSU and had to miss the next two games after he had surgery to insert a screw and help the fracture heal. He was a starter again by the end of the season, but wore a protective cast the rest of the way. In a private moment, Rigg would admit he had a hard time catching passes. It was Rigg, though, who was on the ground and reached out to grab the ball, pull it close, and get the recovery for the offense at the 26 with 3:02 to go.

"The guy on the team with one good hand got the ball?" Goode asked himself.

WVU still had some work to do, and picked up two quick first downs to get to the USF 42, but Smith then made a mistake and took a sack and a nine-yard loss. The offense hurried and gained nine yards back on the next down before an incomplete pass on third down. It was fourth down with 13 seconds left. WVU needed 10 yards for a first down, but probably even more than that to get into Bitancurt's range for a shot at a game-winning kick.

Smith made a call at the line of scrimmage, relied on the years he spent playing with Bailey in high school, pumped slightly to open a window in the middle of the field, and then threw into it. Bailey leaped on the run and caught the ball with his oversized hands, the type of catch that words don't do justice. Bailey claimed, and rightfully so, "that catch pretty much made our season."

He did everything he could to stretch out parallel to the turf to catch the ball, but he couldn't protect himself as he hit the ground hard, bounced, and rolled to a stop at the USF 26. He was hurt and immediately tried to call a timeout—one the Mountaineers didn't have—before falling back to the ground. The offense hurried to the line of scrimmage, but Bailey was still lying on USF's side of the line and couldn't get himself onto WVU's side. Running back Shawne Alston swooped in and stood over Bailey.

"I saw him lying on the ground and I said, 'Get up, we've got to hurry up and spike the ball so we can get the field goal team out here,'" Alston said. "I don't even think he realized what was going on. I tried to pick him up, but I couldn't. I started dragging him."

Bailey finally got to his feet and lined up next to Alston.

"Then I look up and we're not even in the right spot," Alston said. "We're over the ball, so I get him to back up a little bit. Then we spike the ball."

Alston prevented a disaster with three seconds to spare. If Smith waited and Alston and Bailey never righted themselves, the Mountaineers would have run out of time. In a flash, Bailey was on the sideline wincing and accepting congratulations, and Bitancurt came out and kicked the game-winning field goal for a share of the conference title.

Two days later, Cincinnati was routing Connecticut, scoring twice on defense and then once on offense for a 21–0 lead. The BCS berth was inching closer to WVU, which would finish in a three-way tie with Louisville and the Bearcats, but win a tiebreaker by being ranked highest in the BCS standings. The celebration was on and the Mountaineers couldn't ignore it. Left tackle Don Barclay and left guard Josh Jenkins, who missed the season with a knee injury, decided to watch the game with Urban and right tackle Pat Eger at their place.

"We were going crazy," Barclay said.

They were thinking about the Orange Bowl and the sun and beaches in Miami, but just when it looked like things would turn out for the best for the Mountaineers, there was a scare at the end, the kind of scare that reminds WVU it is WVU. Down 35–12, UConn started to rally.

"They scored and we were like, 'Oh, geez, we better watch this,'" Barclay said. "Then they got the ball and scored and got it down to eight points and it was like, 'This can't happen.'"

For a change, it did not happen. The Huskies never got the ball back, and the Bearcats gave the Mountaineers the necessary bump into the BCS.

Believe it or not—and believe me when I say WVU fans could not believe it—the Mountaineers got all the breaks all the way to the end. It just never, ever happened like that for WVU.

"We never panicked because we're all a bunch of professionals," Holgorsen said. "The whole coaching staff—the *whole* coaching staff—was a bunch of professionals. We never quit believing, and we got that related to our players. That didn't mean it was easy, but we took a deep breath and worked hard to get better."

The outcome of the Orange Bowl was almost inconsequential compared to what happened in the regular season. A Big East championship and the league's spot in the BCS was, in reality, a significant achievement. There were defeats, distractions, and dissatisfactions along the way, the things that often disrupt or destroy teams that are young or imprecise or following a new leader, teams such as WVU in 2011.

Holgorsen had more regular-season wins in his first season than any of the previous 32 WVU coaches had in their first seasons. His roster was largely composed and legitimately compromised by his predecessor, but Holgorsen forced together parts on offense and trusted his coordinator on defense to make it work. While he was far from perfect and would admit and display flaws, he did nothing to empower the people who feared the guy on the bench outside the casino might overshadow the guy with the headset on the sideline. Maybe he didn't wear the team colors, but Holgorsen actually developed and displayed the resiliency and resolve that best define the teams and the people of West Virginia.

And then at the end, when the Mountaineers avoided all the misfortune and embraced every break that they needed, when all the worries about what might be in that first season and beyond seemed to be put to rest, when people remembered Holgorsen was hired to transform the football culture at WVU, they entered the offseason hopeful again that things were changing. That was new, invigorating, and magnificent.

Maybe good luck was finally wearing Old Gold and Blue, and maybe something that seemed so good would end up being just that. Or maybe this was just another tantalizing tease, another step closer to the splendid vision that always disappears when WVU and its supporters reach out to grab it.

20
SEVENTY

So I've shared a bunch of stories and secrets and sidebars that I believe have defined the past several years of West Virginia football. I've told just one lie. A couple pages back, I said the result of the 2012 Orange Bowl would be inconsequential. Allow me to explain.

Look at everything that happened before and then during the season, from when Dana Holgorsen was surreptitiously hired as the head coach-in-waiting, up until the Bowl Championship Series bid was clinched. Then try to understand not only what happened, but also how and why it did.

Winning the Big East and securing the Orange Bowl bid was a very big, very commendable accomplishment for the players and the coaches. The former were made to go along with a new program, while the latter were forced to get along with one another. I'm not sure the final score in the 13th game would, or should, have changed the fact that mattered most, which was that this convoluted plan to position the program for the future had crumbled, composed itself, and still worked. If WVU won or lost against Clemson, it couldn't change that simple premise.

A lot of people thought the 2011 season—preceded by the ill-advised union of Holgorsen and Bill Stewart and the way it fell apart—would be somewhere between underwhelming and disastrous. There were times things trended and maybe even threatened to end that way, but it didn't happen. WVU wound up as the Big East's resilient representative in the BCS, all while acting as if it was too cool for school by fleeing the conference.

That should have served as sufficient proof that the past was the past, the present was good, and the future could be great. Given that Holgorsen seemed to grow so much within the season and Geno Smith and Tavon Austin and Stedman Bailey and others would do the same in the offseason, everything felt fun again—and that wasn't going to be changed by the events of the Orange Bowl.

I'm willing to admit my statement was inaccurate, though.

Now, I still really believe it, and I really believe you'd be lying to yourself if you didn't agree—the outcome of the bowl wouldn't enhance or diminish what was achieved before it. I saw all of these weird things happening late in the season, things I didn't recognize or anticipate, and I often thought, "Well, this doesn't work with the book I'm writing." After all, I was essentially documenting WVU's history of bad things happening at the worst time.

Yet after the events late in the 2011 regular season, be it the blocked field goal against Cincinnati, the sacks against Pitt, the unbelievable ending against South Florida, or the way the Bearcats toyed with WVU's emotions as they put away Connecticut and gave the Mountaineers the BCS berth, I started to think it all fit. Perfectly. Things were changing. The dread was being defeated.

Everything Athletic Director Oliver Luck suggested, and President Jim Clements approved, was about moving WVU beyond its past. These men, aware of WVU's recent past and witnesses to it on some level, were not spooked by it. They were instead focused on the future, and they were willing to put a whole lot on the line to get there.

Pulling the trigger on hiring Holgorsen and then jettisoning Stewart, trying to get out of the Big East and then (twice) accepting an invitation to the Big 12, it was always about making WVU a place that could do and be a lot of the things outsiders did not think WVU could do and be. So there was something poetic about the way the regular season ended, and how the Mountaineers did unto others as so many others had done unto them. You can safely assume WVU and its fans were among the doubters. To be so wrong had to feel so good.

And then came the bowl game, the once-guaranteed annual occasion of WVU's shame, where the team would go to park the car for the offseason but always seem to bump into the garage and mess up the paint job. There were clues it might again go badly against a Clemson team that was ranked No. 14, had been 8-0, and twice defeated Virginia Tech.

Dustin Garrison, the bright freshman running back who had taken control of the position with his performance against LSU and then rushed for 291 yards a week later, tore up his left knee in the team's first practice in Miami and would miss the game. That only weakened a wobbly backfield that saw two running backs, including Vernard Roberts, who for a time was the top player at the position, leave the team after the end of the regular season. A few days after Garrison was hurt, Connor Arlia, a walk-on freshman who had impressed during the early bowl practices and was going to play in the game, broke his right leg, cracked two ribs, bruised a lung, and lacerated a kidney in a jet skiing accident at a team function.

The Mountaineers were understandably disappointed by the news, but they wouldn't be beaten. Not only did they play better than they had in previous bowls, they were by many measures better than anyone to ever play in any bowl. Not bad for the school that went 16 years and eight bowls between postseason victories.

The Mountaineers actually scored more points than any team in the history of all bowls. You think about that.

It was a 70–33 final score and, if such a thing can be said of such an uneven outcome, it really wasn't that close. Never mind Clemson once led 17–14. WVU was just indisputably better. A long list of records were set along the way, with Smith passing for six touchdowns and 401 yards, better than Orange Bowl bests set by Matt Leinart and Tom Brady. Only Chuck Long had thrown as many touchdowns in a bowl game, when he led Iowa to a victory against Texas in the 1984 Freedom Bowl. Austin set a record for all bowls with four touchdown catches. The same team that had made a habit of slow starts, that scored only 68 points in 12 first quarters and had trailed at halftime five times and was tied another time, scored 49 points against Clemson before halftime. Never before had any bowl team done that. Thirty-five of WVU's points came in the second quarter alone.

In one incredible sequence the Mountaineers were both who they'd been at the end of the regular season, and who they wanted to be throughout the season. The defense made impactful plays, and the offense was unstoppable. It began with the Tigers near WVU's end zone and just three yards away from what looked to be an inevitable 24–14 lead. Doug Rigg, the linebacker still playing with one hand in a protective brace, managed to pull the ball out of the running back's grasp. Safety Darwin Cook sneaked into the pile, grabbed the ball, and returned it 99 yards for a touchdown. Cook punctuated the play by tackling the Orange Bowl mascot, Obie.

"Obie doubted us, too, so I had to tackle him," Cook said, referring to another ESPN poll that gave WVU no chance, this time one that showed 73 percent of the country thought the Tigers would win. Clemson was never the same after that play. The Mountaineers knew it.

"What we saw on film was when Clemson gets down, they have no fight left in them," safety Eain Smith said after the game. "That's exactly what we saw tonight. I saw it when Cook took that fumble back. I saw their body language go way down immediately. I looked at their faces and I looked at the sideline, and I saw their body language and I knew they didn't want to play the game."

WVU's defense knew a whole bunch of other things about Clemson that proved true during the game. Cornerback Keith Tandy said Clemson quarterback Tajh Boyd would sometimes telegraph passes and force throws late in a half or a game. Late in the second quarter, with his team down 35–20, Boyd threw a pass that Pat Miller picked off to set up a touchdown. Other defensive players knew Boyd would run a few times throughout the game, but that he would expose the ball. On the very next drive, defensive end Bruce Irvin ran some 20 yards from the left side of the field to track down Boyd on the right side. He tackled Boyd, swiped at the ball, and knocked it loose.

The officials said Boyd was down. Irvin disagreed and the play was reviewed. The replay overturned the call, gave Irvin the fumble, and put the ball in Geno Smith's hands for one more touchdown before halftime.

"That was the only time at halftime we sat in there and said, 'Well, I guess we don't have any adjustments,'" Holgorsen said.

WVU's fans, whether they were in the stands or at home, nevertheless wondered how they'd lose this game and how much it would hurt to see a fine first-half performance and a 49–20 lead disappear. That is a game-day tradition, as indelible as the band playing "Simple Gifts" before a home game and the crowd singing "Country Roads" after the win.

Instead, the Mountaineers' two best drives of the game were probably the first two after halftime. The offense countered whatever counters Clemson's defense offered and raced down the field twice in a row to make it 63–20 in the third quarter. Those halftime anxieties were gone, replaced by a serious conversation about when Holgorsen would remove his starters, who might get the ball two more times in that quarter, and, who knows, possibly score 77 points and really challenge the boundaries of sportsmanship.

Really, these were the thoughts WVU fans were having. In a bowl game. The fourth quarter was a party in the stands for the many who braved the travel and the economy and the calendar and made the trip. WVU didn't sell the majority of the tickets allocated by the Orange Bowl, but it might not have that problem again for a few years.

For a place that will likely forever be haunted by 13-9, the Orange Bowl victory served as a counterbalance. The whole 70-33 thing took on a life uniquely of its own. It peaked when the university purchased billboard space on Interstate 79 and Interstate 68 and posted a message to remind anyone from anywhere about what happened in Miami. On the left side was a large "70" with an orange standing in for the zero. To the right was a sentence that said, "It's not just our speed limit." Just below that was a photograph of the final score on the scoreboard.

There was one blow that the business of college football could land in the afterglow of the victory. Rich Rodriguez had been hired as the head coach at the University of Arizona on November 22, and he'd pieced together much of the old gang he had at West Virginia and then at Michigan. He never hired a defensive coordinator, which built obvious concern and speculation that the choice would be Jeff Casteel.

Rodriguez had tried once and failed to lure Casteel away from WVU, but he figured to have better luck the second time. Holgorsen and Casteel coexisted in 2011. There were no indications they didn't get along, but similarly there were no indications they much liked one another. They quite likely worked and succeeded in spite of one another.

No one on the outside ever knew the true nature of their relationship because there were no obvious, ominous signs of the sort of awkwardness or even contempt that could have complicated their arrangement. Even with the way Stewart went out, that sort of peace was to be expected, and not because Holgorsen said at his first press conference that his top priority was to "keep Jeff Casteel happy." No, Casteel was the good guy at WVU, the one who'd not only remained with Stewart years earlier because his family and his friends and his players and his state meant so much to him, but who had also remained above the fray through some pretty adverse circumstances in his 11 years with the Mountaineers. He never publicly bad-mouthed Rodriguez or Stewart or Holgorsen or anything that happened once those two were together. He never campaigned for a raise or more control or less interference. Even the occasions he had to consider other jobs, most notably as Vanderbilt's defensive coordinator after the 2010 season and after Holgorsen had arrived and been promised the future, were private and quiet. People respected him for that as much as they did for his unquestioned success.

It was impossible not to see his exit coming, though. He'd outgrown WVU, not because he'd gotten too big, but because it no longer fit around him. He left WVU for Arizona a week after the Orange Bowl. He brought with him longtime defensive line coach Bill Kirelawich, who Rodriguez had moved from the sideline to behind a desk when he started at WVU in 2001, and cornerbacks coach David Lockwood. Though Casteel took a lower salary, though Kirelawich had been at

WVU for 32 years, though Lockwood had played and coached at WVU before Stewart brought him back in 2008, they left for a better situation. No one on the defensive staff was guaranteed anything beyond the 2011 season—and people forgot that while Casteel had signed a three-year contract in 2011 and his three assistants signed two-year deals, Holgorsen was initially scheduled to take over and have the final say beginning in 2012. He could have cleaned house and brought in his own guys. So it made sense for Casteel to leave, to look out for his own best interests, and for Kirelawich and Lockwood to do the same.

Oh, it did bring back some of the old anger aimed toward Rodriguez, the very feelings that had been put in storage as he was shamed at Michigan, and when he tried to restore some goodwill in West Virginia. Some were mad at Casteel for associating himself with Rodriguez again after Casteel had blossomed on his own and with teams that really relied on and won with his defense. It saddened most to see Casteel leave after such a good run at the school, but this was also the guy whose credentials were routinely questioned because of his unorthodox 3-3-5 scheme. It didn't matter how good his defenses were for years and years in a row. It wasn't a 4-3 or a 3-4 and that, for some reason, bothered some fans, who were relieved to see Casteel and his scheme head out West.

Plus, the Mountaineers had Holgorsen. You could say what you want about the defense, but while Holgorsen had just coached a team to 70 points, Casteel had, in reality, coached the defense that allowed the third-most points in a season in school history. Timing is everything in sports, and WVU had Holgorsen at a time when points per game was the statistic most closely linked to wins in college football. In a way, the program was able to press the reset button. With Holgorsen it could get back to the high-speed, high-powered offense it had with Rodriguez and there was something therapeutic about that. If there was a proper way to end a year on a high that would overshadow every low that came before it and any one that might one day follow, the Orange Bowl was it. WVU and everyone behind it entered the offseason unusually optimistic. Never before had the past seemed so

WAITING FOR THE FALL

far away, and never before had the future appeared so bright and shiny in the distance. It couldn't arrive soon enough. WVU was once again ready for what was next, as Smith said when he woke up the echoes from not long ago.

"The sky," he said, "is the limit."

300

Epilogue

West Virginia football bravely entered a new world on July 1, 2012. After 21 years in the Big East Conference, the Mountaineers joined the Big 12 Conference with guns blazing. A celebration on campus included all the coaches and student athletes, and pretty much everyone else who had something to do with the athletic department. The Mountaineer mascot, Jonathan Kimble, was beckoned to the front of a packed room at Touchdown Terrace. There, the president of the university goaded Kimble into leading the crowd in a "Let's go ... Mountaineers!" chant.

This, mind you, took place just feet away from newly installed Big 12 Commissioner Bob Bowlsby, a universally respected athletic director at multiple schools who had also served on the United States Olympic Committee (USOC). Kimble jolted Bowlsby and everyone else into the reality that the Mountaineers had not merely arrived, but that they intended to be heard in the Big 12.

The party was a formality, just the period at the end of the last sentence on the last page of the last chapter of a quirky story. The Mountaineers, despite a dubious twist powered by political pandering, had been bound for the Big 12 since October 28, 2011. The consummation of that relationship ended a rather brief courtship of only about a month.

Prior to that, WVU had spent months anticipating and reacting to conference realignment throughout collegiate athletics, and the Big 12 had been doing the same. Both had been reactive rather than proactive, but that was about all they could do at that time.

Pitt and Syracuse were accepted into the Atlantic Coast Conference on September 17, 2011, which doomed the Big East. Days later WVU was in play. The Mountaineers got a boost in the Big 12's direction thanks to a forgotten hero of the past, one who didn't so much put the

Mountaineers on the map as much as he made the map.

"I called Don Nehlen and said, 'Coach, would you mind putting a call in to your old friend Chuck Neinas?'" WVU Athletic Director Oliver Luck said, explaining for the first time the process that led WVU to the Big 12.

It started with Nehlen reaching out to his longtime colleague and the Big 12's interim commissioner at that time.

"I didn't know Chuck all too well, and I certainly didn't know him the way that Coach Nehlen knew him," Luck said. "Fortunately, they had been great friends over the years, so that gave us an opportunity to reach out and get things going."

Neinas had a lengthy history with the Mountaineers, beyond being contracted by WVU (but never utilized, owing to Bill Stewart's sudden hiring) to help the school replace Rich Rodriguez in 2007. At that time, under the Neinas Sports Services banner, he was a headhunter who consulted schools in coaching searches and told them who might be interested and who would be a good fit. Prior to that, though, he was commissioner of the old Big Eight Conference from 1971–80 and then the executive director of the College Football Association from 1980–97. He built a rather round Rolodex through the years and knew everybody in the business. If Neinas didn't know you, chances were you were a nobody.

Neinas knew WVU beyond Nehlen. When Neinas was running the Big Eight, he employed an associate commissioner named Dick Martin, who would later be WVU's athletic director. Martin had hired Nehlen to coach at WVU before the 1980 season. Martin left WVU in 1981 and was replaced by Fred Schaus, someone else Neinas had known previously. Gordon Gee was WVU's president at that time, and would later move on to lead Brown, Vanderbilt, Colorado, and Ohio State, but Neinas would remember him as the man who was put in charge of WVU before the age of 40.

So when Nehlen placed his call to Neinas and spoke of the Mountaineers, Neinas had plenty of past knowledge to reference.

"A lot of people who I trusted spoke very highly of West Virginia," Neinas said.

Nehlen would tell Luck that Neinas wanted to talk to WVU, and the Mountaineers were suddenly in the game. WVU then put on the blitz, arranging a call from Gene Budig, another former university president Neinas knew and revered. Then the present WVU president, Jim Clements, used a back channel to arrange an appointment to call and sway Neinas.

"Jim Clements is a pretty good salesman," Neinas said, echoing the words Luck used to describe how he came to be convinced he could have success at WVU.

What Neinas knew about the Mountaineers was one thing in the university's favor, but one thing WVU did not know was perhaps more important. The Big 12 was already researching WVU. It was in the midst of an independent evaluation of the Mountaineers, as well as other schools, but at least WVU wasn't asking the Big 12 to start from scratch. Many of the things WVU's ambassadors said were things Neinas and the Big 12 were aware of already.

The Mountaineers appeared to be a good fit for the Big 12. WVU is a land-grant institution, a flagship university like other Big 12 schools. There was additional commonality in that WVU and other Big 12 schools rallied around natural resources and agriculture. And WVU had a pretty good football program, and an athletic department that made itself available at an opportune time for everyone.

"We had an expansion committee and we actually retained three outside consultants to help us with an objective view of potential candidates, and we also had input from our two television partners, plus our own evaluation," Neinas said. "We researched it very well and soon it became obvious that, along with TCU and their program and location, West Virginia was the strongest program that was interested. And we were interested in them. There was no question bringing them in was going to strengthen the conference."

On October 24, the Big 12 decided to formally invite the Mountaineers as its 10th team.

"I remember exactly where Jim and I were," Luck said. "I was sitting in the Coliseum interviewing Jerry West. He did a book signing on a Monday. He and I were on the floor of the Coliseum, kind of doing a Charlie Rose interview. There were a couple thousand people there, a really good turnout. Jim and his wife, Beth, were sitting in the front row, maybe 10 or 15 feet away. I could tell Jim's phone rang and it turned out he got a message and it was positive news; Chuck called and said, 'Hey, I'd like to invite you to our conference.'"

Clements would save that message for some time, perhaps just to serve as a reminder throughout the unbelievable affairs that unfolded the rest of that week that Neinas did indeed call and that Clements had not imagined it. Eventually, the Mountaineers were in and rescued from whatever suffering and indignity they might have experienced as a leftover in the Big East.

So many people believed WVU's move was about athletics, and while that's largely true, it's not entirely true. Luck had witnessed similar conference shifts in the past and the side effects they caused, particularly and most directly while working in Houston. He tried his hardest to help WVU avoid becoming collateral damage.

"If you take a program like ours that has had the record of success we had, I think that being able to ultimately find ourselves in a power conference was crucial to what we do," Luck said. "I've been very sensitive to this and you've probably heard me say this as well having lived in Houston, but this happened to the folks at SMU, Houston, and TCU when all of a sudden the Southwest Conference fell apart and they were left out.

"That not only affected the athletic programs at, say, the University of Houston, but it affected the entire university. Perception is not always reality, and people looked at that university as a second-tier school and would say, 'Well, it's not Texas A&M,' only because Houston wasn't in the Big 12. If you look at the metrics, it's every bit as good a school.

"What it boiled down to was this existential issue: Can we continue to maintain the things we do, can we continue to support a lot of Olympic sports, continue the many things we do in academics and not just athletics, without the benefit of having a strong football program, which is the engine that moves the bus along? Without having a football program in a power conference and a great home schedule and sold-out games and great bowl opportunities and more television dollars, all those other things maybe aren't possible."

WVU neither won nor lost its legal battle against the Big East in February when the university agreed to a $20 million settlement. It was a costly expense, but it allowed for an immediate escape. WVU was ultimately responsible for $15 million of that—the Big 12 contributed $10 million and asked only that $5 million of that be paid back over time. The debt wouldn't vanish completely until WVU had been in the Big 12 for eight full seasons, but given the alternative, it seemed like the sum was easily accepted and thus dismissed.

That may have been the most bizarre development of all. Fans don't like it when WVU jerks with their ticket prices or donation levels or parking fees. They didn't like it when John Beilein didn't have to pay all of his buyout, they raged when Rich Rodriguez suggested he wouldn't have to pay his, and they cringed at what little money WVU could make staying in the Big East as opposed to being in the Southeastern Conference or, in the end, the Big 12. Fans want what's theirs to be theirs and what's WVU's to be WVU's.

So the idea of paying the Big East to get out before the roof collapsed, and then leaving a whole lot of earned revenue behind as they fled the burning building, figured to sting—particularly because so much of this move was about having more revenue. Certainly, the money lost was going to eventually come back from a number of directions, but surely the fans would be asked to fill the coffers one way or another.

Yet the alternative, the scenario explained by Luck and feared by all Mountaineers, was just too grim to consider. What could a Big East be without Pitt and Syracuse and whoever was able to get out next? How long could that league live, considering the fixes made after the Atlantic Coast Conference's first raid in 2003 stuck for just a few years?

WVU didn't have to worry about it any longer, and that gave people a reason to smile so bright that most couldn't see the consequences to consider them. The satisfaction of the Orange Bowl and the excitement for life in the Big 12 was like a tall, shiny can of Red Bull to power people through the offseason. And really, hadn't everyone earned that feeling?

A lot of the offseason was spent quietly cleaning the house, rearranging the furniture, and buying new pieces so WVU could be the most excellent host possible in the Big 12. And then one day, a new threat appeared off in the periphery.

Neinas was just the interim commissioner of the Big 12 and the conference really outdid itself when it hired Bob Bowlsby—and not Luck, who was rumored to be a candidate, but who would nevertheless be asked to shoot down rumors again and again. Bowlsby was seen as a star in the business of athletics, so much so that he'd twice been trusted with assisting the USOC, in addition to successful years spent as the athletic director of Northern Iowa, Iowa, and Stanford.

You know Stanford, right? On a list of hypothetical dream jobs for an athletic director, Stanford is right at the top. Colleges win team and individual conference and national championships in the sports they sponsor, but the broadest and most valuable award is called the Directors' Cup. The Cup goes to the most successful athletic department in the land. Stanford won it for Division I schools in 2012 and each of the 17 years before that. When you're the athletic director at Stanford, you want for nothing, except maybe more years to have so much fun.

One reason people respected Bowlsby so much was his bold hire of a Football Championship Subdivision coach to turn around the Cardinal program. That coach was Jim Harbaugh, who nurtured and developed an elite quarterback to take the Cardinal to the top. That quarterback was Andrew Luck, who gave his dad reason to be in Palo Alto, Calif., many times through the years—opportunities to get to know the president and the athletic director and the coaches and the administrators at Stanford. The dots almost connected themselves, and right away, Luck's name was on the short lists sportswriters and bloggers put together predicting who might follow Bowlsby.

Would Luck do it? Before you could answer that question completely and accurately, you had to ask if he could leave his alma mater at that moment. Honestly, the answer was yes. He'd already done so much and positioned the athletic department in such a way that he could depart for a truly premier position, content in the knowledge he'd left the Mountaineers better than he'd found them. When he arrived in June 2010, the unquestioned top priorities were getting the Mountaineers into a power conference and positioning the bus-driving football program for future success. He'd done both inside of two years, as well as smaller things that would make money or make life better for other parts of the athletic department.

Did he have other stuff he wanted to do? Did he want to see more things through to the end? Absolutely. But if he left for the Stanford job, those who would begrudge him would not do so for very long.

One day in the middle of May, Luck was spotted in San Francisco, not far from Stanford, for what turned out to be a previously arranged speaking engagement. Still, the people who were getting used to not worrying about the gold and blue rug being yanked from under their feet were suddenly reminded what that felt like. Surely something was afoot, and this was a precursor to Luck accepting the Stanford job and making sure he was on campus to be the athletic director as his two daughters got their college educations right there with him.

The apprehension didn't come merely from those most prone to pessimism. There was an awareness right at the top of the university. Clements was getting phone calls and emails from people he knew and people he'd never met. He was getting stopped on the street or on the way from one point on campus to another. Quite frankly, he was getting tired of it. It wasn't anything he had against Luck or Stanford or the situation, as ambiguous as it was. It was just time to settle it. The two met and Clements asked the question he needed to ask and Luck supplied the answer Clements wanted to hear.

"I knew his name had come up for Big East commissioner, the Big 12 commissioner, it had come up for Stanford, so I said, 'I'm just asking in general, because I know the next big university, like Texas, is going to need an A.D. and your name is going to be on the list, so I need to know because we've got a lot going on here,'" Clements said.

"He said, 'Jim, I love it here, I love what I do. I think we're making great progress. This is my alma mater and this is where I want to be.'"

A few days later, Clements sat in his office and started calling sportswriters who cover WVU, one by one, to tell them his athletic director would remain his athletic director. This was as unusual as it sounds, but Clements thought it was necessary. Though he was still relatively new to the culture, he felt he understood the way people felt about this uncertainty.

"We know how much West Virginia means to everyone, and I don't want Mountaineer Nation to continue to be stressed out about it," he said. "I don't want Oliver distracted from his work or me distracted from my work. I'd rather just squash the rumor."

That piece of positive news was topped first by an announcement that WVU and reigning national champion Alabama, Dana Holgorsen and Nick Saban, would be squaring off in the Chick-fil-A Kickoff Game to start the 2014 season. Then Luck fired his baseball coach, a truly quirky source of happiness to people who follow Mountaineers baseball, and hired an assistant coach from very successful TCU. Twice before Randy Mazey had been a winning head coach, but never on a stage quite like the one Luck was assembling.

Prior to hiring Mazey, Luck and WVU announced a plan to build a new baseball stadium off campus and fund it through tax-increment financing, which meant only a little would come from the school. Mazey was given a salary nearly three times that of his predecessor to at least keep him in the same zip code of his Big 12 peers. Mazey spoke glowingly about the assurances he'd received from Luck that together they'd work to make baseball big in the new conference. Luck was in charge, and he was on a roll.

Then came a tragic reminder about life and sports, and how they are intertwined, but also separate. Bill Stewart died, suddenly and unexpectedly, after a heart attack suffered during a round of golf on May 21. He was playing with his old friend, former WVU athletic director Ed Pastilong, in the annual West Virginia Hospitality and Travel Association event at Stonewall Jackson Resort, in Roanoke, West Virginia.

On the golf course, old Billy Stewart was doing what he did best. He was telling stories and making people laugh when, literally right in the middle of one of his tales, his life was cut short. Morgantown, West Virginia, and college football fans everywhere who came to know Stewart during his 59 years were thrust into a prolonged period of mourning. There were magnificent memorials, beautiful eulogies, and unforgettable tributes to the man. While the occasion brought everyone's thoughts back to a strange and sad time for WVU football, it redirected attention away from the way Stewart's time as head coach ended. Instead, it reminded people how it began. Stewart's death forced fans to take in the whole of the man's life, how he lived it, and how it came to be defined during that magical time to end the 2007 season.

Admittedly, Stewart and I were not great friends or close confidants during or after his final season. But for a lengthy time, I liked and admired him very much. I'd like to think that whatever differences we had—that however our professional relationship changed in accordance with the questions asked and the answers given relative to our job titles—my opinion of him as a husband, father, friend, and mentor had not much changed. Those were the impressions pressed into my mind when I first got to know him as an assistant coach, when life was different and he was so happy to talk about the quarterbacks or fullbacks or tight ends or special teamers he coached and liked so much.

For whatever reason, Stewart took a sincere interest in my life, and my career as a young guy that had graduated from the school he loved and was later lucky enough to cover its sports. I was engaged in the summer of 2006 and Stewart would often ask me about my fiancée or my wedding plans or whatever else popped into that mind of his. The night Rich Rodriguez made that unmistakably angry phone call from Lakeview Golf Resort & Spa to the *Statewide Sportsline* radio show, to hammer the hosts for perpetuating the rumors of Rodriguez going to Alabama, was the night my employer at the time, the *Dominion Post*, had its holiday banquet at Lakeview.

During the evening, Stewart passed the doorway to the banquet room. And, being Bill Stewart, he went back, engaged his curiosity, poked his head inside and looked around the room. After the game the next night, right after WVU beat Rutgers in double overtime to deny the Scarlet Knights a spot in the Bowl Championship Series and earn its own way to the Gator Bowl, Stewart wanted to talk with me. Not about the job his backup quarterback, Jarrett Brown, did in relief of injured starter Pat White, but about the night before.

"Was that your bride?" he said.

I replied that the woman I would marry in August was indeed my guest for the banquet.

"You outkicked your coverage, buddy."

I'm not special in this regard; this is the kind of story that countless others could tell, similarly, about Stewart. But he made me feel special. That was Bill Stewart, as a person.

Bill Stewart, as a head football coach, was the guy who would later botch the ends of games or muddle press conferences or do the things he did and was accused of doing after his job was taken from him. The two were different people.

Stewart's reputation took an immense hit upon and after his resignation. Though it should never have happened the way it happened, his death calibrated the thoughts people had of him and they framed his life appropriately. People would again and forever remember who he was, as opposed to what he was.

I happened to be on vacation in Antigua when Stewart died. In the days that followed, natives who are consumed by cricket and have few attachments to American sports, let alone college football, knew about Stewart's death and were sad that he had gone so young. Think about that for a moment and ask yourself this: would that be the case if not for what he did at the Fiesta Bowl? Would WVU football have been so identifiable, so prominent that complete strangers on a small island in the West Indies could recognize and relate to the Mountaineers?

And that ought to evolve into a larger question: what if Stewart hadn't picked WVU up in December 2007 and carried it to glory against Oklahoma? It's impossible to know for sure, but what Stewart did was guarantee the Mountaineers left Arizona with respect and admiration, and in the end that's all Stewart ever really cared to do. If the Sugar Bowl sent WVU hurtling into the future, Stewart and the

Fiesta Bowl made sure the program would not fall apart as so many others had as they tried to make a similar journey to the top, only to be derailed by a coach's exit.

College football became an even more volatile business in the seasons that followed that Fiesta Bowl. While WVU was shaken at times and just plain shaky on other occasions, it also maintained relevance. The Mountaineers were still on television and in bowl games. They recruited talented players, including the core of the Orange Bowl team and the one that would follow, and remained attractive for imaginative and capable coaches, and to a conference like the Big 12. That should not be overlooked.

The Mountaineers entered their new league still in possession of the respect and admiration they had earned, evidenced most clearly when the preseason Coaches' poll ranked them No. 11—as close to the top 10 that they had been since the second game of Stewart's first season. Days later that distinction was complemented quite fittingly when *Newsweek* ranked WVU as its No. 1 party school.

And what's not to celebrate? Now, Holgorsen has a full season as head coach to his name. The veterans on his roster know who he is and how he operates. Those facts are vastly underrated; people often forget that when Holgorsen first arrived, he wasn't supposed to become the head coach until 2012.

There's no way the Mountaineers would have had the same momentum and reputation entering the Big 12 if Holgorsen was just starting out as the head coach. The quality of the continuity on the sideline and on the roster, mostly on offense, propelled WVU to second place in the Big 12's preseason poll put together by the conference's media members. Quarterback Geno Smith, not Oklahoma's Landry Jones or Kansas State's Collin Klein, was named the preseason offensive player of the year. Truth be told, this didn't really surprise people, least of all the Mountaineers.

"I expect to win every game like I expect to complete every pass and make every read," Smith said. "Will that happen? No, but that's the standard I hold myself to. If you shoot for the moon, you may land among the stars."

Holgorsen and his players were popular guests at the Big 12's annual media days in Dallas. On the opening day of the two-day event, Oklahoma's players and head coach, the preseason favorites, strutted down a hallway on their way to meet the media. Looking on from the side, mascot Jonathan Kimble spoke up from beneath his coonskin cap and fired a warning shot—not from his musket, but from the heart, deep inside his buckskin outfit.

"Hey, Oklahoma! See you in Morgantown November 17," Kimble said.

Bob Stoops, coach of the Sooners for 14 years, one national championship, and seven conference titles, heard it and made sure everyone would remember the exchange.

"We'll be there," he said.

Out of nowhere, it was clear: WVU and everyone else in college football couldn't wait for the fall.

Acknowledgments

A disclaimer: This is the last thing I wrote for this book and even though it's the part I probably thought about the most, what follows is my best attempt at, but in no way, a conclusive list of people I have to thank.

I want to and need to begin with my parents, Marie and Gene. They let a high school kid moonlight as a newspaper reporter and keep ridiculous hours when he was a junior and a senior chasing a dream. They let me come home from my part-time job way after midnight when I had school the next day. They let me travel to parts of Virginia I'd never been to so I could cover softball or basketball or whatever was thrown my way. They let me do something at an early age that I truly wanted to do when I became older. They let me go to college out of state because West Virginia University had a journalism school I really liked. They put up with my screwed-up schedule for holidays and birthdays and anniversaries and Mother's Day and Father's Day and other family occasions after I graduated. They always understood and never, ever complained about how a bowl game or a basketball tournament compromised plans for Christmas or a wedding or just a weekend in the fall when it would be fun to get together. There is no way I can possibly thank them enough for everything. A paragraph seems so preposterous, but without them, none of this would have happened.

My family has always been great for me. There's not enough space for me to mention everyone and why they matter, but thanks to my sister, Devon, for a lifetime of laughs, stories, and experiences probably only we can understand; to her husband, Mike Possanza; to my grandma Teddy, my grandpa George, my grandmother Dorothy, my Uncle George and Aunt Linda; my Uncle Butch and Aunt Pat, my cousin Edward and his wife, Diane; my cousin Patti, my cousins Donna, Doug and Lindsey, my cousins Barbara and Bill and their children, Kara, Leah, and Drew; as well as Chip and Jan, friends of the family who are much more like family than friends. These people didn't write a word or edit a page in this book, but every one of them had some impact on me—and most of that impact has been good.

I got married in 2007 and officially added a whole bunch of new family members, but they took me in years before that. My in-laws, Alan and Joanne, are a whole lot like my mom and dad and treat me so much more like a son than a guy who married their daughter and then promptly used his job to keep her hostage for long parts of the year. Thanks to them and to my talented brother-in-law, Josh, his wife, Jessica, and my nephew, Hunter.

Thanks to the *Manassas Journal Messenger* for hiring me when I was in high school and letting me work as a stringer. Thanks to Nick Hut, Lewis Forrest, and Mike Doser for taking me in and giving me my first look at life in a newsroom and how much fun you could have at work.

I was extraordinarily fortunate to work at the *Dominion Post* for seven years. That place gave me every opportunity to do my job and to show me how to do it. That's the newspaper that let a 22-year-old me cover a Division I basketball team and spill my mind twice a week in a column. I'm a beat writer, but I won an APSE award writing columns there and I'm still immensely proud of that.

I was just as fortunate to have the *Charleston Daily Mail* hire me in 2007. We've been to a lot of places and covered and broken a lot of stories, and I can't accurately express my appreciation for the opportunities given to me. This is the place that rolled the dice and decided it would be a good idea to let me live and work 160 miles from the office and have a blog where I could write unfiltered. This is the place that let me write a book while covering a monumental football season. I've always tried to live up to the faith they have in me.

To all three newspapers and the people charged with making it work, a heartfelt thanks for everything.

Then there's the audience, which is the most important part of the newspaper business. Thanks so much to the folks who have read and followed my stuff through the years, especially the men *and* women who drive my blog at the *Daily Mail*. I can't say they only read it or comment on it because they really do keep it running. I love it and I hate it and for the same reason—the people there are funnier than me.

Professionally, there's been no one more important to me than Bob Hertzel. It's impossible to try to explain it here. Just know that a guy who for so many years was as good as there was at what he did decided, for some reason, to take me under his wing. It was and continues to be unbelievable. He helped me get out of, and helped me stay out of, trouble at times I wouldn't have been able to do it on my own. He showed me how to do this inside and outside the office. I can't say enough.

Then there's Jack Bogaczyk. He, too, took a shot on me. Just like Hertz, Jack helped me more than I can explain. I found a whole new way to cover sports and games and stories. I found a whole new way to be a beat writer and a columnist. Jack showed me a new way to do the same old job.

I hope people understand this: I lucked out and worked for two of the best.

I've been lucky to make great friends and acquaintances in this business. Remember, this isn't a job where you meet a lot of good people and make a lot of good friends. I have both. Justin Jackson was the best man at my wedding for a reason. I'm very lucky Colin Dunlap was on the WVU beat for two years. I haven't known him nearly as long as I've known many of my other friends, but Colin is one of the best friends I have. He'll tell you this, so I might as well get it out there: he changed the way I do this job. In addition to Justin and Colin, I'm happy to say I spent fun times next to Mike Cherry, Duane Rankin, and Dave Hickman through the years. You spend a lot of time on press row and in press conferences with your peers, but it's been fun sharing all the other times with them, too.

I've worked with and learned from a lot of coaches and want to thank Mike Carey, Marlon LeBlanc, Jeff Casteel, Jeff Mullen, Jeff Neubauer, Matt Brown, John Bowers, John Kelly, Tom Yester, and Linda Burdette, who was the longtime gymnastics coach at WVU and the first one to really let me in with a team. You might not believe this, but Rich Rodriguez was good to me. He was fun to cover. He knew where I was going with stories and he usually helped with quotes and anecdotes. Things changed at the end and we grew to stand for and believe in different things, but that's the way the game goes. I got that. I think he did, too. Bob Huggins has taught me a few things about how to do my job, but I'm better for it. He has a reputation for his dealings with the media, but I have to say that just doesn't match what I've experienced working with him. This is not to brag, but to my recollection, he's returned all of my calls except one. He wasn't sure whether he'd returned that one or not, so he followed up by finding me on the sideline before a game.

Dana Holgorsen and I got to know one another under, shall we say, bizarre circumstances, but as best as I can tell it didn't affect our working relationship whatsoever. I thank him for that and for trusting me in some moments when it would have been difficult to trust anyone, most of all someone with my job.

And finally, John Beilein was the best thing to happen to my career. My first day covering his team was his first day running the team and I was lucky enough to spend four years covering him at a time when not a lot of other people were covering him. I learned a lot about basketball and statistics and strategy by being around him and talking to him and I learned a ton more about how to conduct myself as a person and as a professional. I'm not ashamed to say this: he was a hell of a role model for me. You're just not going to find a better guy than him. I'll be forever grateful for things I'm not even sure he knows he did for me.

I'd also be dumb not to thank Jarmon Durisseau-Collins, Johannes Herber, Kevin Pittsnogle, Pat Beilein, Mike Gansey, D'or Fischer, Frank Young, Darris Nichols, and Tyrone Sally. It was with them that I figured out how to work a beat. They also took me on the best experience of my career and made it fun when our feet were on the ground.

I have a lot of "sources" who I have to thank, too. I can't name them, of course, but there's a bunch of them. They know who they are and they know I don't get a lot of my stories without them. I want them to know I appreciate them. One thing I'm most proud of is that I have a list of people from a variety of places inside and outside of WVU who trust me to use their information responsibly and to protect their identity valiantly. It's extremely redeeming after all these years.

I've been lucky to have great, great friends. I'd like to think everyone I've mentioned is, on some level, a friend, but there are so many others who I haven't named and who I must name. In Morgantown, West Virginia, I met Brett and Jessica Nuckles, Jay Baldwin, B. J. Painter, Jay Glassick, Cam Bordman, Chris Richardson, Chris and Melissa Elliott, Casey Quinlan, Scott Rohrer, Chris Schreiber, Tony and Katrina Curia, Rob Rossi, Mike Pehanich, Sam Wilkinson, Jennelle and Jeremy Jones, Gregg and Sabrina Cave, Tara Curtis, Courtney Jennings, Christie Zachary, Jason Martin, and so many others. I'm sure I forgot people, but if those people are my friends, then they know I'm forgetful.

Growing up in Manassas, Virginia, I met awesome friends in Dave Smock, Brian Swenson, Mark Townsend, Jon Shachter, Kaleil Cherry, Matt Feldmann, Eric McDermott, John Henkel, Mark Brzozowski, Toby Mergler, Nick Peterson, Su-Hou Chen, and my first writing partner, Dave Rao. We shared a byline in the school newspaper for a column called "Why We Hate ..." What started in that little classroom in Osbourn High under the watch of Dottie Priddy, what I found to be so fun while sharing strange hours with people like Kaleil and Rao and Adam Russell and Rachelle Sawal, somehow ended up here. I think that's pretty damn cool.

Also, thanks to Julie and Mark Thalman. They don't even know it, but they made a big difference for me. They bought Town Hill Tavern in Morgantown and Julie told us once, "I didn't buy a bar so my friends could drink for free." Thanks so much to them because now I can say, "I didn't write a book so I could give it to my friends for free."

Thanks to Mike Patrick for the terrific foreword. In all honesty, he's the first name that came up when we started to talk about who should write it. We did think of other candidates who could do it differently or come from another angle, but not one of those alternatives made as much sense as Mike. All those names did was convince me Mike was the right guy. I think he proved it. True story: Mike wrote the foreword by hand on three pages of yellow legal pad paper. You should see the scribbling and the edits he made. It shows how much the topic means to him.

I'm literally not here right now without Peter Bodensteiner and Zone Read. I never wrote a book before this. I tried once and it fell apart, though that was out of my control. The entire thing discouraged me and I hadn't thought about getting into a book again until the summer of 2011. I had offers and discussions with some people, but everything with Peter and his company was right. Peter's put up with a lot of emails and ramblings and typos and attempted murder on the English language, but here we are, with a book published by a company that had unwavering confidence in a guy who sometimes struggles to write 15 inches.

One little lady must be mentioned because I know she's reading and I know she's wondering how I've gotten this far and haven't explained the profound impact she's had on my life and on this book. So thanks to my dog, Lilo. I put a lot of miles on her legs walking around town and organizing my thoughts in my cluttered head as I tried to write this thing. I also work from home and constantly cramp her style. I can't say enough about her patience.

In all seriousness, my wife, Erinn, is the best. She puts up with a lot. My job sometimes asks things of people that probably shouldn't be asked. The schedule is lengthy and sometimes demanding. It's hard to make plans. It's harder to put up with the hours. Writing a book only added to that. Erinn was married to a ghost for a long time in 2011, and I can only think of one word to describe the way she handled it. Coincidentally, it's her favorite word: tremendous. She knows how I feel about her because I tell her all the time and I know how she feels about me. On my best days and on my worst, when people want to pat me on the back and when people want to wring my neck, I'm with my wife and I'm just Mike. That can't be beat.

Publisher's Note

In my mind the origins of this book lie in 2007. After the incredible drama of West Virginia's season that year I thought somebody, somewhere, ought to document it with a movie, a book, a graphic novel—something. But the chaos didn't stop then; if anything it reached new heights with the events of 2011.

About that time I found out the *Charleston Daily Mail*'s Mike Casazza was considering writing a book. I emailed him right away, and our conversations led to the book you're reading. In our discussions we were hard-pressed to think of any team, in any sport, that had experienced so much insanity over its recent history. Naturally, Mike's book had to cover all the mayhem of the last decade, a period punctuated by events that would be impossible to believe had we not lived through them. Only by explaining where the Mountaineers had come from and where they might be going could the true intensity of the story be conveyed.

My Mountaineer fandom dates back to that magical season of 1988. I was a sophomore in high school; my family had moved to Morgantown from Oklahoma the year before. Despite seven formative years spent in that football-mad state, I had never really caught the college football bug.

But then I found myself sitting in the sun at my first WVU game, watching as Major Harris and perhaps the best WVU team ever assembled absolutely destroyed their hapless opponent in the season opener. I was hooked from that point forward—how could I not be? With season tickets (thanks, Dad) about 10 rows up from the Pride of West Virginia, we hunched under a rain poncho as the Mountaineers made up a 14-point deficit against Maryland, watched the Maj run circles around Penn State, and cheered when the team carried Don Nehlen off the field at the end of the school's first undefeated season.

Like all Mountaineer fans, I was devastated by the loss to Notre Dame in the Fiesta Bowl. Unlike many of you, though, that was only the first time I experienced the true nature of the cult I had joined, the whipsaw of emotions that all West Virginia fans know well. If you're a Mountaineer fan you know that for every Major Harris miracle there is an Alex Van Pelt comeback, for every Amos Zereoue sprint there is a Tremain Mack punt block, for every Patrick White scramble there is a Marvin Graves beanball. You can say those painful memories make the good times sweeter, but I'll bet that Graves still gets an earful whenever he encounters a true-blue Mountaineer fan.

When Rich Rodriguez left for Michigan, my greatest fear was that the team's ascent toward becoming an elite program would be halted, that the Mountaineers would return to mediocrity. That's exactly what I felt was happening under Bill Stewart. Others, like our foreword writer Mike Patrick, thought Stewart got a raw deal, that he certainly had been successful enough that he deserved to stay on. Our difference of opinion encapsulates this tumultuous and often-painful period for WVU's passionate fan base—with so much raw emotion on tap, such disagreements were inevitable. The decisive Orange Bowl victory of January 2012, we all hope, will help heal those divisions. With a new coach and a new conference, the future looks bright. But as Mountaineer fans, we know better than to fully trust that optimism.

— Peter Bodensteiner, founder of Zone Read

About the Author

Mike Casazza is an award-winning reporter and the beat writer for the *Charleston Daily Mail* and has been covering collegiate athletics since 2002. He's covered NCAA Tournaments that have ended in the Final Four, Elite Eight, and Sweet Sixteen, and numerous football bowl games, including three BCS games. He's broken stories and been around breaking news along the way, and has learned more about coaching searches, coaching contracts, litigation, and the legal side of sports than he ever predicted.

Born in Hamilton, Ohio, in 1980, he graduated from Osbourn High School in Manassas, Va., in 1998 and attended West Virginia University. He was a magna cum laude graduate in 2002, when he was named the Most Outstanding News-Editorial Student and Top Scholar in the Perley Isaac Reed School of Journalism.

He began his work in a newsroom at the *Manassas Journal Messenger* in 1996 and moved on to WVU's *Daily Athenaeum* in 1998, the Morgantown *Dominion Post* in 2000, and the *Charleston Daily Mail* in 2007. He's won a list of awards from the West Virginia Press Association, including first-place awards for sports news writing in 2009, 2010, and 2011, and was the recipient of an honorable mention honor from the Associated Press Sports Editors for column writing in 2003.

He resides in Morgantown, West Virginia, with his wife, Erinn, and lives a quick sprint away from Mountaineer Field, in case news ever breaks. Of course, it often breaks when he's on vacation—or perhaps *because* he is on vacation.

Made in the USA
Monee, IL
14 October 2024

67528850R00187